The Insolent Slave

William E. Wiethoff

University of South Carolina Press

© 2002 University of South Carolina

Published in Columbia, South Carolina, by the
University of South Carolina Press

Manufactured in the United States of America

06 05 04 03 02   5 4 3 2 1

Library of Congress Cataloging-in-Publication Data

Wiethoff, William E., 1945–
  The insolent slave / William E. Wiethoff.
    p. cm. — (Studies in rhetoric/communication)
  Includes bibliographical references and index.
  ISBN 1-57003-414-1 (alk. paper)
  1. Slaves—Southern States—Language. 2. Invective—Southern States—
Social aspects—History. 3. English language—Discourse analysis. 4. Slave
insurrections—Social aspects—Southern States. 5. Slaves—Legal status, laws,
etc.—Southern States. 6. Slavery—Law and legislation—Southern States.
7. Plantation life—Southern States—History. 8. Southern States—Race relations.
9. Gentry—Southern States—Attitudes—History. 10. Gentry—Southern States—
Language—History. I. Title. II. Series.
E443 .W6 2001
305.5'67'0975—dc21   2001001836

The Insolent Slave

Studies in Rhetoric/Communication
Thomas W. Benson, Series Editor

For Jim

Contents

Series Editor's Preface ix
Acknowledgments xi

    Introduction 1

PART 1   THE LEGISLATIVE PERSPECTIVE
1 "Subordination Not Susceptible of Any Modification or Restriction" 15
2 The Master of Westover 42

PART 2   THE BUSINESS PERSPECTIVE
3 "A Perfect Understanding between a Master and a Slave" 57
4 The Polk Overseers 86

PART 3   THE SOCIAL PERSPECTIVE
5 "An Offence Which Consists of Inconsistency" 101
6 The Reluctant Mistress 117

PART 4   THE MORAL PERSPECTIVE
7 "The Crowning Glory of This Age" 133
8 The Judge and Patriarch 149

    Conclusion 161

Notes 171
Bibliography 199
Index 219

Series Editor's Preface

In his analysis of "the insolent slave," William E. Wiethoff discovers a highly elaborated system of fear and repression in the words and works of Southern slaveholders. Slave insolence, perceived as a dangerous mode of resistance to the authority of the master, took on legislative, business, social, and moral meanings in the writings of slaveholders, according to Wiethoff. Insolence was a verbal activity, a communicative accomplishment exercised primarily through language that expressed disrespect for the master and, at least indirectly, denial of the legitimacy of his authority. Southern slaveowners reported sharply increased levels of insolence beginning at about the time of the Revolutionary War and continuing in the first decades of the nineteenth century. In some areas, slaveowners responded to their perceptions of slave insolence by attempting to proscribe it through laws; in other areas, judges created remedies. Slave insolence was interpreted as a business problem, affecting the organization and deployment of capital assets, and directly influencing profit and loss. In his examination of what he calls the "social perspective," Wiethoff demonstrates how slave insolence was regarded as a threat to men's honor and women's virtue. Even looks and gestures could constitute insolence to these elements of the social order. Insolence was regarded as a moral failing on the part of slaves, who were regarded as obligated to respect the divinely assigned authority of their masters and mistresses. These four dimensions—legislative, business, social, and moral—are examined by Wiethoff through a series of case studies utilizing a wide variety of contemporary documents, constructing something like a rhetorical theory of insolence and providing a fresh look at the experience of slavery—for both master and slave—as partly constituted through communication and through competing understandings of communication. This is a deep, subtle, and astonishing book, revealing the contradictory rhetorical theories and everyday discursive practices that supported the institution of slavery in the American South.

THOMAS W. BENSON

Acknowledgments

The tireless efforts of librarians and archivists made this project manageable. Professor Ann Puckett, Director of the Law Library at the University of Georgia, John White at the Southern Historical Collection, and Wayne Moore and Julia Rather at the Tennessee State Library and Archives were especially gracious.

Insightful editing and reviews made this project cogent. Barry Blose and two anonymous reviewers for the University of South Carolina Press were always constructive in their criticism.

The love of a good woman made this project possible. Thank you, Carolyn.

The Insolent Slave

Introduction

By word and deed, slaves challenged the world view and self-concepts of their masters in the American South. As an object of scholarly inquiry, slave resistance has prompted research on both macroscopic and microscopic levels, from demonstrating political significance,[1] to deciphering personal motives.[2] Prompting related inquiries into the evolution of race relations, including "the nation's racist pathology,"[3] the study of slave resistance informs our understanding of historical attitudes and habits. A special mode of resistance, insolence, forced the Southern gentry to acknowledge a unique power among slaves: their speech. As immediate or delayed responses to insult or injury, voluntary or involuntary, slave insolence shamed the gentry despite its utterance by mere chattels. Prompted to control this discourse if not extinguish it through legislation, the gentry attached business, social, and moral meanings to this insolence, thereby acknowledging and illuminating four troubled dimensions of plantation society.

In this book, I assess the driving force behind legislation against slave insolence. As revealed in their expressions of unreflective judgment, self-persuasion, and sectional propaganda, the gentry expressed an understanding of the insolent slave—a singularly misshapen piece of the larger puzzle that was slavery. The institution itself gradually changed over the years, making slavery all the more puzzling. I make less sweeping claims about the motives or meanings of insolence for slaves. Indeed, as often as not, slaves may have involuntarily engaged in behaviors perceived by the gentry as insolent. The slaves' story remains to be told fully and accurately as more of their genuine discourse is discovered, edited, and interpreted. Rather I have concentrated on the several explanations that members of the planter class used to clarify for themselves—and ultimately justify to others—their coping with slaves' disagreeable exercise of discursive power. Especially noteworthy among these explanations are the related thoughts of overseers and plantation mistresses who were forced to cope with an intermediate position between the higher authority exercised by masters and the special manipulation directed at them by their slaves.

Insolence has always held a significant meaning in western civilization. Aristotle first speculated on its discursive functions in his Rhetoric when he analyzed human emotions. Insolence, or insult, was classified among slights that excite anger. More significantly in the present analysis, Aristotle defined insolence as a form of slighting that causes shame for the receiver and pleasure for the sender. Particularly in a relationship of unbalanced power or status, people discursively gain the upper hand over other people by treating them insolently. For example, he observed, people expect to be respected by their inferiors; rulers demand the respect of the ruled; people who think they ought to be rulers demand the respect of others whom they think they ought to be ruling. Insolence is felt most intensely in a longstanding relationship such as that between masters and slaves in the American South. People become angry, Aristotle explained, with those who have usually treated them with honor but suddenly behave insultingly, because they are perceived to feel contempt or they would still be behaving as they did before.[4] Expecting to be treated as absolute rulers, and usually treated that way by their slaves, the gentry reacted strongly to perceived slights.

Not Aristotle's precepts specifically—although proslavery discourse in the American South has been characterized as obedient to Aristotle's rhetorical and logical doctrines[5]—but the general regimen of a classical education guaranteed the gentry's sensitivity to rhetorical norms.[6] As a result of this education, members of the gentry regarded highly Hugh Blair and George Campbell, eighteenth-century British rhetoricians who elaborated on the classical precepts about purpose, subject matter, and methods in insolent discourse. Fundamental to this theory, and especially meaningful for the gentry, was Blair's warning that ridicule can produce great mischief in unskilled hands.[7]

The proper purposes of insolence were limited to refuting grossly flawed beliefs and restraining auditors from silly or foolish actions.[8] Although some members of the gentry acknowledged doubts about the peculiar institution of slavery, they did not regard their slaveowning as foolish. Thus, slave insolence lacked a canonical purpose. The proper subject matter of insolence was limited to criticism of comic flaws such as awkwardness, rusticity, foppery, and affection.[9] Yet the gentry denied slaves the standing to criticize these flaws in their masters because slaves themselves were perceived as embodying traits such as rusticity and affection. Moreover, Blair only grudgingly acknowledged that native peoples whom he considered barbarous and rude might possess the ability to appreciate sophisticated rhetoric. It was more likely, he opined, that a proper taste for rhetoric would be found among the citizens of a civilized and flourishing nation like his own.[10] Finally, the proper methods of insolence were covert and oblique. Properly insolent rhetors could appear to argue in favor of an idea that they actually despise, draw absurd conclusions from premises that have not been thoroughly examined, or disentangle themselves from embarrassing situations by offering odd excuses.[11] To the gentry's dismay, slaves perfected these methods.

The gentry's sensitivity to rhetorical norms, illustrated by consternation over slaves' command of artful insolence despite their supposed incapacity, guaranteed a tortuous rhetoric of proslavery ideology. Thomas Jefferson, for example, expressed an ideology of freedom only with difficulty alongside his defense of slavery.[12] George Washington provided for the emancipation of his slaves and those of his wife but nonetheless deplored the likelihood that they would become "insolent" if they anticipated freedom.[13] More precisely, the gentry had to cope with what they perceived as brutes who nonetheless possessed what classical authorities from Isocrates to Cicero had proclaimed as the "power" of speech.[14] This discursive power could not be denied no matter how attractive the outcome of denial. As South Carolina's John Wardlaw remarked grudgingly, at law the "words of a negro are at least as significant as the cry of a brute animal."[15] The scholarly debate whether racism was the cause or the effect of enslaving Africans has not been resolved;[16] scholarly analysis of the gentry's convoluted response to slaves' power of speech remains inchoate for similar reasons.

Close analysis of the language in which the gentry expressed their perceptions of insolence reveals legislative, business, social, and moral meanings. That this discursive facet of the peculiar institution had a range of meanings is scarcely surprising. By the 1820s, Jeremiah Jeter understood that the debate over slavery in Virginia was based on recognition of its "many evils, economical, social, political, and moral."[17] Slavery "was not an isolated economic or institutional phenomenon"; rather it was "a way of society's ordering its members in its own mind."[18] Just as slavery in the ancient world cannot be understood without reference to "social, economic, political, and religious conditions,"[19] specific regulation of slave speech in the American South—for example, its admissibility in criminal trials—rested on "legal traditions, religious values, the imperatives of social subordination, racism, and even property interests."[20] And so the gentry attached several meanings to the sauciness of their human chattel. Yet the precise words and deeds of slaves that amounted to insolence by the gentry's standards have not previously been identified, classified, and interpreted for their significance. These discursive elements, the "doing" of resistance in postmodern terms,[21] signified disruptions in the master-slave relationship.

Although slaves had voiced their discontent for many decades, slave insolence did not become a vexing concern until the late eighteenth century, as reflected in legislation, case law, and various types of white and black narratives. The more obvious of two factors explaining this phenomenon was the slave experience of the American Revolution. Difficult to assess, this experience nonetheless included a "vigorous circulation of the idea of freedom."[22] Acknowledged as significant in the development of slave resistance generally, these wartime experiences have not been examined for their influence on insolence.[23]

Slaves had wartime contacts with their masters' enemy that reduced or destroyed entirely their sense of futility in bondage. John Weems reported to his superior in Maryland that he had "posted gards at the most Convenient places to prevent the Negros from going to the Enemy."[24] But these measures were not always effective. John Linton, for example, advertised in the *Maryland Journal and Baltimore Advertiser,* Extraordinary that his slave George Parker had run away "to join part of the British Army, in order to get off the Continent."[25] The results were no less troubling to the gentry when their slaves failed to "get off the Continent." Six months later, Hugh Young advertised in the same newspaper that his runaway slave Dick would "endeavour to pass himself for a freeman, and a disbanded soldier, as he wore a British soldier's coat."[26] Elsewhere in the Chesapeake region, the story was similar. Sam, Simon, and Robin had run away from John Mayo in Virginia "about the time of the invasions of this State by Phillips and Arnold"; Abraham Green advertised that his slave "WENT to the British in July, 1781, and was with them at York-Town"; and, at the same time, a nameless "large black man" had defected and "joined the British at Portsmouth."[27] In the Deep South, Richard Walter advertised in the *Charleston Royal Gazette* that his slaves Somerset, Jemmy, Pompey, Mingo, Ellick, Sambo, Joe, Hercules, Riner, Charlotte, Bella, Statira, Melia, Judy, and Dolly had run away when the city had fallen—finding refuge "in the Quartermaster-General's different Departments"; and similarly James Skirving advertised that his slave Johny had been "employed in the Commissary-General's Department some time ago for several months."[28] Having defected to the enemy, all of these slaves had tasted a measure of self-control and freedom that would have been unimaginable before the war and increased the chances of their being insolent after the war.

Other slaves were seized against their will. The State Council of Maryland routinely awarded tax relief to masters such as Basil Williams, Empson Bird, and William Currer for the loss of their slaves in British raids.[29] Equally troubling to Benjamin Eaglestone of "Patapsco Neck, about 6 miles from Baltimore-Town" was the likelihood that his runaway slave Peg would "endeavour to pass for a free Negro" after she had been carried off by "some rogue, perhaps a soldier."[30] Seizure of their slaves was serious enough that the gentry extracted a British promise, in Article 7 of the Treaty of Paris, to retreat without "carrying away any Negroes."[31] These contacts with the British, although involuntary, made slaves aware of alternatives to the plantation system if not persuading them that their masters were not all powerful.

The Revolutionary War also opened the eyes of slaves who, by serving their masters under arms or by enlisting in the American army, experienced a different political climate.[32] Abram was one of these slaves. He "was a servant to an officer during the late war and travelled a good deal, chiefly in the northern states." But most bothersome for his master was the probability that Abram would "pass for a free man" after his wartime experiences.[33] The slave Seffe had already succeeded in passing as free when Thomas Mumford advertised for his return: Seffe "formerly made such an attempt, and enlisted in the division of Colonel Jolly Parish of Goochland County, as a substitute, by the name of William Jackson."[34] Increased awareness of the world outside their captivity made the more discerning slaves conscious of their own potential. At a practical level, the Revolutionary War introduced slaves to protocols and opportunities that had never before been apparent. At this level, the local gentry would understandably be alarmed when vacant military barracks were being used as "a Rendezvous for Negroes in the Night."[35] At a more abstract level, slaves may have taken to heart the same ideology that was dear to the hearts of select Northerners: live free or die. It is tempting now to attribute this level of consciousness to late-eighteenth-century slaves but, if they had drawn lessons at a merely practical level, the Revolutionary War exerted a massive influence.

Combined with enhanced language skills, wartime experiences created a slave population that never before had seemed as insolent to the gentry. Newly arrived Africans, a substantial portion of the slave population of the Deep South until the nineteenth century, had no English language skills unless they had also labored in British-controlled areas of the Caribbean. A slave's acquisition of the English language became an important measure of acculturation as well as job aptitude.[36] Although younger slaves learned more quickly, "it took most of the older ones several years to add a few English words to their vocabulary."[37] Lacking a command of English, slaves could not readily be perceived as saucy.[38] During the late seventeenth century, for example, William Fitzhugh did not complain about insolence among the slaves on his extensive tobacco plantations. The reason may be plainly evident in a complaint Fitzhugh made to another influential colonist about "your dumb Negro that you sold me." Seeking at least a partial refund of this slave woman's purchase price, Fitzhugh argued that the seller "knew her qualitys, which is bad at work worse at talking."[39] Ironically, this woman was defective in Fitzhugh's eyes for a language skill that empowered later generations of slaves to irritate and threaten the gentry. In fact, slaves might confound the normal functions of colonial institutions with their silence: during the 1665 Maryland trial of the slave Jacob for the murder of his mistress, the court clerk noted with chagrin that the slave merely stood "in a manner mute" before the jury.[40]

No precise date can be calculated for the linguistic empowerment of slaves. By 1745, for example, three different advertisements for runaway slaves in Virginia attributed three different levels of proficiency in English to the fugitives. First, Margaret Arbuthnott advertised that two of her slaves, both named Jack, "understand no English"; they were "new Negroe Men, imported from Gambia." Second, Michael Sherman noted that his nameless, thirty- to forty-year-old "Negro Man . . . talks pretty good English" despite his African heritage; he bore the distinctive "Marks of his Country," that is, tribal identifications that left scars on his temples. Finally, Philip Lightfoot advertised that his twenty-five-year-old "light-complexion'd Mulatto Man" named Ben "talks good English."[41] As these advertisements illustrate, linguistic proficiency was closely related to the length of time spent in America. The most articulate slave, Ben, being a mulatto, had most probably been born in the colony. Furthermore, linguistic conditions had not changed toward the end of the century. In 1786 D. Sans advertised for his "east India negro man called JEAN," prominently identifying this slave's command of both "French and English." One year later, Charles Jones described his middle-aged slave Jack as "outlandish" and speaking "broken English."[42] In these two instances, neither slave was native born, but Jean had prior exposure to British culture.

Random extremes of linguistic proficiency can be similarly measured up and down the Atlantic coast. In Maryland, 1748 advertisements draw a prominent contrast between Swilli, who was "outlandish" and "can't speak very intelligible," and Peter, who was "a Molatto man" and "well spoken";[43] 1790 advertisements offer a similar contrast between the middle-aged Lancaster, who "talks a little broken," and the teenager Jim, who "speaks good English."[44] In these instances, youth and mulatto characteristics accounted for the slaves' fluency. Surprisingly, as late as 1836 in North Carolina, A. H. Richardson advertised that his slave Jack spoke merely "broken English."[45] In Georgia, ten advertisements published during 1764 and 1765 are split evenly between slaves who spoke little or no English and other slaves who were fluent in the language.[46] Then again, seven of eight runaways identified in George Houstoun's 1787 advertisement are said to "speak very good English"; only the slave Bonam "speaks thick, and not easily to be understood."[47] In most of these instances, the slaveowners provided scant details that explain the differing degrees of fluency.

Variations in regional trends and in patterns of importation further complicate the task of understanding slaves' development of English language skills.[48] Although sharing a common African stock of "ideas and practices" and perhaps a common linguistic stock as well, slaves had different histories in the Upper and Deep South.[49] Nonetheless, their relative command of English often dictated in significant ways how they were perceived by the gentry. In 1724, the Reverend John Bell saw as "infidels" the many slaves "that understand not our language." That same year, the Reverend James Falconer opined that adult Africans would never be able "to speak or understand our language perfectly." More than a century later in the Deep South, John DuBose of South Carolina observed that local slaves "have hardly learned to speak intelligibly" and William Harrison agreed that they "still jabbered unintelligibly in their Gullah and other African dialects."[50]

This bewildering variation in English proficiency complicated the gentry's practical dealings with slaves as much as it now confounds an academic appreciation of developments in slave insolence. By 1841 in Mississippi, slaves' ability to "understand the English language sufficiently well to conduct ordinary affairs" complicated the trial of "Isham, a slave, for the murder of Wilford Hoggatt." Appealing Isham's conviction on the grounds that his confession had been coerced, appellate counsels Montgomery and Boyd successfully argued that slaves remained "woefully ignorant of what few rights they possess in common with free men" despite their speech skills.[51] Ironically, their eventual mastery of English made slaves liable in the gentry's view for a comprehension of rights and duties that in reality remained substantially arcane—including of course their liability for insolence.

Yet more controverted is the 1849 case of *Blanchard v. Dixon* in which Louisiana's high court awarded seven hundred dollars in damages to a slave-owner for injuries to his wandering slave. The overseer of a neighboring planter had accosted the slave on "the high road" and challenged him to produce a pass from his master authorizing his travel. But a language barrier caused trouble. "The answer of the slave was in french, and was not understood by the defendant, but the latter, judging from the tone of the slave, conceived it to be disrespectful." When the slave fled the overseer pursued and shot him, "fracturing his knee."[52] In this instance, a slave's failure to speak English late in the antebellum period—despite the French heritage of Louisiana—affronted his captor. This overseer demonstrated a tendency toward brutality shared by many of his peers, but the slave suffered a fate not usually shared by his non-English speaking peers in earlier decades.

While developing their language skills, slaves also learned when to use these skills and how to disguise expressions of criticism and contempt. Current scholarship on "code-switching" provides valuable insights into slaves' communicative prowess.[53] Sociolinguists agree that the ability to adopt differing codes or speech patterns (also called "style shifting") to gain favor or avoid disfavor requires a sophisticated command of communicative processes.[54] From this perspective, a code transcends mere language although codes are often switched within the same language family as part of the process.

The paradigmatic study of code-switching focused on subjects for whom English was a foreign language.[55] As analyzed in subsequent chapters, slaves not only learned a foreign language but also developed verbal and nonverbal devices to mask their insolence. They switched codes when addressing members of the gentry, overseers, and other whites. Indeed, slaves addressed each other in varied patterns because of cultural and experiential differences within their ranks—a skill that is the focus of recent research in intraracial communication.[56] Among other issues raised in an illumination of slave insolence is whether it nurtured the roots of an African American skill in code-switching.

Generalizations about the causal influences of slaves' revolutionary wartime experiences and linguistic proficiency are mitigated by the arbitrary or intuitive process by which the gentry detected insolence. However, just as the peculiar institution itself mutated over the years, a measurable change occurred in the master-slave relationship late in the eighteenth century and early in the nineteenth century. Reports of slave insolence increased in various narratives and the gentry began to enact related legislation. The interaction of speech and race that had troubled prior generations of planters became an increasingly thorny issue for later generations, reaching a previously unimaginable degree of intensity.

My analysis and interpretation of this interaction of speech and race consists of four parts. Each represents a perspective on the interaction, ranging from those based on the legislative and business concerns of planters to those shaped by the social and moral norms that it was assumed slaves would obey. Within each part, a case study illustrates related perceptions, self-persuasion, and sectional propaganda by large and small slaveholders, plantation mistresses, and overseers. The Old South had a more diverse population than planters, overseers, and slaves, but those were the people whose everyday interaction prompted these perceptions, persuasion, and propaganda. Taken together, the perspectives and case studies illuminate related legislation about slave insolence.

Part 1, "The Legislative Perspective," traces the development of Southern statutes proscribing slave insolence. This legislative process was rooted in a volatile clash of fear and arrogance: the dread of servile insurrection and a presumption of black subordination. Volatility in the process also ensured unpredictability. Some states and territories never enacted precisely relevant statutes, instead discouraging slave impudence by extralegal custom or judge-made law. Legislators in other jurisdictions invented discursive offenses and their remedies that reflected both the characteristic concerns of constituents and the peculiarity of slavery as an institution.

This section includes a case study of William Byrd II, the master of Westover. Grounded in a relentless pursuit of order, but replete with double standards and idiosyncrasies, Byrd's management of slave insolence illustrates a pattern that became pervasive across the South. Ironically, due to his extraordinary accomplishments outside plantation management, Byrd scarcely represented a role model for planters in other respects.

Part 2, "The Business Perspective," examines the gentry's mercantile calculations of work-related insolence. These calculations reflect genuine, pragmatic concern about profits as much as self-persuasion about the gentry's role in preserving their way of life. The planting business involved a complex hierarchy of human relations with which not every slaveowner or overseer could readily cope. Inept and brutal management of slave misconduct on the job was widespread. Ineffective responses to slave complaints and denials, or their assertions of independence and equality, or their insults and threats, wasted valuable assets. In turn, the slaves' tactical affronts to their supervisors—especially overseers—identify considerable sensitivity to the dominant culture in which blacks would never be invited to participate fully if at all. Particularly noteworthy for their revelation of gender roles in the dominant culture, interactions between slaves and the mistresses of plantations merit special attention. In fact, except for their exclusion from the legislative process, women figured prominently in constructing all other meanings of slave insolence for the gentry.

The case study of James and Sarah Polk's overseers in part 2 illustrates factors in the planting business that prompted overseers to respond harshly to slave insolence. Prominent among these factors were the disagreements over management policies between planter and overseer and the constant scrutiny of overseers' conduct by a bewildering variety of business consultants. Reacting to oppression and stress much like the slaves, overseers sought the most satisfying but least risky outlet for their feelings.

Part 3, "The Social Perspective," analyzes the social deviance perceived by the gentry, men and women alike, in slave insolence. At best, most expressions of this perspective reflect self-persuasion about enforcing selected norms. Based on norms such as male honor and female virtue, offensive speech by slaves was adjudged as a threat to the social order. In fact, slaves could not be sure of avoiding sanctions even when they grounded their discourse in white social norms. Outstanding sources of annoyance for the gentry included drunken slave utterances, complaints and insults, affronts to women, and the unspoken insolence of look and gestures. Readily distinguishable from insolence in the workplace, these types of speech branded slaves as socially disruptive in the minds of planters.

The case study of Fanny Kemble in part 3 emphasizes that, notwithstanding her moderately abolitionist leanings, she agonized over slaves' prospects for achieving full social communion in the American South. Her recollections of the four months she spent on her husband's Georgia plantations bespeak deeply ambivalent attitudes toward slaves, including admiration for their power of speech but also disgust at their lack of social graces. Based on class consciousness more clearly than racism, Fanny Kemble's journal records her impressions of slaves' verbal complaints and nonverbal insolence as emblems of social deviance.

Part 4, "The Moral Perspective," identifies an alliance between the myth of paternalism and the moral meaning of slave insolence. The most abstract of the four meanings, this moral dimension was articulated only with difficulty and finally was converted into less than credible arguments against abolition. In its more authentic manifestations as self-persuasion, this moral perspective included the notions that masters deserved respect because they were divine agents, that a familial attachment between masters and slaves prohibited insolence, and that bonds of friendship similarly discouraged impudence by slaves. This latter notion, the least reliant on formally religious doctrine, occasionally made the moral perspective palatable to slaves as well as masters.

The case study of Joseph Henry Lumpkin, small slaveholder and Chief Justice of the Georgia Supreme Court, completes my illustrations of the gentry's perspectives on slave insolence. Although notably reliant on moral principles to resolve personal and professional problems, Lumpkin might just as readily be cited to illustrate any of other three perspectives. While authoring a substantial portion of his state's common law of slavery, he consciously protected business interests and social norms. However, he also consistently articulated a paternalistic view of slaves that defined their insolence as a moral failing and endorsed the primary duty of masters to be disciplinarians.

The conclusion assesses the interaction among the four perspectives: legislative, business, social, and moral. I conclude that business concerns were dominant in those jurisdictions that enacted laws against slave insolence. Where this type of legislation was absent, social and moral concerns were dominant. Above all, the threatening specter of the insolent slave illustrated the awe with which members of the gentry estimated the power of speech.

Because reconstructing the meanings of slave insolence is an enterprise riddled with scholarly perils, this introduction would not be complete without a brief note on sources.

Legislative minutes and statutory language draw attention to the measures envisioned by the ruling class to regulate slave insolence. Reports of cases identify remedies for the civil and criminal wrongs perceived in slave insolence. Equally valuable, however, both of these sources contain accounts of verbal and nonverbal affronts to the gentry when they perceived that slaves were abusing their station in life. Legal materials, however, must be interpreted within their institutional function of providing formal, satisfying responses to the felt needs of legislators' and judges' constituents—none of whom were slaves.

White narratives in the form of letters, diaries, plantation journals, and assorted publications by agricultural societies report experiences and related judgments by the people who were offended by slave speech. A bigoted view of slaves' characters and habits is unmistakable in these sources, but bias illuminates the meaning of insolence for white narrators. To observers removed in time and place, the complaints or assertions by many slaves scarcely rise to the level of intensely offensive discourse that would prompt harsh exchanges or brutal whippings. Equally informative is the relative infrequency with which slaveowners mentioned their slaves when committing their daily experiences to writing. A silent, submissive slave was no more worthy of mention than commonplace tools or other tangible assets. On the other hand, overseers and the mistresses of plantations routinely mentioned their experiences with slaves. These accounts indicate that slaves had considerable control over human relations in the plantation community, notwithstanding the barriers to communication erected by the aloofness or absenteeism of large-scale planters.

Other white narratives, such as travelers' accounts and journalistic reports of the master-slave relationship, mention slaves sparingly and vaguely unless the narrator strongly favored abolition. These third-party narratives express a wide range of preconceived notions about slaves and slavery, some being informed and others lacking personal knowledge or experience.[57] Most valuable in these sources is the quotation or paraphrase of words addressed by slaves to their overseers and masters. Whether partisan or neutral, third-party narrators had little incentive to distort slave speech or to disguise their perception of its significance.

Runaway slave advertisements are especially useful guides to identifying the emblems of insolence because the gentry had a strong incentive to describe their slaves accurately. They identified the physical marks left on their slaves by punishment or neglect just as readily as they described the language and facial expressions by which their slaves normally communicated. Advertisements for runaway slaves are frequently valuable resources,[58] but these documents cannot always be cited as representative or accurate.[59]

Black narratives in the form of hundreds of antebellum biographies and autobiographies offer alternative accounts of slave insolence but not all of these accounts can be taken at face value.[60] Aside from those sources now devalued as fictitious or sheerly propagandistic, others were composed with significant contributions by abolitionist editors if not ghostwriters.[61] Moreover, interview data collected from ex-slaves under the auspices of the Freedmen's Bureau in the 1870s and the Federal Writers' Project in the 1930s reflect varying degrees of accommodation by the respondents to their white interviewers' preferences and expectations.[62] The letters written by slaves to a variety of correspondents, from their masters to the leaders of anti-slavery organizations, display similar accommodations.[63] Yet black narratives substantially confirm that the words and gestures decried as insolent by the gentry were actually used by slaves. Equally significant, these narratives confirm that silence was as highly valued by slaves as it was by their masters.

The potentially insidious effect of slave insolence was not lost on the gentry. Whether explained to them in theoretical terms by classical rhetoricians or manifested pragmatically in ordinary interactions, the gentry perceived significance in verbal and nonverbal affronts by their slaves. At the heart of the matter was an undesirably unsettling pressure on a desirably stable calculation involving race and power. A serious but manageable problem near the end of the eighteenth century, slave insolence increased in scope and intensity after the Revolutionary War had altered perceptions, both white and black, and proficiency in English had become more common among slaves. The gentry's growing apprehension of slave insolence revealed itself in realms as divergent as legislative initiative and moral fulmination, as well as in the intervening realms of business policy and social etiquette. Despite their masters' renewed devotion to the maxim that silence is golden, slaves kept speaking until they no longer could be heard over the din of war.

PART 1
The Legislative Perspective

1

"Subordination Not Susceptible of Any Modification or Restriction"

Statutory regulation of slave insolence in the American South, and the meaning of this legislation for the gentry, resist analysis for at least two reasons. The historical and intellectual contexts are partially obscure. Moreover, the several legal and extralegal options for addressing insolence made the legislative process itself as peculiar as the institution of slavery.

Twenty-first-century minds appreciate only with great difficulty that the gentry never questioned the need for absolute subordination of millions of African captives who inherited the roles of the "20 and odd Negroes" bartered at Jamestown in 1619.[1] Questioning this basic precept would have rendered meaningless the laws of slavery—criminal codes, police regulations, and lesser ordinances. Enactment of these laws also represents whites' fear of blacks as potentially dangerous brutes whose claims to equal rights had to be prevented because remedies were inadequate. For legislative purposes, slave insolence meant words and deeds that not only violated a basic legal presumption but also threatened state security.

Second and more tangibly, the array of options for regulating slave speech discouraged an orderly process of legislation across the South. From the master's casual administration of justice on the plantation to the precise legal process required by statute for prosecuting insolent slaves, various alternatives abounded in the South. Not only did statutory definitions of who might be punished for insolence vary widely, measures also varied for immunizing whites against civil suits after they had assaulted or killed insolent slaves.

Presumption and Fear

While North America was being settled, the gentry specifically adopted a precept that Africans were inferior as a matter of law.[2] South Carolina enacted the first comprehensive code of slave laws in 1690,[3] using as a pattern the code devised earlier to regulate slaves in Barbados.[4] Earlier, less sweeping legislation in Maryland and Virginia nonetheless set the tone of absolute black subordination. Maryland lawmakers in 1664 decreed the perpetual bondage of "all Negroes," following the paternal line, as well as a coeval term of bondage for any shameless white women who intermarried with slaves "to the disgrace of our Nation."[5] Despite the troubling occurrences of interracial sex, a 1671 Maryland statute encouraged "the Importacon of Negros and Slaves into this Province," and explicitly protected masters against misguided claims to freedom by baptized slaves.[6] More pertinent to insubordinate behavior, Virginia legislators specified in 1680 that, "if any negroe or other slave shall presume to lift up his hand in opposition against any christian," this offender should "receive thirty lashes on his bare back well laid" as soon as minimal proof was offered through official channels.[7]

Early legislation expressed partially but emphatically the presumption of subordination. By law in several colonial jurisdictions, persons of color were slaves for life. Black males drew their white wives and offspring into the same perpetual submission. They could not escape their bondage merely by entering the Christian fold, and they could not oppose their degraded treatment—certainly not by threatening a white (in Virginia, the only authentic "christian"). Absolute, all encompassing, and irresistible as a matter of law, black subordination constituted an essential precept within "a wider legal framework designed to give [the colonial] world a civility and structure."[8]

"There Is No Remedy"

Emblematic of this precept was Thomas Bacon's 1753 sermon to slaves in Maryland that they should submit even to the most wicked overseers because they had "no remedy in this world."[9] As slavery became more controversial during the late eighteenth century—a surprising development for respectable, pious Anglicans such as Thomas Bacon—black subordination and its ideological counterpart, white supremacy, gained more substantial expression in legislative acts. As South Carolina's John Wardlaw declared in *Ex Parte Boylston*, the slave was "subject to despotism" by "the very nature of things." And so legislative acts traditionally "contemplate throughout the subordination of the servile class to every free white person, and enforce the stern policy which the relation of master and slave necessarily requires."[10] By 1806, for example, Louisiana lawmakers explained that the degraded condition of slaves rested legally on their "absolute" subordination. "Not susceptible of any modification or restriction," this subordination entailed "a respect without bounds, and an absolute obedience."[11] The circle was complete. Slaves were debased because they had no rights, and they had no rights because of their degraded nature. There was no remedy.

The language of sermon and legislation is robustly bipolar, thriving on the extremes of denial and affirmation. The exclusion of any "remedy" and the denial of any "modification" expresses an unshakable, a priori belief in black subordination. However, these negative flourishes are wedded to an equally thriving positivism in defining the slave's duties under law: "respect without bounds, and an absolute obedience." By this mode of expression, the gentry announced impermeable barriers in the white-black relationship, including forbidden forms of speech.

Regardless of race, everybody supposedly understood the permissible bounds of slaves' words and deeds. Thomas Jones implied this understanding in 1763 when advertising in the Annapolis *Maryland Gazette* for the return of two runaways, Juba and Jack. "They are extreme artful sensible Fellows," Jones believed, "and can give as ready and pertinent Answers to Questions ask'd them as most of their Colour."[12] Wyatt Ballard seconded this notion in 1804 when advertising in the Raleigh *Register and North Carolina Weekly Advertiser* for the return of his slaves, Davy and Tom. According to Ballard, both Davy and Tom were "free spoken and humble, with as much reason and submission as the most of Negroes."[13] Qualified specifically by their race, Juba, Jack, Davy, and Tom could be expected to speak up—and cleverly at that—but not to cross the racial line of submissive behavior. If slaves needed to vent their more uproarious feelings, then they had an audience of peers. Lunnon, for example, assumed "an air of importance among other negroes," according to the 1821 advertisement for his return in the Salisbury *Western Carolinian*; but Lunnon knew that, "when spoken to by a white person," he should display "a great deal of politeness."[14] Moreover, these slaves were perceived as similar to "most" of their kind. Indeed, in 1835 when E. J. Hale advertised in the Fayetteville *Carolina Observer* for his runaway slave, Jim, he declared simply that there was "nothing remarkable either in his appearance or manners."[15] Like other slaves, Jim had learned not to draw attention to himself with outlandish looks or unruly behaviors.

Equally robust expressions of the presumption favoring black subordination spiced litigation. Mr. Legare called Mr. Eden a "mulatto" in South Carolina, and earned himself a sizable fine for slander in 1791. According to Chief Justice Rutledge, these "words themselves were, in this country, actionable."[16] This ruling was based on the civil rights that Eden might have lost if Legare's words had been accepted as true by the authorities, but more visceral feelings lurked behind the legal reasoning of John Rutledge. In a secure state, he doubtlessly felt, members of the subordinate class must be known with certainty so that the forms of their debasement can be administered confidently.

More notorious among judicial pronouncements on this presumption is Thomas Ruffin's 1829 opinion in *State v. Mann*. John Mann shot and wounded Lydia, a slave whom he had hired from Elizabeth Jones, when Lydia ran away during a beating. A North Carolina jury found Mann guilty of battery because he was not Lydia's owner, but Justice Ruffin reversed this verdict on appeal. By way of explanation, he initially described his personal struggle "between the feelings of the man and the duty of the magistrate" before finding that Lydia owed an equal subordination to her hirer as a temporary master as well as to her permanent owner. But the judge had much more to say: "The power of the master must be absolute to render the submission of the slave perfect." Confessing his "sense of the harshness of this proposition," he allowed that the perfect subordination of slaves could be repudiated on idealistic grounds but that "in the actual condition of things it must be so. There is no remedy."[17] Bipolar rhetoric again dominates: affirmatively, the slave owes "perfect" submission; negatively, "there is no remedy." Executing duties that elsewhere required both a preacher and a judge, Justice Ruffin efficiently expressed the gentry's presumption of black subordination. At the same time, he acknowledged the strain on that presumption growing out of the abolition movement. The result of his opinion, he predicted, would be more desirable than the outcome of "any rash expositions of abstract truths by a judiciary tainted with a false and fanatical philanthropy."[18]

Other facets of black subordination can be read in and between the lines of judicial opinions. For example, although free blacks held a handful of civil rights in South Carolina, John B. O'Neall did not envision different types of subordination for the free and the bound. "Free negroes belong to a degraded caste of society," he opined in *State v. Harden*, and "they ought, by law, to be compelled to demean themselves as inferiors, from whom submission and respect, to the whites, in all their intercourse in society, is demanded."[19] Scarcely subtle, Justice O'Neall delivered an opinion for which he would never have anticipated a rejoinder. The law was clear, he thought. Blacks, free or bound, had an affirmative duty "to demean themselves as inferiors." On the other side of the relationship, he further thought, whites had a duty to keep blacks in their place. In *State v. Maner*, Justice O'Neall held that Jonathan Maner got what he deserved at trial when a jury found him guilty of "assault and battery with an intent to murder a slave named Phil." Legally, the defendant was properly charged as a felon for his misconduct; on other grounds, Jonathan Maner deserved punishment for being "on terms of intimacy" with Phil.[20] In this instance, it was a white who had crossed the line in black/white relationships. If the white had not encouraged the black to act casually and friendly, then their quarrel would not have happened and Jonathan Maner would not have shot Phil.

Advocates supplied judges with arguments favoring black subordination in Mississippi. In *Isham v. State*, Messrs. Montgomery and Boyd formed part of the team representing the slave Isham in appealing his conviction for murdering Wilford Hoggatt. Isham's master had been prevented from testifying at his slave's trial because of his likely bias toward protecting his property. But Montgomery and Boyd argued that, in addition to a legal precedent in Tennessee, Isham's master should have been allowed to testify because a slave is typically unable to help in his own defense. "Habitually accustomed to submit . . . naturally timid and submissive," the advocates observed, a slave will fail to "show that firmness and independence when accused of crime which is usually displayed by the weakest and most unprotected freeman." Chief Justice William L. Sharkey agreed. He reversed Isham's conviction and ordered a new trial.[21]

A consensus on the core value of submissive slaves can be seen underneath the otherwise fractious opinions in *Caesar v. State*. About 11 p.m. on August 14, 1848, Caesar had struck and killed Kenneth Mizell with a jagged piece of fence rail after Mizell and a white drinking buddy had whipped Caesar and begun beating another slave, Dick. A North Carolina jury convicted Caesar of murder, despite his attorney's plea that the extenuating circumstances supported merely a verdict of manslaughter. For Richmond M. Pearson, the evidence showed that Caesar was "an obedient slave, submissive to white men," who yielded to "a generous impulse" in defending his fellow slave—an impulse that reduced white culpability at common law to manslaughter. "The law requires a slave to tame down his feelings to suit his lowly condition," Justice Pearson held, "but it would be savage to allow him, under no circumstances, to yield to a generous impulse."[22] An unlikely accident of diction, Justice Pearson's opinion announced his motive of rising above savagery in deciding the fate of Caesar.

Frederic Nash concurred, perhaps to avoid sharing a savage status with the defendant. However, Justice Nash explicitly restricted his focus to a restraint on judicial discretion. "Is it not a legislative act," he asked rhetorically, "to dispense with a rule of the common law which, in mercy to human frailty, has been adopted to save life?" He then rejected stylishly the prosecutor's argument that "policy and necessity" required a path different than the common law when dealing with slaves: "Necessity is the tyrant's plea, and policy never yet stripped, successfully, the bandage from the eyes of Justice." Unmasking justice would exhibit the race of the defendant in this case as well as pay undue deference to policy considerations. Ultimately fleeing the larger issues, Nash took refuge in the "well-known principles of the common law." He refused "to wander in the mazes of judicial discretion."[23]

These two judges essentially decided that Caesar's violence against a white antagonist did not significantly injure the gentry's expectations of black subordination—expectations that normally would lead to a verdict of murder rather than manslaughter. One judge found admirably extenuating circumstances; the other judge rhapsodized on beauties of the common law. But then Justice Ruffin dissented.

Echoing the tenor of his opinion in *State v. Mann*, Thomas Ruffin observed that slaves should not be encouraged in any degree to forget "their vast inferiority." Showing humanity to slaves had a practical limit: "the safety of the citizens." Judicial deference to the common law was desirable, but the common law made no provisions for the institution of slavery. Thus, Justice Ruffin opined, the court should shed its reluctance to adjust a rule of law "not suited to the actual state of things and not calculated to promote the security of persons, the stability of national institutions and the common welfare." In other words, the court had a duty of "enforcing a subordination to the white race." Otherwise, the court must admit that "slavery is fundamentally wrong." Scarcely expecting this admission from his brethren, Ruffin concluded his dissent with a flourish. "The great mass of slaves—nearly all of them," he expounded, "are the least turbulent of all men." Granting these normally docile creatures the right to pick and choose which whites should be obeyed and which ill treatment should be suffered silently is "dangerous to the last degree" and a step toward the unthinkable—granting blacks a voice that they would use "in denouncing the injustice of slavery itself, and, upon that pretext, band together to throw off their common bondage entirely."[24] Exploiting the rhetorical license allowed in dissenting opinions, the judge speculated on violent uprisings that were a lively and dreaded topic among the gentry.

His colleagues expressed less fear about servile revolt than Ruffin. For Richmond M. Pearson, disagreement came painfully. "If after examining a subject," he later wrote to Ruffin, "the conclusion to which I had arrived, agreed with yours, I rested upon it with entire confidence, and it gave me no further trouble."[25] Justice Pearson was not a large slaveholder and he ultimately opposed secession.[26] Nonetheless, during Reconstruction he publicly declared his belief in "the superiority of the white man" and his inevitable hegemony over former slaves through his "innate power and vigor."[27] Frederic Nash, who had written the report of the commission appointed to revise and consolidate North Carolina's statutes in 1836, also valued Ruffin's jurisprudential sense and his advice in general.[28] Ruffin's philosophy of race relations falls outside the scope of the present analysis, but his close attention to his plantation and his concern over having "the domestics kept in due order" should be noted.[29]

The three authors of *Caesar v. State* differed in their immediate apprehension of slave insurrection, but they expressed a common base of ruling class beliefs.[30] Despite an exchange of fear appeals and their disagreement over the type and scope of exceptions to a rule, the judges endorsed the basic purpose of enforcing black subordination. They did not dispute Justice Ruffin's claim that "the security of persons, the stability of national institutions, and the common welfare" were paramount. As a priority, state security merited legislation. To be appropriate for its end, this legislation must prevent the erosion of security and stability. There would be no suitable remedy once violent revolution had begun.

Insolence as a Prelude to Revolt

In the minds of many articulate Southrons, they were one step closer to revolution each time a slave was insolent.[31] There was no remedy for slave insolence; it had to be prevented. Once an insult or challenge had been uttered by a member of the degraded caste, the damage was done. The gentry did not want to bridge the gap between white and black—a racial chasm that was troubling only when it lost sharp definition. For example, unlike Legare's experience sixty years earlier in South Carolina, slurring a white man's racial superiority in Georgia in 1853 could lead to more than a mere fine. Only a few days after Newton J. Carr complained that George W. Youngblood had talked to him "worse than if [he] was a negro,"[32] Carr killed Youngblood in a duel.

Not only their self-conception as the ruling class but also a perceived threat to their security prompted the gentry to enact regulations of slave insolence.[33] Security was an abiding concern. During the seventeenth century especially, there was "endemic disorder."[34] Major attacks by native Americans in 1622 and 1644 motivated British settlers in Virginia to make at least some provisions for defense. But the cost and effectiveness of building and maintaining this defense establishment irritated gentry and yeomen alike, resulting in a 1676 rebellion that was symptomatic of continuous "law, order . . . and upheaval."[35] Nathaniel Bacon's shortlived rebellion against the colony's royal governor, Sir William Berkeley, anticipated a wider but also economically motivated revolution one hundred years later. But the participation of approximately 10 percent of the colony's slaves in Bacon's rebellion, with promises of freedom from both sides for the slaves' loyalty, injected a novel virus into the body politic. Ironically, in their face-to-face encounter at the statehouse, Berkeley expressed outrage at Bacon's "insolency" before storming off.[36]

Endemic disorder might also be interpreted in the seventeenth-century statutes and case law related to unruly speech by whites. While the very survival of "James Citty" remained uncertain in 1624, the royal council stripped Richard Quaile of his military rank—as well as threatening to cut off his ears unless he paid a hefty fine—for his "speeches" derogating the colony's administration. Later that same year, the council sentenced Richard Barnes to run a gauntlet "of 40 men" and to be banished for his "base & detracting speeches concerning the Govno^r."[37] Shortly after Maryland's royal governor had complained of William Clayborne's "contempts" and "insolences" in 1638, the colony's Assembly proscribed "Scandalous or contemptuous words" against the lawful authorities as "Enormious offences."[38] Forty years later, Edward Husbands ran afoul of this durable law and received a whipping for menacing and cursing the government.[39] Unruly speech by whites drew sufficiently strong sanctions in the seventeenth century to indicate clearly that similar insolence by a degraded class of people would be suffered no less grudgingly and sanctioned no less harshly.

Actual servile revolts, large and small, are well documented in early America. But determining whether the gentry's expressions of related fear— as distinct from the objects of their fear—represented reality or rhetoric for them remains as challenging as deciphering generally the meaning of slave insolence. Personal correspondence, newspaper reports, and travelers' accounts sustain Herbert Aptheker's conclusion about "increasing straining by the Negro people against the degradation and oppression of their enslavement" during the 1850s.[40] Related fears expressed by women at the time no doubt exacerbated matters. Emily Burke claimed to express the fear held by other white women in Georgia,[41] and Mary B. Chesnut's *Diary* publicized the murder of a South Carolina woman by her slaves.[42] Then again, Louisiana's Rachel O'Connor narrated an 1831 account of a completely unfounded insurrection scare in her neighborhood—suggesting that rhetoric occasionally subdued reality. One of her peers, Mrs. Pirrie, "had been told that all the Negroes on little Robert Barrow's plantation had armed themselves and claimed their liberty." The terrified woman "instantly started screaming and crying." But when the patrollers investigated, they "found the overseer and the Negroes very busy at gathering the crops, as peaceable as lambs, and not one word of truth in the report." On the contrary, Rachel O'Connor observed the slaves were behaving well "but shockingly frightened at the patrols being ordered out."[43]

Contradictory accounts notwithstanding, a number of violent uprisings contributed to a revolutionary climate throughout the early decades of the century.[44] In fact, the wealth of evidence for major revolts in the nineteenth century, such as those led by Gabriel and Nat Turner in Virginia, and by Denmark Vesey in South Carolina, has tended to obscure similar uprisings in the eighteenth century—other than the 1739 uprising at Stono, South Carolina.[45] Yet during the first quarter of the eighteenth century, from New York City to New Orleans, whites armed themselves against rebellious slaves.

Southrons addressed this threat to state security early in their legislative history. In 1695 the Maryland Assembly deliberated on "An Act restraining the frequent Assembling of Negroes." By 1712 a committee in the House of Delegates recommended even more extensive measures so that "no Negroes should be allowed to travel and gather together in Companies to the Terror of the good People of this Province."[46] In a preamble to their 1696 Act, South Carolina lawmakers decreed more expansively that: "The said negroes and other slaves brought unto the people of this Province . . . are of barbarous, wild, savage natures, and as such renders them wholly unqualified to be governed by the laws, customs, and practices of this Province; but that it is absolutely necessary, that such other constitutions, laws and orders, should in this Province be made and enacted, for the good regulating and ordering of them, as may restrain the disorders, rapines and inhumanity, to which they are naturally prone and inclined; and may also tend to the safety and security of the people of this Province."[47] No claims of actual revolution are asserted in the early legislation; legislators relied on their own educated guesses about a link between congregations and conflagrations. Had "Companies" of slaves provided substantive grounds for the "Terror" felt by Maryland gentry, or were the legislators only fearing the worst? South Carolina lawmakers freely announced that they were trusting their sense of slaves' "natures" and asserted without specifications that slaves were "naturally prone and inclined" to "disorders, rapines and inhumanity."

The gentry became especially skittish about "tumultuous meetings." In fact, North Carolina's 1669 Constitution had banned whites from attending

"Assemblies, upon what pretence soever of Religion" that did not conform to Anglican ritual. Already suspicious of impious and/or revolutionary assemblies of whites, legislators readily prohibited black gatherings. These assemblies were apparently perceived as politically subversive although, for blacks, these meetings served religious and social functions complete with meals, singing, conversation in African dialects, and "tumultuous" music from banjos, fiddles, flutes, horns, and drums.[48] Members of the clergy took particular offense at these sensuous parties, and accounts of slaves' public dancing and singing proliferated across the South during the nineteenth century.[49]

Virginia legislation illustrated in 1680 that these "frequent meetings of considerable numbers of negroe slaves under pretence of feasts and burials" were perceived as "dangerous" without specific instances of harm, and merited "prevention" rather than remedy.[50] Yet slave conspiracies were reported in 1687, 1694, and 1703 without further legislation.[51] Then in 1710, a verified plot by slaves in three Virginia counties prompted the government to take suitable measures. According to Governor Spotswood, "freedom Wears a Cap which Can Without a Tongue, Call Together all Those Who Long to Shake off the fetters of Slavery." In his opinion, even legally mute slaves could rally their fellows to revolt. Such a revolt, he considered, "would surely be attended with Most Dreadfull Consequences" and so the legislature must be active in "providing Against it."[52] The governor's dire prediction took root in many minds so that, by 1766, Robert Munford listed as a defining feature of his runaway slave, Jack, his "promoting the late disorderly meetings among the Negroes."[53] Ten years later, confirming the gentry's worst fears, John Greenhow advertised that the runaway slave Emanuel had "laid violent hands" on his master.[54]

Seventeenth-century legislative speculation was confirmed by eighteenth-century events in Virginia and, as always, the legislative watchword was prevention. Notwithstanding more notable uprisings, the experience of Charles Crenshaw illustrates an everyday concern of the gentry. Slaves in Hanover, Virginia, had secretly organized a "negro frolic" at Christmastime, 1811. Feasting was the order of the day, but Crenshaw led two companies of patrollers to break up what he determined was an "unlawful" activity. During an 8 p.m. raid, the patrollers captured sixty black revelers—immediately releasing all women and children, and sitting up all night with the male prisoners, because nothing could be done with them until the following day. In the meantime, Crenshaw persuaded a captured woman to reveal the hiding place of the victuals that would have been served at the party. He reported in a public broadside that she impudently declared that, first, a slight delay in the raid would have forced the patrollers to confront twice as many revelers and, second, "she would have had as elegant a supper set out as Charles Crenshaw ever saw." White perception of danger in this gathering was intensified by the female captive's haughty speech.[55]

Even when relevant legislation was enacted, some of the gentry feared to anger their slaves by enforcing the laws strictly—as was the case in South Carolina. The number and conduct of slaves in South Carolina scarcely justified the harsh police code of 1696 that was based on Barbadian experience. But the unwillingness or inability of the gentry to use their police power over slaves, coupled with attractive offers of freedom to runaway slaves by the Spanish governor of Florida, may have motivated the Stono revolt of 1739.[56] South Carolina legislators rectified their past mistakes in 1740 with a new slave code.[57] Once again, practical experience of servile insurrection appeared to validate whites' prior forebodings.

In the same year, Maryland's governor issued a proclamation of "several Laws . . . to prevent the Tumultuous meetings of Slaves." However, unlike earlier legislators' apparent speculation, his Excellency Samuel Ogle cited the "Depositions of several Negroes in Prince Georges County relating to a most wicked and dangerous Conspiracy having been formed by them to destroy his Majestys Subjects."[58] Shortly afterwards, as soon as slavery was permitted in Georgia, legislative restrictions on slave meetings were enacted as "absolutely necessary to the Safety of this Province." Lawmakers acknowledged the frightening effect on whites whether slaves brandished "Wooden Swords and other Mischievous and dangerous Weapons" or merely "Drums Horns or other Loud Instruments" at their gatherings. Moreover, masters and overseers should be fined if they allowed "any Public meeting or feastings of Strange Negroes or Slaves in their plantations."[59] By 1755, then, instruments for making tumultuous noise were as fearsome to Georgia's gentry as weapons, and slave gatherings were suspected of harboring outside agitators. After the Stono revolt, conspiracy was everywhere.

As the evidence of actual revolts mounted in succeeding decades, legislators began to integrate relevant statutes into their codes. Tumultuous meetings gradually became proscribed as riots, unlawful assemblies, and other terrifying acts. Seditious speech by slaves was also outlawed, but this proscription should be studied within the broader frame of the gentry's disfavor for anti-establishment messages after the Revolutionary War.

Virginia's 1785 prohibition of "riots, routs, unlawful assemblies, trespass and seditious speeches" by blacks eventually took root across much of the South.[60] Verbatim legislation in a 1798 chapter of its slave code would be expected in a client territory such as Kentucky,[61] but the same prohibition—excepting the offense of "trespass"—appeared in the 1804 slave codes of Louisiana and Missouri.[62] In 1805 and 1806 respectively, Alabama and Tennessee enacted sections in their slave codes that included "trespasses" among the prohibited conduct, although Alabama legislators made a separate provision for slaves who might "conspire to rebel."[63] Florida's territorial assembly enacted its statute by 1828.[64] Virginia retained this type of prohibition in its criminal code until the question of slavery was resolved by war.[65]

Not relegated merely to a slave code, this Virginia legislation also merits notice for its explicit attention to slave speech. In the other jurisdictions, elements of slave codes that prohibited fearsome slave gatherings also were durable.[66]

The legislative attention to slave speech is noteworthy although, except in Virginia, insolence was not classified among criminal offenses. Legislators verbally transformed weekend and holiday parties of slaves into riots, and finally to insurrections—with sedition as the common base of motivation. Growing fear of insurrection throughout the South elicited extremes of vigilance, making less than remarkable an 1835 event in Livingston, Mississippi. A "vigilance committee" lynched five whites as well as a dozen blacks upon report of an insurrection plot. One surviving white charged with conspiracy was not only a justice of the peace but also the cousin of William L. Sharkey, later chief justice of the state's supreme court. The future jurist managed to save his cousin from hanging but never questioned the authority of the vigilance committee.[67]

On the other hand, fear of slave insurrection did not unduly trouble all Southrons. There is evidence that apprehension of white violence—such as Bacon's rebellion—was more compelling in the eighteenth century.[68] In the mid-nineteenth century, even moderate abolitionists ridiculed the fear of black revolution among the Southern gentry. "Every two or three years," Richard Hildreth critically observed, "the report of an insurrection, real or imagined, spreads the most frantic terror through the southern states." It was not necessary that these reports include sightings of armed slaves: "Half-a-dozen unintelligible words overheard and treasured up by some evesdropping overseer" were sufficient. Complete fabrications of seditious speech "by some miscreant" were also effective at inducing "public alarm . . . commotion, and . . . agony and sleeplessness to hundreds of thousands."[69] Hildreth's criticism stressed hysterical reports rather than actual events, active imaginations rather than measured deliberations, and scurrilous if not malicious motives.[70] However, as an outsider and obvious critic of the peculiar institution, his credibility suffered.

More credible and more intriguing was Justice O'Neall's roughly contemporaneous argument in *Ex Parte Boylston* dismissing slave insolence as a prelude to revolt: "Has insolence of language any thing to do with raising or attempting to raise an insurrection? Some of the most faithful and devoted slaves have been remarkable for their liberty of speech. Indeed, insolence is but another term for sauciness, and who has ever dreamed that an open-mouthed, saucy negro, is the deep intriguer calculated to raise, or attempt to raise, an insurrection?"[71] In effect, O'Neall argued that the gentry should not be permitted legally to embrace both the presumption of subordination and the fear of insurrection. True belief in white supremacy should leave no room for fear of a servile revolt; either slaves were brutish and submissive property or they were cunning and fearsome enemies. Unlike outsiders and abolitionists, this native son enjoyed a credibility drawn from his slaveholding and distinguished legal career in South Carolina: he inherited "Springfield" plantation from his grandmother in 1820, "adding to it many adjoining farms," and in 1848 he authored *The Negro Law of South Carolina*.[72] But O'Neall's heavy reliance on formal devices such as rhetorical questions, and his unspecified references to exceptional slaves, rendered his argument in *Ex Parte Boylston* more piquant than persuasive. His dissent remained merely colorful, and the South Carolina gentry remained legally entitled to their fear as well as their presumption.

The gentry expressed their presumption and fear about slave insubordination in ways that invigorated this conceptual merger. Its long lifespan is illustrated in *Gordon v. Hines*. Hines was a judge of the Police Court in Warren County, Kentucky, and in 1858 he ordered ten lashes for several slaves—unless their owners paid fines and court costs—for "disorderly conduct by blowing horns and beating tin pans."[73] Disapproval and fear of tumultuous meetings died hard. More striking yet is evidence that white concern about noisy slaves outlived the war between North and South. As illustrated in the 1866 case of *State v. Broadnax*, William Duncan had beaten Thomas, a slave, for continuing to "dance and sing" along with "his sister . . . and some small children" after having been ordered to stop. Thomas struck back and his conviction for "felonious slaying and killing" of his former overseer was affirmed on appeal. As a slave at the time of the beating, Thomas was not legally entitled to behave so violently "in defence of his own life" much less in defending his noisy playtime.[74]

As war approached, "complex and contradictory" portraits of slave character illuminated the legal merger of presumption and fear among whites. The docile "Sambo" and the rebellious "Nat" represented extreme stereotypes: the comforting image of Sambo appeared most often in Southern literature because invoking the specter of Nat would have further alarmed an already vigilant readership. Sambo's image also presented a convenient means of refuting Northern abolitionists. Just as significantly, Sambo was the type of slave whom the gentry would prefer to find on every plantation, if they could not have a more dependable, hard-working type. The problem for legislative analysis, just as it has represented "the horns of a dilemma" for literary and historical analysis,[75] has been choosing one of the images as paradigmatic. Yet the two images of Sambo and Nat variously may have sustained judicial reasoning,[76] and their interchange may also illuminate what the legislative regulation of slave insolence meant for the gentry. Most likely, legislators sensed that Sambo was becoming Nat.

Legislative Developments

The gentry presumed black subordination and feared servile revolt. Their solidarity, though never perfect, prompted legislation on slave insolence that reflected similar imperfection. Plantation justice was not supplanted as the typical venue for dealing with cases of "saucy behavior,"[77] but this level of jurisprudence needed statutory authorization as much as any other. Indeed, "the law of slavery in general was largely statute law."[78] These statutes reveal that the gentry saw explicit threats as well as intolerable insults in slave insolence, but they also embraced alternative legislation as a means of authorizing their discipline of insubordinate slaves.

Explicit Threats

Early legislation addressed implied threats by slaves. The 1680 Virginia "act for preventing Negroes Insurrections" prescribed twenty lashes for any slave attending the fearsome meetings "under pretence of feasts and burialls" without written permission "from his master, mistris or overseer." These slaves were to be sent to "the next constable" for immediate execution of sentence, without any statutory requirement of investigation and hearing. At common law, the facts might speak for themselves. In statutory context, the legal process and sanctions were identical for slaves who were found carrying "any club, staffe, gunn; sword or any other weapon of defence or offence." Also included within this act was the enhanced sentence of thirty lashes for any slave who might "presume to lift up his hand in opposition against any christian." However, for this offense, "due proofe" was required in the form of an "oath of the party before a magistrate."[79]

Virginia's 1680 legislation illustrates the merger of presumption and fear by sanctioning the counter presumption of a slave "to lift up his hand," and by textually linking insurrections, slave meetings, and threats. Logically enough, sanctions were lighter for the implied threat of slaves' wandering about or arming themselves than for the explicit threat of shaking their fists in the face of a christian. Furthermore, because explicit threats might easily be more private and fleeting than implicit threats, a more substantial legal process was required for disposing of the case.

The Virginia legislation satisfied felt needs. It was reenacted in 1705, retaining the same legal process and sanction but expanding the class of offenders to include "mulatto, or Indian, bond or free" and excluding these persons from the class of victims.[80] This same statute migrated to the Kentucky code in 1798.[81] More precisely than when they had identified only slaves as the subjects of regulation, legislators had begun to locate the source of fearsome conduct and they more emphatically measured the racial distance between victims and perpetrators. Virginia's legislative treatment of the explicit threat remained identical in 1748, although conditions warranted a relaxation of the ban on implicit threats: "all negroes, mulattoes, and Indians, bond or free" were permitted to keep and bear arms "at any frontier plantation" if a license was obtained from the local justice of the peace.[82] Since the time of Bacon's rebellion, the gentry needed protection in their westward expansion. Rather than expanding the scope of slaves' prerogatives, the 1748 legislation affirmed a means of protection that the gentry had long been demanding.

The gentry wanted protection, not threatening gestures from their slaves. Thus the ban on lifting hands was reenacted in 1819, excluding Indians from the class of offenders and providing a "defence" if the "negro or mulatto was wantonly assaulted."[83] By contemporaneous standards, the conditional defense appears generous. Retreat or absolute submission, as a matter of law, could not be interpreted by a drunken or crazed white as threatening. But whether lifting a hand against white attackers was a purely defensive act could complicate even the rudimentary legal process afforded blacks. Of course, their legal incapacity to testify against white attackers kept the process simple enough to modify the apparent liberality of the 1819 conditional defense. Reformed to read "menacing gestures" and provide a maximum sentence of "thirty-nine" lashes, the statute continued in effect through the antebellum period.[84]

The Deep South followed Virginia's legislative initiatives but several variations in classifying potential offenders, in requiring legal process, in levying sentences, and in recognizing claims of self-defense illustrate key issues for the white electorate. Who were the sources of threats? Which level of jurisprudence should be required in dealing with these offenders? How grave was the problem? Were any exculpatory conditions feasible or desirable?

The legislative identification of potential offenders varied widely. Early nineteenth-century statutes in Arkansas, Louisiana, and Alabama are exemplary: Indians were excluded from the expansive roster of negro and mulatto offenders, "bound or free," in the 1804 Arkansas territorial code;[85] Indians were also excluded in the 1804 District of Louisiana code;[86] the 1806 Alabama code applied only to slaves.[87] However, Alabama legislators repealed this section of the state code in 1814. As the frontier was moved further west and native Americans became more thoroughly pacified or exterminated, the exclusion of Indians from the ranks of likely offenders is understandable. Restricting offenders only to slaves in Alabama makes sense in light of that region's aversion to continuing residence by free blacks. However, repealing the statute indicated that the gentry no longer wanted to be burdened with legal process in disciplining their slaves. Louisiana's later restriction of likely offenders to slaves refects the nineteenth-century growth of the peculiar institution as well as the distinctive tradition of race relations in that jurisdiction. The 1807 territorial code was amended to apply only when "an overseer or other white person, representing the owner of a plantation, is threatened . . . by any slave of the said plantation." This amended language survived in virtually the same form throughout the antebellum era.[88]

Later legislation in Mississippi, Florida, and Texas articulates an equal measure of variety in identifying the perceived sources of threats. In 1822, "any negro or mulatto, bond or free" was subject to legal action for lifting a hand against a white in Mississippi; by the late 1850s, only "slaves" could be held guilty of this threatening behavior.[89] The Florida territorial code of 1828 identified negroes and mulattoes.[90] Although the 1837 code of the Republic of Texas identified "any slave or free person of colour" as a potential offender, by 1853 only a "negro" could be a culprit.[91] These statutes illustrate no consistent pattern of expanding the classification as warfare approached, or restricting it. Unlike other jurisdictions in the Deep South, the tendency of lawmakers in Mississippi, Florida, and Texas to equate persons of color with slaves is the most parsimonious explanation for the varied identification of offenders. The gentry had determined that race made a fundamental difference in their lives, forcing them to draft legislation on the type and scope of "color" in their world. They now faced the task of racially defining the unacceptable sources of threats. Simply put, the general complexity of drafting laws based on racial hierarchy complicated the specific drafting of threat regulations.

Every jurisdiction in the Deep South required at least some level of legal process before slaves could be punished for their threatening behavior. Like Virginia and Kentucky, a hearing before a justice of the peace was mandated continuously in Arkansas, Alabama, Florida, and Texas. The requirement in Louisiana's codes shifted as the form of government changed, from "any justice of the peace of the district where such offense shall be committed" (1804), through "the judge and inhabitants, who are by law charged with the punishment of crimes committed by slaves" (1807), to the appropriate "tribunal" (1852) or "court" (1860). A similar shift occurred in Mississippi statutes, from "justice of the peace" (1822) to "the court trying the offender" (1857). Clearly, then, plantation justice was preempted in favor of more formal proceedings in all jurisdictions that legislatively addressed threatening behavior by slaves—or, more expansively, by persons of color. The gentry were hard pressed over the years to draft any law that clearly and consistently articulated a racial hierarchy; by always requiring conspicuous legal process, they were more successful in expressing their shared feeling that slave threats were significant.

Statutory sentences match the requirements of legal process in revealing the perceived gravity of slave threats. Virginia set an early norm by providing for sentences of "thirty lashes" (1680 and thereafter) as did Kentucky (1798). Then, more solicitously, Virginia lawmakers defined thirty as the maximum number of stripes (1819), and finally they left the actual number up to the "discretion of the court or justice by whom the offence is tried, so as not to exceed thirty-nine at one time" (1849 and thereafter). The statutory language indicates that, after major slave insurrections in the East during the 1820s and 1830s, being solicitous in punishment was out of favor. An unlimited number of sessions, during which thirty-nine lashes could be administered, was a considerable enhancement of the one session including an absolute maximum of thirty lashes.

Once again, however, variations across the Deep South are noteworthy. While the 1806 Alabama code permitted a maximum of twenty lashes, the 1804 Arkansas code permitted thirty. As a federal district, Louisiana sentenced offenders to a maximum of thirty lashes but, as a territory and state, made the sentence discretionary for whatever tribunal had jurisdiction. The sentences in these three jurisdictions were distinct from the maximum of thirty-nine lashes approved in Florida (1828). Mississippi also sentenced offenders to thirty-nine lashes in its 1822 code, but later made the number discretionary. Texas stood alone by initially permitting between twenty-five and one hundred lashes in 1837 and then reducing the maximum number to thirty-nine by 1853. Although these statutory sentences varied remarkably, they consistently underscored whites' agreement that slaves must suffer—perhaps enduring permanent disability or death—for explicitly threatening their putative racial superiors. Combined with the uniform requirement of legal process, statutory sentences emphasized the perceived gravity of these threats.

A serious problem, the gravity of slave threats was not widely or easily modified by claims of self-defense. As noted above, Virginia permitted this defense by the early nineteenth century in tandem with the appearance of statutes regulating slave abuse by whites. The Territory of Arkansas, the District of Louisiana, and the Territory of Florida contemporaneously recognized this defense. The language in these statutes, based on Virginia legislation, allowed an exception "in those cases, where it shall appear to such justice, that such negro or mulatto was wantonly assaulted, and lifted his or her hand in his or her defence."[92] Available to offenders but strictly limited, claims of self-defense could be raised only when a white attacker had committed the statutory crime of assault, aggravated by wanton disregard for the slave's life. Mississippi used the same language in 1822, but by 1857 had modified the legislation to emphasize limits on the defense: the slave might lift his hand "in self defence if wantonly assaulted, and then only so far as may be necesary to defend himself."[93] Simple but effective, the device of repetition was inserted to stress that a slave's "self defence" meant only those few actions "necesary to defend himself."

Despite the trend in other jurisdictions, Alabama legislators did not provide for self-defense—instead limiting punishment to twenty lashes.[94] The Republic of Texas was even less solicitous: the claim of self-defense was not recognized and offenders were liable to "stripes not exceeding one hundred nor less than twenty-five." Later state law also did not provide for the defense.[95] Not available everywhere in the Deep South, the claim of self-defense offered scant relief to offenders when it was recognized by law. Mississippi legislators, with their rhetorical flourish of repetition, may have provided the best clue to understanding a fundamental concern they shared with colleagues across the South: explicit threats by slaves in the form of raised fists—much less riots and sedition—seriously violated the presumption of black subordination and heightened the gentry's fear of servile revolt. Identifying prime offenders by racial characteristics was unavoidably complicated. Much simpler was the drafting of standard provisions for legal process and harsh sentences that together underscored the gravity of the offense.

Intolerable Speech

Human dynamics resist scientific explanation. For example, the human perception of a division between words and deeds has never been explained with necessary or sufficient accuracy. Southrons did not routinely grapple with this problem as much as they worried about agriculture and engineering, but the dynamics of their presumption and fear prompted them to fashion slavery laws about intolerable speech as well as explicit threats. In fact, statutes that addressed slaves' rioting or lifting of their hands against whites often regulated slave insolence as well.

In 1747 the Maryland Assembly authorized constables in Anne-Arundel and Talbot counties to administer up to thirty-nine lashes if "Negroes and other Slaves . . . behave impudently" when ordered to disperse from tumultuous meetings.[96] This mid–eighteenth-century version of a statute regulating slave insolence illustrates that the gentry were seeking institutional solutions to a problem they had recognized even earlier. For example, Mary Mulloy—most likely an indentured servant—had been formally tried in 1686 and sentenced to twenty lashes for uttering "lying and scandelous words" about one of the gentry.[97] However, as the peculiar institution of slavery developed, common-law prosecutions of slaves could not be justified as readily as those of indentured servants.

Eventually legislators had to enact more legally sustainable measures. The earliest statute of this type apparently was an 1806 Tennessee regulation of "free negroes, mulattoes, and slaves." This law linked "insulting or provoking language" by slaves with "riots, routs, unlawful assemblies, trespasses and seditious speeches," and authorized any number of "stripes at the discretion of a justice of the peace, and he or they who will, may apprehend and carry [the slaves] before such justice."[98] Legal process was minimal. For example, in 1841 the Davidson County First Circuit Court affirmed the "exclusive jurisdiction" of a simple magistrate for such offenses. In this case, the slave Charles was tried for "throwing rocks at Robert Bradfate and giving him ill language."[99] Nonetheless, Tennessee lawmakers ruled out plantation justice and authorized potentially severe whippings for an offense grave enough to rank with riot and sedition. This statute survived into the 1850s because it secured local and immediate satisfaction for the gentry while preserving at least some formality in the process. By 1858, a justice of the peace alone was authorized to pass sentence on insulting or provoking offenders.[100]

The 1819 Virginia statute that addressed Negroes and mulattoes, whether enslaved or not, who lifted their hands against whites also proscribed "at any time" their use of "abusive and provoking language."[101] This link with explicit threats fell short of equating insolence with riot and sedition, but the law addressed a longstanding need in Virginia. Almost a century earlier, a slave had been tried for precisely this combination of offenses. Two whites complained in 1729 that "a negro man named Cook . . . had threatened to burn" one of their houses, as well as cause other injuries. As further aggravation, Cook had "an impudent & churlish manner."[102] In 1745 "Tom a Negro man Slave" received twenty-five lashes for his "threatening language" to James Gordon.[103] Virginia legislators reformed their approach late in the antebellum period: they identified slaves alone as potential offenders, defined the offense as "provoking language or menacing gestures," linked this offense with riot, sedition and several other misdeeds such as carrying weapons and administering medicine, and raised the maximum allowable punishment to thirty-nine stripes.[104]

Elsewhere in the Upper South, North Carolina's 1836 revised code may have generally allowed for the prosecution of insolent slaves,[105] but a specifically relevant statute was not enacted until 1854. By this law, slaves were liable to receive up to "thirty-nine lashes" for being "insolent to a free white person" or uttering "mischievous and slanderous reports about any free white person."[106] Thirty-four years prior to this legislation, however, the state's supreme court had held that slave insolence was legally significant for whites. In *State v. Tackett*, the appellant had been sentenced to death for murdering Daniel, a slave. Tackett had been intimate with Daniel's wife, Lotty, and the slave had repeatedly been belligerent and threatening, once telling a witness that "if [Tackett] did not let his wife alone he would kill him," and another time stating "that the devil had been to pay" for Tackett's behavior. Furthermore, Daniel and Tackett had occasionally scuffled in public. Ordering a new trial, John Louis Taylor held that the trial court had erred in refusing to hear testimony that Daniel "was a turbulent man, and that he was insolent and impudent to white people." Evidence of Daniel's general reputation for "turbulence and insolence," even if not directed at Tackett individually, would have increased "the probability that [Tackett] had acted under a strong and legal provocation."[107] At the time, Daniel could not legally have been whipped for his insolence. Nonetheless, according to Chief Justice Taylor, Daniel's choice of words offered a meritorious defense to his alleged murderer.

Missouri enacted relevant legislation by 1845,[108] and although Kentucky had no related statute, insolent speech by slaves at least indirectly contributed to an actionable offense. In *Williams v. Greenwade*, Williams was ordered at trial to pay $100 in damages "for falsely and maliciously uttering and publishing the following words;—'negro Jude said that Mrs. Greenwade was a drunken whore, and it is rumored every where.'" The verdict was reversed on appeal because of an erroneous evidentiary ruling by the trial judge. Although his opinion benefitted Williams, Chief Justice Robertson was not especially pleased with the results "Such a social organization as ours," he volunteered, "will not . . . permit a white person to justify the injurious repetition of a negro's slander."[109]

Early efforts to curb intolerable speech by slaves in Tennessee and Virginia, variously influential in the Upper South, set a model for related legislation across the Deep South. By 1822 Mississippi had its own statute linking "abusive and provoking language," either by free or enslaved blacks, with the explicit threat of lifting a hand to whites.[110] As sectionalism grew more intense, Mississippi lawmakers addressed slaves alone as potential offenders, defined their offense more expansively as "abusive, provoking or insulting language," and linked it with both explicit threats and riot.[111] In Florida, "abusive and provoking language" by Negroes and mulattoes was linked to explicit threats.[112] When Georgia finally enacted similar legislation, lawmakers proscribed "insolent or improper language to a white person" in the same section of a slave code that addressed "indecent or disorderly conduct in the presence and to the annoyance of free white persons."[113]

Elsewhere in the Deep South, several idiosyncrasies within this body of law warrant further attention. Early burdens of proof upon white complainants were relaxed or entirely removed, and the scope of potential offenders was expanded. In another jurisdiction, whites were authorized to administer punishment without any legal process. Equally striking was the substantial line of prosecutions in yet another jurisdiction despite the lack of clear statutory authority.

Historical case law in Louisiana illustrates the gentry's felt need for a proscription of slave insolence. In the 1743 case *Re Jeannot*, a slave "was suspected of murder and accused of abuse of his master." Included in the slave's alleged misdeeds was a threat to set fire to his master's cabin "on the left bank of the river, below New Orleans."[114] In *Lemoine v. Raphael*, Charles Lemoine sought legal satisfaction in 1745 when "a negro named Raphael and his wife Fanchon . . . attacked him and insulted him without cause." Indeed, Lemoine complained that he had been "followed and pelted" by the couple's children.[115] The complainant's need to plead that he was bothered "without cause" is significant. Lemoine had to deny the causes historically available to free blacks in Louisiana for justifying their words and deeds. The divide between slave and free was wide enough to make a difference in actions for insolence and threat.

Two years later, this difference was vividly illustrated in *Re Larue*. Although the testimony was conflicting on some points, it appears that Larue (or La Rue), "a free mulatto," argued and fought with three soldiers on sick leave in New Orleans. One of the soldiers initially taunted a demonstrably drunk Larue with the salute, "Goodnight, Little Lord Negro," to which he responded "Goodnight, Little Lord Jack Fool." Next, one or more of the soldiers reproached

Larue for insulting them without having been insulted himself. Larue did not stop speaking to them in an abusive and threatening manner, despite having been slapped and warned to go away. The three soldiers asked for help from a passerby, who arranged for a corporal of the garrison to lead Larue off to prison. He obeyed "without any resistance" until he asked permission to change his clothes. The corporal refused and Larue fired one of his concealed pistols, injuring himself and his captor.[116] Again in this case, the complainants had to testify that Larue lacked cause for insulting them. Even then their testimony might not have been compelling if Larue had not shot the corporal.

In any event, an 1816 digest of Louisiana law implies that, because free blacks were under close scrutiny, slaves certainly had to control their speech rigidly. "Free people of colour," the digest recites, "ought never to insult or strike white people, nor presume to conceive themselves equal to the whites." Moreover, free blacks should "yield to them on every occasion, and never speak or answer them but with respect, under the penalty of imprisonment."[117] By 1842, plantation slaves explicitly were liable if their overseers and other whites acting as agents of planters were "insulted," explicitly threatened, or assaulted.[118] By the 1850s, Louisiana's black code clearly set out the restrictions on unacceptable speech by all people of color. The section dealing with slaves' insults to overseers remained intact and both "slave" and "free person of color" was liable for an "insult or assault" of "any white person."[119]

A noteworthy Texas penal code also made slaves liable for their speech. The link between threatening conduct and "insulting or abusive language" to whites by "any slave or free person of colour" in 1837 Texas legislation was later expanded to include the standard proscription of riot and seditious speeches.[120] Furthermore, 1859 legislation authorized immediate sanctions without recourse to legal process. The penal code authorized "a free white person . . . whether such person has lawful control over the slave or not" to chastise a slave for "insulting language or gestures" as long as the chastisement was "reasonable." A separate section in another title of the penal code clarified the standard of reasonableness in chastising slaves. A "white man" was authorized to inflict "moderate chastisement, with an ordinary instrument of correction" for slave "insolence" as long as the correction was administered "at the time when the insolent language" was used or "within a reasonable time after." Outlawed was "excessive battery, as with a dangerous weapon." Moreover, in yet another section, Texas legislators listed several offenses that merited chastisement and defined the ordinary instrument of correction as "moderate whipping." The offenses included "improper language," "indecent or turbulent conduct," "insulting language or gestures," and drunken disturbances.[121]

Identifying all free whites in Texas as potential complainants was consistent with many other Southern codes, but authorizing on-the-spot sanctions was unique among jurisdictions that enacted regulations of slave insolence. More typically phrased in negative terms, this type of statute defined the conditions under which irate or financially injured owners could not initiate prosecutions or civil suits for the battery of their slaves. Only the first of the related sections cited above fell into this category; it belongs to part of a chapter in the Texas penal code that addressed "Cruel Treatment of Slaves." But the other two sections—progressively more specific in defining slave misconduct and lawful degrees of chastisement—affirmatively create a power instead of negatively proscribing battery on slaves. From a legislative viewpoint, these sections made the empowerment of whites a matter of state policy.

Power of another sort flowed to whites in South Carolina, despite uncertain authority. Justice O'Neall declared, in his *Ex Parte Boylston* dissent, that "the Legislature have not thought proper to declare [slave insolence] to be a crime." In fact, he claimed that as of 1847 he was "wholly ignorant" of prosecuting slaves for "insolence" in the magistrate and freeholders' courts, despite his being "tolerably familiar with the administration of justice in this State, for the last 33 years."[122] Whether he was accurate in his declaration and disclaimer remains moot.

In terms of legislation O'Neall was correct—if a longlived regulation of slaves' apparel is discounted. Slaveowners, according to this century-old statute, could not provide garments to their chattel that were "finer, or of greater value, than negro cloth, duffils, kerseys, oznaburgs, blue linen, check linen, or coarse garlix, or calicoes, checked cottons, or Scots plaids." Only the typically gaudy uniforms of "liverymen and boys" were protected from forfeiture to the "constables and other persons" charged with policing slaves' wardrobes.[123] This statute has been analyzed for its role in illustrating the "public dimension" of slave law in South Carolina:[124] the white public had become incensed at slaves' display of fashionable clothing on Sundays and holidays—garments that expressed self-respect and thus spoke insolently to the gentry. However, the legislation regulated only nonverbal communication outside a statutory context of explicit threat and riot.

South Carolinians had seriously considered enacting early proscriptions against slave insolence, but the measures fell short of passage. In 1737, the Assembly did not endorse granting patrols the right "to kill any resisting or saucy slave"; in 1741, the Assembly did not pass a bill for the imprisonment and "corporal Punishment" of any slave who behaved in an "insolent abusive Manner" on market day.[125]

Prior case law more clearly sustained Justice O'Neall's declaration about a lack of statutory authority. In *White v. Chambers*, a 1796 case cited in *Ex Parte Boylston*, the court held that "in all cases where a slave behaved amiss, or with rudeness or incivility to a free white man," the complainant should first seek redress from the slave's owner or an authorized agent of the owner, turning to legal process only if not satisfied. In this instance, a slave had dutifully refused to allow a white the use of his master's canoe, "some high words passed between them on both sides," and the slave was beaten severely. Despite counsel's argument that "unless this speedy and summary mode of redress was allowed, this class of people could never be kept in order and due subordination," the trial judge and the high court agreed that self-help in the form of slave beating was not justified under "the principles of the law."[126] Justice O'Neall accurately pointed out that this early case confirmed a lack of statutory authority for prosecuting slave insolence. However, the majority in *Ex Parte Boylston* argued "that if express legislative authority cannot be found for it, this is only because the usage has never been questioned."

O'Neall could not rely for authority on a trial judge's instructions to jurors. Otherwise, he might have cited Judge Colcock's charge to the jury in *State v. Porter*. A magistrate and freeholders court had convicted Amy Lapier, a free black, for "slandering and insulting" a white woman. The issue at trial was whether the magistrate was liable for not forwarding to proper authorities the ten-dollar fine paid by Lapier. Judge Colcock charged the jury in Charleston that "no words, however abusive, used by a person of color, whether free, or a slave, would amount to an offence, punishable, by indictment." Therefore, since the proceeding itself lacked authority, the magistrate could be found guilty of extortion. The jury agreed, returning a guilty verdict. On appeal, counsel for the magistrate used the sweeping but customary argument that black insolence harmed "the root of the peace and security of society"; the attorney general rebutted technically that the 1740 "negro act" and its progeny did not authorize prosecutions for insolence. Although the appellate court granted a new trial, at least some of appellate justices "were of the opinion the [magistrate and freeholders] court which tried the woman of color, acted very properly."[127] Unfortunately for Justice O'Neall, several appellate judges in *State v. Porter* laid the groundwork for the majority opinion in *Ex Parte Boylston*.

Notwithstanding O'Neall's disclaimer, much less a lack of statutory authority, slaves were occasionally prosecuted for intolerable speech. Arguably mistaken for the "negro, mulatto, or slave" covered by the 1740 act, Thomas Gray protested that he was a "free Indian." But his protest did not forestall his 1824 trial for "insolence" in *Gray v. Court of Magistrates and Freeholders*.[128] In 1846, a magistrate and freeholders' court convicted the slave, Tom, of "rude and insolent behavior" upon hearing evidence that he had exposed himself to Mary Manus and offered her a dollar for sex. The gentry's well documented distaste for sexual advances by blacks to white women may have been mitigated in *State v. Tom:* Mary Manus had lower class status, and Tom received only twenty-five lashes.[129] Moreover, in *State v. Harden*, Justice O'Neall had volunteered his opinion "that words of impertinence, or insolence, addressed by a free negro, to a white man, would justify an assault and battery."[130] As sufficient exculpatory evidence in whites' trials for assault and battery, why would not slave insolence merit formal sanctions? Each of the initial two cases can be distinguished because slave insolence is not precisely the issue at bar, and Justice O'Neall articulated in the final case a technically unrelated opinion, but their combined tenor suggests a legal climate in which blacks were formally at risk for their sauciness.

After the ruling in *Ex Parte Boylston*, whether it was noticed or not, lower courts in South Carolina clearly took jurisdiction over prosecutions for slave insolence. For example, Anthony was tried for his "gross insult" to Turner Turket while doing roadwork; the slave received a hundred lashes after his owner gave no "satisfaction" to Turket. The slave John also received a hundred lashes for ignoring repeated warnings against trespassing on Francis McKleduff's yard and for declaring "he would be god damd if he did not go where he pleased"—as well for his part in the ensuing brawl with McKleduff. For "improper or unbecoming language" to a patrol, in which he asserted "his Equality with any man" because "all men was made of flesh and Blood," Solomon (or Sole) received two hundred lashes.[131] Of course it also was actionable for a slave to utter "improper language" about a white person in wartime.[132] In all of these post-*Boylston* cases, the magistrate and freeholders' courts indicated little reluctance to prosecute slaves for their language. By custom rather than legislation, the "due subordination" of slaves and the "security of society" prevailed as justifications for the regulation of intolerable speech.

Most Southern states eventually legislated against slave insolence. The dual forces of presumption and fear dominated these jurisdictions, and the regulation of intolerable speech seemed to fit comfortably among statutory proscriptions of explicit threats. Indeed, Texas authorized the direct sanction of slave insolence without legal process. Rare among the Southern states, South Carolina joined Kentucky in resisting this type of legislation despite a long-lived debate among its judicial officers over the need for a statute that would authorize related prosecutions of slaves. Furthermore, South Carolina had legislated against brazen slave wardrobes since the mid–eighteenth century. But South Carolina, and several other jurisdictions, already could rely on legislation that practically obviated the need for designing formal means of regulating slave insolence.

Sufficient Cause

The Texas statute that authorized whites' immediate chastisement of insolent slaves simply codified longstanding custom across the South. Anecdotal sources need not be consulted for evidence of this customary chastisement; case law in all Southern jurisdictions records the physical punishment meted out to slaves sooner or later by aggrieved whites. When early-nineteenth-century lawmakers crafted statutes that authorized minimal legal process in punishing insolent slaves, they reaffirmed the rule of law without removing a speedy balm for their constituents' fear and anger. Heightened social awareness of the slaves' plight and the abolition lobby made the historical alternative of assenting by silence to slave abuse politically unattractive. But legislators had another alternative: modifying the sections of criminal codes that regulated slave abuse.

An early version of this alternative appeared in a 1788 Virginia statute that repealed a 1723 law insulating masters from criminal liability for killing slaves while punishing them—unless at least one credible witness would testify that the slaves were killed "willfully, maliciously, or designedly."[133] More directly, this alternative had been used in Georgia as soon as slavery was permitted in that colony. Persons who had "beaten Bruised Maimed or Disabled" any "Negro or other Slave" who was lawfully employed in his master's service were liable to fines of several types (or jail "if he she or they shall produce no goods on which the said penalty and Damages may be levied"), unless they had "sufficient Cause or Lawfull Authority" for their actions.[134] In legislative context, this defense to an indictment for slave abuse immediately preceded regulations of the fearsome "Assembly or meeting of Slaves."[135] The language of this 1755 statute and its system of fines implied that slaveowners and their authorized agents were not included among potential offenders. However, casual slave abuse by all other persons was financially risky unless mitigating circumstances could be pleaded. Subsequent legislation clarified the meaning of "sufficient Cause."

The state assembly of Georgia, in an 1817 statute, more precisely defined potential offenders and mitigating factors. Slaveowners were explicitly exempted; any other person could run afoul of the law by "whipping or wounding a slave or . . . beating, whipping, or wounding a free person of colour, without sufficient cause or provocation." Convicted offenders were to be "fined or imprisoned, or both, at the discretion of the court."[136] The meaning of sufficient cause was clarified by adding "provocation" as an equivalent mitigating factor: contemporaneous references in other state codes to "provoking" language by slaves could scarcely be ignored if, for some reason, the trial judge was not easily persuaded that slave speech could provide a sufficient excuse for slave beating. Exempting only a slave's owner and permitting considerable judicial discretion, this statute served the gentry's needs for a generation.

By 1837, a more expansive Georgia statute addressed both state and private interests in restraining slave abuse. The "owner, overseer, or employer of a slave" was exempted from its provisions but everyone else could be indicted for the misdemeanor of slave abuse if they would "beat, whip, or wound such slave; or . . . a free person of color, without sufficient cause or provocation." Upon conviction, the fine and/or imprisonment remained discretionary with the court but, in a revealing addendum, the statute also permitted slaveowners and the legal guardians of free blacks to "recover in a civil suit, damages for the injury."[137] Finally, lawmakers had explicitly acknowledged that unmitigated slave abuse harmed private fortune as well as public welfare.

This meld of public and private interests underscored related legislation in neighboring South Carolina. More significant in the present analysis, this 1822 law may explain why South Carolina never enacted a proscription of slave insolence. The statute authorized compensatory damages as well as a punitive fine of "one dollar and twenty cents"—to be devoted to poor relief—for each offense in which any person "not having sufficient cause, or lawful authority" beat, bruised, maimed, or disabled a slave who was lawfully employed in his master's business or under the lawful charge of another person.[138] These provisions discouraged the unmitigated abuse of slaves as offensive to the public good as well as harmful to private investment in slave property. But when sufficient cause or lawful authority justified the slave beating, no offense existed. Given this legislative context, proscribing slave insolence was superfluous. Whites could rely on immediate self-help when a slave spoke insolently to them. Generations of South Carolina judges had found slave insolence to be sufficient cause for slave beating, making it unlikely that whites would incur criminal jeopardy for their immediate correction of these unruly slaves.

Not surprisingly, two other jurisdictions that lacked statutory proscriptions of slave insolence also recognized complete defenses to indictments for slave abuse. The "Criminal Jurisprudence" title in Arkansas's 1837 code authorized prosecution for whites' assaults on slaves "without considerable provocation."[139] This language matched the qualification in a later criminal code's provision for the prosecution of assault and battery generally.[140] The key term of "provocation" was modified to require a "considerable" mitigation of the offense but, in an era when simple insults between whites could end in a duel, slave insolence would certainly qualify as considerable provocation.

Similarly, in 1839, the Alabama assembly provided for the prosecution of "any person" who "without just cause" committed "an assault or an assault and battery on the body of a slave, such person not being legally appointed patrol, or not being the owner, or overseer, or other agent, of the owner." Convicted offenders were to "suffer the same kind of punishment as if the offence had been committed on the body of a free white person."[141] The operative term "provocation" was missing from this Alabama statute but slave insolence would remain a likely "just cause" for slave beating when conviction meant that offenders would be punished just as severely as if they had assaulted a white.

Drawing conclusions from negative evidence cannot replace relying on positive clues. Nonetheless, the statutory treatments of exculpatory factors in slave abuse are noteworthy because they appear in the laws of three Southern jurisdictions that did not enact proscriptions of slave insolence and in a Georgia code that did not proscribe such insolence until 1861. These statutes required careful crafting and recrafting in order to meet constituents' needs:

slaves had to remain liable to immediate correction for their insolence; several types of persons had to be excluded completely from liability for excessive correction; and, most significant in the present analysis, complete defenses had to be available for white offenders. These defenses, especially "provocation," tracked the language in other jurisdictions' codes that defined an outstanding characteristic of unlawful speech by slaves—that it was "provoking."

The lone exception, an 1813 Tennessee statute that authorized indictments of "any person or persons" who "without sufficient cause" beat or abused someone else's slave,[142] draws critical attention once again to the larger issue. Authorizing the same punishment for offenders "as for a similar offence committed on the body of any white person," Tennessee legislators retained this statute throughout the antebellum period.[143] Yet slave insolence, a notably sufficient cause for slave beating, had also been proscribed in Tennessee since 1806. What did it mean to enact this type of proscription, especially when alternatives such as statutory defenses to slave abuse were also available?

The gentry's presumption of black subordination and collateral fear of servile revolt account generally for the statutory regulation of slave insolence, verbal and nonverbal. These statutes reflected whites' beliefs that the African race was degraded, or should be as a matter of law. Words and gestures contrary to this perceived degradation offended the state, as represented by the constituency of planters. Moreover, fear of slave insurrection heightened the sense that black words and gestures must be scrutinized for their potential contribution to disorder.

Several variations in these laws can be traced to regional and local customs and preferences. The 1859 Texas code, for example, authorized self-help by whites so that they could immediately correct insolent slaves. This authorization—qualified only by what whites themselves would perceive as the reasonable limits of chastisement—indicates merely that legal process was unwieldy and inconvenient in the wide open spaces wrested from Mexico. Differences among other jurisdictions in the statutory identification of potential offenders and the severity of punishments also reflect local needs.

Other regulatory variations remain challenging but tractable. Prominent among these tractable variations is the explicit linking of insolence to threats and riots in several jurisdictions—for example, the early proscription of slave insolence in Tennessee. These links are missing in the codes of states such as Virginia and South Carolina where actual, large-scale, and notorious slave revolts occurred during the eighteenth and nineteenth centuries. Slave unrest increased late in the antebellum period, but major or concerted attacks on the gentry have not been documented in most of the Southern jurisdictions. If abolition-minded observers and selected jurists are to be believed, the absence of firsthand experience was no bar to powerfully worded legislative discourse. Fear and the visions it conjures prompted the building of discursive bridges between insolence and servile revolt.

Tractable also is the lack of proscriptions in several jurisdictions. Lawmakers in Alabama and Arkansas enacted remedies for slaves' explicit threats—for example, lifting their hands to whites—in very early codes. But rather than proscribing the implicit threat of slave insolence, these legislators defined mitigating factors in slave abuse. In effect if not in codification, whites' immediate correction of unruly slaves was authorized; the statutory proscription of slave insolence was superfluous. South Carolina provides the most striking illustration of this process because of related case law. Trial and appellate judges acknowledged the absence of statutory authority for criminal proceedings against insolent slaves, but magistrates nonetheless agreed to preside over these proceedings. Moreover, with rare exceptions, high court judges found justifications for these proceedings in custom or policy.

Yet other regulatory variations raise questions that cannot be answered without reference to the meanings of slave insolence from business, social, and moral perspectives. A cynical critic might wonder whether the continuous adjustment of slave codes reflected more of self-perpetuating bureaucracy than a profound commitment to the peculiar institution. Continuously adjusting statute law to developments in the basic meld of presumption and fear, were lawmakers generally voicing the gentry's antipodean definitions of its perceived power and its real insecurity? Were the legislators specifically addressing Northern as well as homegrown critics of slavery? Or was the regulation of slave insolence aimed at both of these targets? State law notwithstanding, slaves did what their family, friends, or individual nature dictated. As a result, they did not always modify their communication and were subject to beatings or worse. Leaving cynicism aside, critics may ask to what extent statutes reflect legislators' commitment to protecting slaveowners' investments in their human chattel.

2
The Master of Westover

William Byrd II (1674–1744), a Virginia legislator and planter, coped with his presumption and fear regarding slaves in ways that illuminate how slave insolence troubled the early Tidewater establishment. During the period in which "any negro, mulatto, or Indian, bond or free" was prohibited by statute from lifting up his hand against a white, Byrd served in the Council of State and flourished as the master of Westover as well as other plantations along the James River. Moreover, he repeatedly dealt with cases of unruly slaves both as master and judge of the General Court.

Byrd's father sent him to England for formal schooling and the equally important task of courting highly placed patrons. There the teenaged Byrd developed life-long habits of literary composition and scientific observation, as well as political maneuver—all of which he practiced with poignant flaws but remarkable acclaim. His personal library was noteworthy,[1] and his voluminous writings continue to engage scholarly critique. He was called to the bar after residing at the Middle Temple, 1692–1695, and was elected to the Royal Society in 1696. His political career began with his election to the House of Burgesses at the age of eighteen. Upon his father's death in 1704, he returned to Virginia, replacing the elder Byrd as the colony's auditor and receiver of royal revenues. Before his own death he had won the presidency of Virginia's Council of State.

Biographies, large and small, of Byrd are abundant.[2] Tracing various influences on Byrd's life and times, these works do not measure the influence of slave threats and insolence on his legislative and planting careers. Yet unruly slaves and their speech punctuated his politics and his planting.

Thanks to his English patrons, Byrd gained a royal appointment to the Council of State on August 20, 1708 (though he was not formally seated until September 12, 1709).[3] His political platform was simple. Continuously resisting the absolute mandate of the colony's lieutenant-governor and then governor, Alexander Spotswood, he endorsed the gentry's share in legislative power. In this regard he followed his father who had initially supported Bacon's rebellion in 1676. Ingeniously, however, his father had "emerged at the victorious governor's right hand and was soon appointed a member of the royal council."[4] The younger Byrd was more plodding in his politics, remaining at odds with Spotswood until the governor was removed in 1722. This mirror image of his father's political career is relevant here only for Byrd's connection with Bacon's rebellion—an early instance of slave revolt during which the younger Byrd was sent away for his safety. The mature Byrd dealt with slave threats directly as a lawmaker and judge.

Despite the fear of slave violence he shared with his peers, Byrd articulated his equally shared presumption of black subordination by matter-of-factly addressing the need for human chattels in the colony's development. Here too his father's legacy was instrumental. In addition to acquiring land and slaves, the elder Byrd had invested heavily in the business of slave trading—eventually outfitting his own slave ship, the *William and Jane*.[5] Thoroughly capitalizing on his inheritance, Byrd touted the back country for others' development as well as expanding the family's own plantations. Far from civilization, Byrd staked out the areas of Richmond and Petersburg for settlement in the 1730s. By that time he had also increased his inheritance of "above 43000 acres of Land, about 220 Negros, with a vast stock of every kind."[6] Moreover, he bequeathed this estate to his own son, William Byrd III, without emancipating any of the slaves.[7] Administering slave property could be difficult, especially when it talked back, but its monetary worth for Byrd outweighed any sentimental value he might have attached to long and faithful service. This pragmatism was also a central feature in how the legislator viewed the slave.

A Pragmatic Legislator

Byrd's thoughts and actions identify his viewpoint as pragmatic,[8] a perspective inherited from a father who ultimately pledged allegiance to establishment virtues after initially plundering his neighbors during Bacon's rebellion.[9] Byrd's self-conscious recording of commonplaces—a standard rhetorical regimen of cataloguing pithy sayings for future use in composition or speechmaking—identifies his preferences in human behavior. His legislative career largely confirms his translation of principles into practice.

"The great misfortune of giddy & inconstant Persons," he wrote in a commonplace, "is that they act by humour & passion, and seldom by good sence." In contrast, Byrd wanted to be a person whose conduct "is always uniform, always the same." Dominated by the rhetorical scheme of epistrophe, Byrd's commonplace announces his preferred mode of conduct in less than delicate style: "always uniform, always the same."[10] Using simple repetition, he concluded his clauses with hammer blows of practical wisdom. Yet seeking this constancy in his public life, he fell short of perfection. On November 21, 1710, for example, he composed a lampoon of the House of Burgesses for resisting a bill that he had co-authored in Council. Three days later he anonymously deposited these "verses" at the burgesses' meeting hall, creating an uproar that would have led to his official censure if he had been discovered.[11] Like many other rules in the gentry's relationship with slaves, there was a double standard. Byrd indulged in the sauciness that was denied to slaves.

Recording a maxim about public leadership, he observed that a "harebrained Minister of State is by so much more pernicious than a Guide that is blind, or a Pilot that is drunk." Unlike errors committed in the private sector, "the mischief he occasions is more general and extensive."[12] This comparison also asserts the ideal of prudence: a blind guide or a drunken pilot were useless in staking out new plantations or sailing tobacco-laden sloops to market. Analogously, as Byrd would also have observed, a foolish legislator was more generally destructive of the plantation-based economy. Especially harebrained would be legislative tolerance of an unruly work force.

Another of Byrd's commonplaces articulates his suspicion about the contrasting sources of impudence and humility. "Most people," he wrote, "bear adversity with a better grace than they do Prosperity, the last is apt to make them insolent, but the first makes every creature, but a French man, humble."[13] British-French tensions aside, this commonplace reveals a bias toward complacency that locates insolence in those whose every need is being satisfied. Unlike the planters who faced ruin almost yearly from natural disasters or marketplace quirks, plantation slaves enjoyed relative prosperity from Byrd's point of view. Ironically, their confident expectation of being provided with food and shelter tended to make them insolent. The only adversity they faced—the only source of humility—was bondage itself. Thus, planters faced a dilemma born of presumption and fear: being reducing to slavery was presumably a humbling experience for blacks, but being maintained in that condition made them cocky.

More of a moralist than a philosopher, Byrd revealed far less idealism than intolerance in his commonplaces. These maxims were "instruments of identity" for him.[14] Continuously redefining himself over the years, his pragmatism would sometimes surface in unlikely contexts. For example, while narrating his labors during the initial survey of the boundary between Virginia and North Carolina, he opined that the most practical method of "reclaiming . . . from barbarity" the native Americans he encountered along the route was to "intermarry with them."[15] He entertained no similar plan for subduing the savagery of African slaves, preferring to legislate measures for their discipline.

Events in Surry and Isle of Wight counties forced Byrd to enact his commonplace principles soon after he took his seat on the Council. Its records for March 21, 1710, proclaim "a dangerous Conspiracy formed and carryed on by great numbers of Negros, and other Slaves for makeing their Escape by force from the Service of their Masters and for the destroying . . . such of her Majtys Subjects as should oppose their design." Almost one month later, the Council offered a reward of ten pounds for the live capture of Peter, one of the leading conspirators, or five pounds if he was dead. Others, however, had not eluded capture. On April 27 "Salvadore an Indian and Scipio a Negro Slave" were sentenced to be executed and dismembered, with their heads to be displayed as a warning to "other slaves."[16]

Byrd was absent for the conspiracy's proclamation but he did participate in the sessions at which the Council offered a reward for Peter and determined the sentences for Salvadore and Scipio. These early experiences, if his commonplaces can be believed, established benchmarks for constancy and good sense in his deliberations. Just as crucial was the contribution the slave conspiracy made to his thoughts on the source of slave insolence. Of course, he was not the only lawmaker having a difficult time fashioning preventatives for slave threats. By November 27, 1710, the House of Burgesses still could not agree on the provisions within "An Act for the better preventing the Insurrections and Conspiracys of Negros & other Slaves."[17] Related threats to the colonists were too complex to permit a simple remedy.

One year later, on December 5th, Byrd had joined other councillors in drafting another "bill about negroes."[18] But then a more pressing concern arose. The Council reported on December 20th that "John Philips a Christian Slave" had testified that "Treweeks, a Nottoway Indian" had disclosed to him a plot by the Nottoway, Seneca, and Tuscarora tribes against settlers.[19] Byrd made a diary entry about the "negro" who testified about this "conspiracy against the English" because he had learned to take these threats seriously.[20] Early the previous October he had noted that Tuscaroras had killed 120 settlers in North Carolina.[21] Slaves were property but they were clever, resolute property. Their interaction with native Americans—a dialogue that itself was suspiciously impudent—created a threat to the gentry that could not easily be forestalled.

The complex threat posed by slavery also involved whites. Indentured white servants had joined Bacon's rebellion along with slaves and this lesson also was not lost on Byrd. In his later years he warned against settling "a great many Servants together in one Body."[22] Nonetheless, he saw an even greater and more complex threat involving the interaction of white and black workers. According to Byrd, mere contacts with slaves "blow up the pride, & ruin the Industry of our White People, who seeing a rank of poor creatures below them, detest work for fear it shoud make them look like slaves." Moreover, the greater the mass of slaves became, the greater severity had to be adopted in regulating them because "Numbers make them insolent, & then Foul Means must do, what fair will not." Bemoaning the lot of masters, especially "a good natured" one like himself, Byrd complained that planters faced the choice of being "either a Fool or a Fury" in coping with the insolence of their slaves.[23]

Commonplace or not, Byrd's belief in the ill effects of "Prosperity" extended to white workers who enjoyed the benefits of slave labor. They were better off, he felt, when constantly challenged by "Adversity." Slaveowners too were handicapped by their disciplinary duties: normally humane masters could be driven to brutality by the unruly conduct of their bondsmen. And at the root of the problem was slave insolence—aggravated as their numbers increased.

It was doubtlessly painful for him to disclose these feelings because, only a few months earlier, he had bragged to a British acquaintance that "Negros are not so numerous, or so enterprizing to give us any apprehension, or uneasiness."[24] But he only carried public relations for the colony so far.

For William Byrd "the private mischeifs" of slave insolence were a prelude to the "publick danger" of revolt, and therefore reason enough to curb the slave trade. He considered that "in case there shoud arise a Man of desperate courage amongst us, exasperated by a desperate fortune, he might with more advantage than Cataline, kindle a Servile War." This hypothetical but fearsome revolutionary leader could be thwarted only by preemptive legislation: "Such a Man might be dreadfully mischievous before any opposition coud be formd against him, and tinge our Rivers as wide as they are with blood. Besides the calamitys which woud be brought upon us by such an attempt, it woud cost our Mother Country many a fair Million to make us as profitable as we are at present."[25] Lacking suitable legislation, colonists faced certain death and Britain faced economic disaster. Thus Byrd heartily approved laws that improved the militia and empowered courts to make examples of dissident slaves. Among his legislative duties was service on the bench of the General Court at Williamsburg,[26] giving him opportunities to apply in specific cases the laws he crafted.

Exemplary opportunities came in 1722 and 1723. At the November 2, 1722, trial of three slaves—Sam, Will "otherwise called Cooper Will," and another Sam—the Court found each defendant "guilty of unlawfully assembling meeting and congregating themselves and with the other said slaves to kill murder & destroy very many" colonists. For their crimes, the three slaves were imprisoned indefinitely until their owners should arrange security for their transportation and sale outside the colony.[27] And then on April 26, 1723, the Court found several slaves—Dick, Tom "otherwise called Bamboo Tom," Sancho, Isaac, Jeffrey, and Rubin—guilty of "unlawfully assembling, meeting, and congregating themselves, with diverse other slaves . . . & communicating, contriving, and conspiring to kill, murder, and destroy very many" colonists. Moreover, Edward Moore testified to overhearing the slaves "since they have been in the Gaol, threaten the lives of John Wormley and John Grymes of the County of Middlesex . . . when the said slaves should get at liberty." Again, indeterminate imprisonment was the sentence—presumably until transportation and sale could be arranged.[28] Byrd himself was less than precise in recounting his judicial experiences involving slaves except when their lives were at stake.[29]

The similar events of November, 1710, no doubt prompted the General Court to deal summarily with later slave conspiracies. Authorized by statute to punish unlawful assembly by slaves, the judges might well have inferred murderous plots in the absence of testimony like that given by Edward Moore. After all, threatening jailhouse conversations were no less impudent than insolence in the fields or on the streets. Particularly for planters like

William Byrd, who perceived insolence as a prelude to revolt, the sentence of transportation and sale was relatively mild.

Byrd was committed to enacting his principles. He adopted a pragmatic stance on slavery legislation and readily exercised his power over unruly slaves. At the same time, he exhibited a presumption of black subordination mixed with a fear of slave revolt that he shared with other members of the early Virginia gentry. This viewpoint survived unabated until warfare destroyed the peculiar institution. Although Byrd found the slave trade repugnant, he would never have dreamed of living without slavery itself. Similarly, in 1862, Colin Clarke exclaimed, "Good God!! who could have dreamed of this," when narrating the unruly conduct of freed slaves in an area north of the York River that had recently fallen to federal troops.[30]

An Authoritative Planter

By his own admission, William Byrd belonged to a "class remarkably concerned with mastery."[31] Only a few installments of the diary he kept have been found and translated from his shorthand code, but these constitute a "form of reassurance and a record of mastery."[32] He cherished authority and expected deference from subordinates. Writing grandly about his life as a planter, Byrd described himself on a par with preternatural chieftains: "Like one of the Patriarchs, I have my Flocks and my Herds, my Bond-men and Bond-women." Nonetheless, he recognized that his elevated station in life required him "to keep all my People to their Duty, to set all the Springs in motion and to make every one draw his equal share to carry the Machine forward."[33] Byrd fancied himself occupying a quasi-divine stature in regard to his slaves, and running his plantations like clockwork made absolute obedience by slaves a practical necessity.

In addition to his role as the mechanically precise operator of Westover, he expected his other achievements to win respect from peers. As commander of the Henrico County militia, Byrd expected a deference coordinate with his rank. He reported contentedly that his officers and troops "showed me abundance of respect" at breakfast and later "respected me like a king" at church.[34] If not divine, he yearned for quasi-monarchial status in his relationships with white peers.

He clearly viewed hierarchy as instrumental in a planter's lifestyle. For example he criticized Henry Duke, another member of the Council of State, for creating the conditions in which he "and his maid were ready to quarrel several times." Colonel Duke "was too familiar" with his maid, prompting her to behave towards him as an equal.[35] In Byrd's eyes, the royal governor had behaved more suitably when he "put Gilbert his coachman into prison for his insolence."[36] Rank, whether military or social, had its privileges only when suitable distance was maintained between unequals. Otherwise, in the case of masters and slaves, interactions could become insulting or provoking and embolden the slaves to join clandestinely in conspiracies against the power structure.

Byrd's sense of hierarchy also extended to his family, and his self-representation as a domineering male has recently drawn predictable indictments from feminist and postmodern critics. These critics have properly treated Byrd as a model of his times. His conjugal quarrels over slave discipline illustrate accurately a planter's craving for authority. His first wife, Lucy, had a complex, often brooding personality and prompted a quarrel with him over her whipping of a young slave, Eugene.[37] Byrd was upset, according to his own explanation, because Lucy had disciplined the slave publicly "to show her authority."[38] A generous interpretation would portray Byrd as being upset over the needless humiliation of the slave but, in context, he was more clearly irritated by his wife's usurpation of his corrective power. In recording a later and related episode, he clearly defined the source of his ire: "My wife caused Prue [a maid] to be whipped violently notwithstanding I desired not, which provoked me to have Anaka [a slave] whipped likewise who had deserved it much more."[39] He was upset with Lucy because she had severely disciplined one slave when Byrd himself had decided not to discipline a more culpable slave. Worse than punishing the wrong slave, Lucy had usurped his decision making.

From Byrd's perspective, slaveowners could not afford insolent behavior by any slave toward any white. Henry Duke, for instance, had prompted criticism because he injured to some degree the authority of all masters by becoming too familiar with his maid. More particularly, an individual slaveowner could permit nothing less than strict obedience and respectful speech from his own slaves to his wife. Accordingly, Byrd protected both himself and his peers when he chased "Tom" with a cane for giving Lucy "bad language."[40] Again the following month, Byrd arranged for "little Jenny" to be "soundly whipped" for quarreling with his wife.[41] All whites, much less his own wife, deserved better.

Acting in the best interests of family and society was desirable, but each planter was legislatively mandated to maintain authority over his own slaves. This mandate involved a complex association of plantation staff. Overseers occupied a niche between master and slave that always complicated matters, and Byrd had his share of trouble finding and retaining trustworthy individuals for positions in middle management. He dismissed overseers such as Joe Wilkinson for being absent without leave, spoiling the tobacco harvest, and pilfering.[42] Lacking job security, successful overseers had to exercise their delegated authority with a deft touch. Yet an overseer was first in line to receive insolence from slaves, and exhibiting anything less than absolute power might foment their disrespect.

Finding the right balance between reward and punishment complicated the planter's direct management of slaves. Here too Byrd learned as much about himself as he did about planting. Celebrating the Christmas season, he "gave the people some cider and a dram to the negroes"; celebrating the hard work of planting on a rainy day, he "gave all the people a dram";[43] simply celebrating Saturday nights, he did the same.[44] Rewarding slaves with liquor was not rare for Byrd despite his occasional punishment of them for becoming drunk.[45] Excessive punishments were as vexing for Byrd as excessive rewards: they lacked the constancy which he prized so highly. Confessing in his diary to being "a little out of humor" one morning, he "beat Anaka a little unjustly," for which he expressed sorrow.[46] At the time he entered this item in his diary, he was most probably feeling a moral twinge; before and afterwards he was more apt to calculate the negative impact of his passionate display on his authority over the slaves.

Further complications in sustaining his authority arose out of Byrd's assumptions about slaves' lying. He indicated repeatedly that he treated most slaves' complaints of injury or illness to be deceitful. For example, he punished "Redskin Peter" for pretending to be sick in January, 1711, by applying a branding iron to "the place he complained of" and forcing him to wear a bit in his mouth.[47] During the planting season of 1712, he repeated the punishment of Redskin Peter for the same offense and "believed [Billy Wilkins] pretended also to be sick."[48] But if a master who strove for constancy assumed that slaves were continually deceitful, when would punishment be appropriate? And when, if ever, should deceit be punished as insolence?

Finally, like many other planters, Byrd compromised his distance from slaves with sexual misconduct. His diary contains frequent confessions of sexual assault on female slaves at his manor house and in his apartment at Williamsburg.[49] If Henry Duke deserved criticism for promoting undue familiarity with female servants, then Byrd's misconduct was at least as reprehensible. His sexual liaisons could readily lead to quarrels, and then to insolence. Moreover, surrendering to base passion violated his principle of always acting with "good sence." Byrd acknowledged privately his moral lapses and described his misconduct as "playing the fool," but he seemed never to have envisioned a causal relationship between promoting sexual intimacy with slaves and inviting their insolence.

To Byrd's credit, he gradually honed his managerial skills to a point where reports of slave insolence became unusual in his diaries. Certainly he did not need to wait for reports of the 1739 Stono revolt in South Carolina to appreciate his need for preventive measures; his judicial experiences in prior decades alerted him to the dangerous outcomes of slave discontent. The more experienced planter, the master who held conversational meetings with "his people" at the end of each work day,[50] had learned how largely to forestall unacceptable slave speech. Until that time, however, his diaries clearly depict a member of the gentry who struggled with the problem.

One facet of the problem involved brazen conduct by slaves when they were being disciplined. In the complex setting of human interaction, slaves had to manage their verbal and nonverbal communication carefully in order to avoid antagonizing their masters. In effect, the master's authority extended to control over the meaning of slave speech. Nurse, a house slave, illustrated this phenomenon in defending her conduct to both her master and her mistress. Early in 1709 Byrd suspected that "Nurse" was having a forbidden sexual affair with "Daniel," and he "threatened Anaka with a whipping if she did not confess the intrigue." More to the point, when he "chided Nurse severely" about the affair, she denied it "with an impudent face."[51] Protective of his authority over all elements of plantation life, Byrd attempted to regulate the sex life of his slaves. Scarcely unusual, this regulation was consistent with slaveowners' financial interest in breeding healthy, productive workers. For Byrd, an unauthorized affair amounted to "intrigue" against him—a legislatively proscribed act. Slaves who were reluctant to inform on other slaves' clandestine affairs might be whipped, and suspected offenders could deny their intrigues only at the risk of aggravating their offense by having their denial perceived as insolence. In this particular instance, Nurse failed to exhibit facial expressions that would soften the impact on Byrd of her verbal denial and forestall his perception of insolence. Instead, she displayed "an impudent face."

Later that Spring, Lucy "could not forbear beating" Nurse for an "impudent" defense of her disobedience. She attended a wedding but "stayed all night, contrary to her mistress' orders." Byrd himself—although Nurse also argued her case to him—did not correct the slave because he felt that he "was in too great a passion."[52] In this instance, the slave may not actually have repeated her nonverbal mistake. Rather, white passions took over. Byrd restrained himself from correcting Nurse based on his principle of avoiding passionate conduct but, by observing that his wife "could not forbear beating" the slave, he also implied that Lucy had improperly indulged her passions. These two episodes involving Nurse illustrate that slave insolence was a complicated medium in which intersubjectivity was prominent. In the master/slave dialogue, white presumption of black subordination always contended with an equally intense fear of servile revolt. Even when slaveowners took a relatively enlightened stance on discipline and consciously restrained their fear, slaves literally faced the difficult task of acknowledging complaints about them without creating nonverbal as well as verbal cues that expressed insubordination to wary members of the gentry. Who was to judge, for example, whether a slave had unlawfully "lifted her hand" merely by shading her eyes from the sun while looking at her aggrieved mistress?

Byrd seldom recorded specifics about slave speech, recounting merely that he "beat Jenny for being unmannerly" or similar observations.[53] However, two or three years after the confrontations with Nurse, another episode at Westover illustrates how difficult it could be for some slaves to avoid insolence when the perceptions and judgments of more than one member of the gentry were involved.

A local cleric had become estranged from his wife and, at Byrd's invitation, she had taken up residence at Westover. Code-named "Incendia" in Byrd's correspondence, she ignited controversy by usurping the services of Westover slaves. In an ironic admission Byrd regretted his dismissal of early warning signs in the woman's speech, that is, her "thoughtless rash way of Reparte, which a Husband jealous of his authority might think intolerable." Nonetheless, he agreed to lodge both the woman and her maidservant after receiving assurances that his own servants would not be bothered. As he narrated the episode, trouble began almost immediately: "But not content with this kindness, she has ever since employ'd clandestinely severall of my servants to the neglect of my business, and the breach of her own engagements. And if any of my People dar'd at any time to neglect her affairs, tho it was to do what I had set them about, by her instigation they were chastis'd and threaten'd after a shamefull manner, & were further given to understand, that if they had the impudence to tell me, they shou'd have their tongues cut out." This problem became worse when Incendia enlisted Lucy as an ally in controlling the slaves and usurped the services of "a Weaver in the House" whom Byrd had ordered "to weave for nobody without [his] express orders." At this point, the last straw had been applied: "The weaver pleaded his masters orders against what she desir'd, & told her plainly he durst not do it. She with abundance of good grace call'd him a sawcy Rascal for disputeing her commands, and assur'd him she had a great mind to break his head. . . . The Weaver lookt so scared when I came home, that I wonder'd what ail'd him. I askt him several times, as I did the other servants, what had betided him: but not one syllable cou'd I get out of any of 'em, so well they had been disciplin'd to secrecy." After threatening the weaver himself, Byrd discovered Incendia's arrangements and discreetly resolved the problem with her so as not to irritate his wife. More importantly in the present analysis, the weaver's conduct illustrates the discursive complications arising out of black subordination. As Byrd observed, "Certainly that servants condition must be most miserable, who is at so unhappy an incertainty whome to obey."[54] The weaver was adjudged "sawcy" for disputing the orders of a white who was not his mistress and who had countermanded his master's orders. Moreover, this slave and others were put on notice by their mistress that revealing the problem to their master would be "impudence." Ultimately, the slave became liable to severe punishment for not disclosing to his master what had happened. For the weaver, insolence was perhaps the only option other than running away.

A later episode of slave insolence illustrates that, if pressed, the gentry preferred surly obedience to cheerful independence among their slaves. Recounting a cold, rainy day in February, 1720, Byrd reported that he "had a quarrel with [his] man Joe and beat him for being very saucy, after which he was very sullen and very good."[55] This episode contains standard features: the master improperly bridged the gap between white and black by quarreling with the slave; the slave was most probably defending his alleged misconduct in a mode that was perceived as insolent; and the slave suffered a whipping. All too predictable, the episode remains noteworthy because of Byrd's notation that "Joe . . . was very sullen and very good" after the punishment. Although surly cues continued, the slave had reverted to a subordinate state. Byrd was content with this arrangement, illustrating that the gentry tended to perceive insolence as a meld of verbal and nonverbal behaviors inconsistent with sensible emblems of degradation.

Whether the slave might have escaped punishment altogether by quarreling in some sort of deferential mode appears plausible because of another episode in April. After an otherwise humdrum day, Byrd "beat [his] man for being drunk and saucy" while returning to his Williamsburg apartment.[56] If Byrd's explicit conjunction of this slave's offenses was intentional, as apparently was his joining of Joe's sullenness and goodness, then drunkenness alone would not have earned the slave a beating. Many whites sought relief from their woes in liquor, and blacks might be excused for doing the same— outside working hours and absent a master's prohibition. But this drunken slave was "saucy" as well—however Byrd perceived this additional misconduct at that time and place.

Further illuminating this necessary conjunction of misbehaviors, a similar incident occurred two months later. Back at Westover and early in the morning, Byrd demonstrated his constancy in discouraging drunken insolence: "I found my man Johnny drunk, for which when I threatened to beat him he said I should not so I had him whipped and gave him thirty lashes."[57] Johnny may not have been whipped merely because he was drunk; Byrd threatened but did not whip his slaves for various types of misconduct during working hours, from leaving the plantation without permission to standing idle.[58] Indeed, Johnny might have escaped the quasi-statutory penalty of thirty lashes if he had not disputed his culpability.

More compelling yet in this regard is a sequence of events during Byrd's maturity as a planter. Early in 1741 he recounted beating a servant because "Tom got drunk and did not what [Byrd] bade him." Subsequent events call into question whether Tom was a slave or an indentured servant, but in any event Byrd's response illustrates his striving for constancy in disciplining workers who exacerbated their drinking with impudence. To draw a beating, Tom had to conjoin disobedience with drunkenness.[59]

Above all, Byrd yearned for preventive measures in his management of slaves. He prided himself on doctoring to his slaves—especially when he could head off debilitating illnesses—and his amateur medical practice was successful enough to attract his neighbors and friends as patients.[60] Maintaining constancy in his disciplinary record was to him the surest means of preventing the spread of less palpable cancers like slave insolence.

The history of legislation on slave insolence identifies the gentry's perception of its threatening nature as the underlying cause of its proscription. Whether replacing earlier statutes banning raised fists or grafted onto statutes banning tumultuous meetings and sedition, the proscription of slave insolence expresses lawmakers' concern about an erosion of white power. These legislative developments are as complex and subjective as the meaning of related verbal and nonverbal behaviors by blacks. The master of Westover actively coped with the threat and its discursive emblems in both his legislative and planting careers.

The types of legislation and verdicts endorsed by William Byrd in the service of colonial Virginia illustrate the gentry's perception of slave insolence as a prelude to insurrection. Byrd prized constancy and responsibility in the Council of State if for no other reason than to sustain generally the gentry's share of legislative power. But the practical wisdom he valued highly prompted him specifically to support laws restraining suspicious assemblies of slaves, and to construe these laws strictly on the bench of the General Court. Personally and professionally, he pursued his ideals vigorously. Nonetheless, he indulged in lampoons and other impudent behaviors that highlight the double standard for whites and blacks.

As a planter, Byrd craved authority and the respect due his status. His regard for hierarchy prompted him to resist egalitarianism in dealing with white subordinates—including family and friends—just as he condemned familiarity in the master-slave relationship. In particular, he saw this familiarity as a breeding ground for slave insolence. But similarly to his legislative career, he did not always live up to his ideals of plantation management. For example, his assumptions about slaves' deceitfulness and his own sexual assaults on slave women ensured imperfection in his planting career.

Both as lawmaker and as master, Byrd sought preventive measures against unruly slaves. The record he kept of his efforts clearly identifies a complex blend of verbal and nonverbal communications that provided the raw materials of slave insolence, as well as specific conditions under which these materials would be perceived by the gentry as having been crafted into the finished product. Most commonly, provoking or insulting language and gestures had to accompany defensive or repugnant behaviors such as slaves' denying their guilt or drinking to excess. In the absence of the underlying conditions, slave speech would not typically constitute a threat. Of course, whites exercised the prerogative of assigning meaning within this process; blacks had the duty of anticipating when their conduct would be perceived as insolent. To ignore their duty was to run the risk of antagonizing masters who were not as introspective and self-regulating as William Byrd II.

Part 2
The Business Perspective

3
"A Perfect Understanding between a Master and a Slave"

The horrors of slavery obscure mercantile decisions that sustained the peculiar institution, yet attending to the business perspective illuminates significant elements in the gentry's understanding of slave insolence. From this perspective, making a profit in staple crops required a good deal of luck as well as hard work. Favorable weather, especially the timing of rains, was a matter of luck. Clearing the land, and planting, weeding, and harvesting a crop were daunting tasks. The greatest drain on planters' mental resources, however, was the contradiction between "goals for plantation communities and their slaves."[1] Each planter faced the dilemma of finding ways to keep profits up while keeping the slaves down.

The planting business involved various classes of people within a complex hierarchy. Federal and state authorities were involved to the extent they regulated and taxed the enterprise. In addition, there were competing planters and other peers who administered the local mercantile and legal institutions. The slaves themselves occupied several levels of a plantation hierarchy, from highly prized artisans and house servants, through foremen or drivers, to lowly field hands. For the majority of slaveowners, relationships with slaves were unavoidably close because only a handful were maintained and they lived nearby, if not in the same rude cabin. For the gentry, the planters who were absentee landlords or who owned hundreds or thousands of slaves, relationships were mediated through overseers—a little understood class of Southrons who were just as likely to be drunken brutes of no particular vision as sober aspirants to their own planting business.

Insolent disruptions of the planting business occurred principally in slaves' discourse with overseers or the mistresses of plantations. In the diverse white population, these were the people who stood to suffer most from slave insolence. Indeed, narratives by both masters and slaves indicate that overseers may have been consciously targeted for insolence; narratives by mistresses identify special tensions created by slaves' impudent behavior. Discourse with masters appeared to have been reserved for more palatable means and ends. Although the need for overseers further complicated an already elaborate business system, the mediating presence of overseers—and analogously the presence of plantation mistresses—elicited clearly definable slave conduct that was perceived as insolent.

Slave insolence has sagely been classified as a "consistent means of resistance" that was especially clever during the colonial period because "it allowed slaves a way to assert themselves and downgrade their masters without committing a crime."[2] As a form of resistance on the job, insolence became a tactic in "the psychological warfare between masters and slaves."[3] Insolence was unsettling enough that "both Marster and Missus taught slaves to be obedient" as a matter of policy.[4] What remains to be understood more precisely are the specific verbal and nonverbal cues that signified resistance to business-minded gentry, and how they interpreted slave insolence through the perceptual filters of their spouses and overseers.

White Policy and Black Custom

The earliest legislative proscriptions against slave insolence signaled the gentry's concern that plantation justice was failing to serve its purpose, that is, "to keep slaves in line within the confines of each unit of production."[5] In a very real sense, law was the servant of the marketplace.[6] John Ashton summarized briefly the gentry's business perspective on slave insolence in his June 15, 1775, *Maryland Gazette* advertisement for the return of Tom. A highly prized shoemaker, Tom may have been encouraged to run away by some of Ashton's neighbors who became "too familiar" with his slaves "to [his] great prejudice." In any event, Ashton offered a reward of six pounds for the return of this slave who had "the look of a rogue when sharply spoken to, and discovers a great deal of assurance and impudence in his conversation."[7] From the business perspective, Tom's insolence reduced his value as an artisan. When he resisted correction with roguish facial cues, he proportionately disrupted the standard way of doing business in the South. When Tom abused his status as an artisan by conversing boldly with superiors, he made matters worse. Moreover, according to his master, Tom may have converted his skills to the service of neighbors. This conversion was a significant emblem to John Ashton of having lost his slave's value, although it was no different in kind than Tom's nonverbal and verbal insolence.

Tom's behavior was extraordinary because of a white policy against black speech. As a business decision, maintaining a nearly silent work force was expedient for the gentry but thorny for the slaves. The dilemmas faced by slaves of the early Tidewater gentry are illustrative. As described in chapter 2, William Byrd's weaver was threatened with punishment for impudence if he complained to his master about his exploitation by a house guest at Westover.[8] Later in the eighteenth century, one of Robert "King" Carter's slaves dutifully adopted an exaggerated posture of submission when voicing a grievance. As related by a tutor on the plantation, an "old Negro Man came with a complaint to Mr. Carter of the Overseer that he does not allow him his Peck of corn a week." The tutor recalled how moved he was by the old slave's "humble posture" as he sat on the floor and clasped his hands together in submission before addressing his master.[9]

By the late 1820s a specific policy against slave complaints had become accepted as an ideal of plantation management. For example, without further explanation, a South Carolina overseer simply published as his policy that any "negro leaving the plantation or field to complain to me is registered and treated as such."[10] Tantamount to a damning performance review in a twenty-first-century personnel file, being registered as complainers might haunt slaves for years, not to mention immediately subjecting them to the painful retooling applied to flawed cogs in the plantation machine. Overseers, of course, exercised substantial control over this punishing process.

Failing to obey orders unconditionally was the passive counterpart to complaining. As a major South Carolina planter decreed in 1833, "a perfect understanding between a master and a slave is that the slave should know that his master is to govern absolutely, and he is to obey implicitly. . . . he is never for a moment to exercise his will or judgment in opposition to a positive order."[11] Scarcely novel, the same policy was also applied to factory workers. Yet this classical theory of business organizations was applied with radical differences in the plantation system, principally because of the unique business perspective shared by the gentry.[12] A planter in Mississippi articulated this mindset clearly in 1851. "Make no laws, give no orders," he advised his peers, "but what you know are right, and then never permit a violation of them . . . for the simple reason that the master has ordered it."[13] Unlike the employers and managers of factory workers, the masters and overseers of slaves felt a duty to justify their business decisions as part of a larger need. They felt duty-bound to defend a way of life and not merely make a profit. As a result they proclaimed "laws" and not merely rules. In a rhetorical parallel with their legislation, the linguistic tenor of their business policies was extremely bipolar. At the affirmative pole, planters sought "a perfect understanding" so that they might manage their work force "absolutely." At the negative extreme, slaves were "never" to question or violate their orders.

Enforcing a policy that favored silence on the job was consistent with the gentry's assumption about slaves' cunning and deceit—an assumption that may have developed from planters' countervailing need to confirm their own sense of honor.[14] In mid-eighteenth-century Virginia, Landon Carter declared curtly that "a negroe can't be honest" and this assumption dictated Carter's management style.[15] Hearing that his slave William claimed to be sick, Carter demanded an accounting during which William "in a violent passion swore he would not be served so by [Carter] or by anybody." William then ran away. After his recapture, he denied that Carter could be his master because no master of his would have dared to treat him so badly. Whipped for his outburst, William nonetheless "went on with his tongue as impudent as possible."[16] These instances, in which a supposedly ill slave retained enough vigor to rail at his master and run away, confirmed planters' suspicions and fostered a distrustful management style.

Illustrating widespread agreement with Carter's sentiment, John Holt restated it more expansively in New York when advertising for his runaway slave. According to the advertisement, Charles was "extremely artful, and ready at inventing specious pretences to conceal villainous Actions or Designs." However, based on his "solemn Promises of his Good Behavior," Charles had been retained by Holt until the slave "villainously abused" his chance for "Reformation."[17] Believing as did John Dorsey in Maryland and Edmund Hatch in North Carolina that slaves would "use every method to deceive" because they harbored "the most cunning malignancy,"[18] planters enforced a business policy that reflected their assumption—much as they enacted legislation reflecting their presumption of black subordination.

By the mid–nineteenth century, planters assumed that work-related resistance and especially complaints by slaves were impudent shams. Thomas R. R. Cobb seized on this assumption about slaves' cunning and deceit to defend the rule of law whereby their testimony was excluded from trials of whites. "The negro," Cobb wrote, "is mendacious, a fact too well established to require the production of proof, either from history, travels, or craniology."[19] Self-evident to planters from their personal recollections and visits with peers, as well as from the astute findings of medical researchers, the assumption of slave cunning was prominent in the purely business perspective on slavery. "The most general defect in the character of the negro is hypocrisy," wrote a Virginia planter; furthermore "this hypocrisy frequently makes him pretend to more ignorance than he possesses," providing the slave with a convenient "apology for awkwardness and neglect of duty."[20] Even the pious Joseph L. Melville grudgingly confessed that "there is a considerable amount of complaining among servants that is merely feigned."[21] The equally religious Keziah Brevard painfully confessed that she perceived a general "deception" among her slaves.[22] Unlike Mr. Melville or the widow Brevard, it was easier for a hard bitten South Carolina overseer to declare that slaves had to be managed cautiously because of their duplicity. Admitting that his judgment was "harsh" but "unfortunately too true," this overseer advised that the "only way to keep a negro honest is not to trust him."[23]

In a notable exception to the rule, William S. Pettigrew not only trusted his slaves but also elevated selected servants to the status of overseers on his North Carolina plantation. Yet silence retained its golden charm for Pettigrew. Among the several attributes of Glasgow, whom Pettigrew had entrusted with an overseer's position, was the slave's habit of being "not too *talkative*"—an attribute underscored by his master as "a necessary qualification."[24] Similarly, a handful of clergymen suggested that slaves be given the opportunity to respond to their masters' accusations. Even then, according to the Reverend A. T. Holmes, a biblical precedent in the Book of Job permitted the slave merely to voice "acknowledgement of the offence, his regret for it, and any palliating fact which he might urge in connection."[25] Part of the clerical reasoning behind a slave's limited right to speak in his own defense stemmed from the master's reciprocal duty to recognize that, with rare exceptions, the slave's "misery is voiceless."[26] Based on this same logic as well as St. Paul's sermon to the Ephesians, a few Southern clerics asserted that the "most efficient government is . . . the most noiseless and quiet."[27] Regardless of their specific status in the plantation hierarchy, a general measure of slaves' value was their degree of mute obedience.

Brutal enforcement of business policy prompted slaves to avoid conduct on the job that might be perceived as insolent and resistant. No less an authority than Frederick Douglass observed that slaves customarily subscribed to the maxim "a still tongue makes a wise head."[28] Douglass, of course, was angry about the maxim's power because gaining slaves' cooperation in keeping silent was one of many tactics bolstering the gentry against abolitionist pressure. However, black subscription to the maxim flourished. At an early stage, slave parents restrained their children's conversation at home as a training ground for their interactions with master.[29] Later, only a daring slave would confide to any white listener that slaves "dare not say anything about being discontented."[30] Much of this story was not told until the peculiar institution became a hazy memory. As Lizzie Norfleet testified when interviewed for the 1930s Federal Writers Project: "The colored was all under bondage and they was afraid to speak till after freedom." Another former slave living in Minnesota recalled that "the slaves bet not conplain to their masters." Yet another former slave, interviewed in Mississippi, confirmed that "We sho' knowed better 'n to grumble 'bout anythin.'"[31]

Remaining silent was not the only method chosen by slaves to hide their true feelings about conditions in the workplace. Trying to allay white suspicion about their cunning, slaves adopted communicative behaviors that could not readily be perceived as insolence or guile. The most thoroughly documented modulation of slave resistance—smiling—later gained a notable status in the American legal doctrine known popularly as "fighting words." In 1941 Justice Page of the New Hampshire Supreme Court devoted part of his opinion in *State v. Chaplinsky* to explaining this doctrine.[32] His explanation, quoted by Justice Murphy when the case reached the United States Supreme Court, identified the significant role played by facial expression in modifying provocative discourse: "The English language has a number of words and expressions which by general consent are 'fighting words' when said without a disarming smile."[33] Slaves appreciated effective tactics for defusing white antagonism and they often chose the disarming smile.

Newspaper advertisements for runaway slaves illustrate how a smiling countenance became a defining characteristic. Especially in combination with a downcast head, a smile disarmed all but the wary master or overseer: "Behind the mask of docility, the male slave was still himself and gave the lie to southern claims of 'knowing' their blacks."[34] Using this skill effectively, four mid–eighteenth-century slaves impressed their Virginia masters. Aaron Trueheart described Will (who was still a youth) as having a "pleasant countenance." John Stith made a point of advertising Tom as "very apt to grin when he speaks or is spoken to." More dramatic yet, Dudley Brooks identified Pompey as a "laughing Fellow." Even very young slaves like Will learned the tactics of disarming white anger, and a tactical smile could soften the image of slaves who by running away had identified themselves as rebellious. Paired with a downcast look, the disarming smile gained greater impact. Thomas Poindexter, for example, explained that his slave Jack avoided "looking in the Face of them he is speaking to as much as possible."[35] This tactic induced a perception that slaves could be deferential if not congenial, despite depriving their masters of their labor.

Contemporaneous advertisements in Maryland confirm a tactical use of the disarming smile throughout the Chesapeake region. Dick was merely a teenager when he ran away from Edward Dyer but the slave had already learned that facial masks were useful. He had "remarkable red Gums," his master advertised, "which he shows much when he speaks or laughs." At the same time, however, Dick had "a sly look, which corresponds very well with his Disposition." Elliner M'Graw was more succinct in describing Tom, noting merely his "smiling countenance."[36] Edward Dyer had arguably expressed the same perception that M'Graw had of slaves, namely that Tom was as cunning as Dick and that both slaves masked their designs with a smile. In fact, "numerous masters learned all too well [that] slaves could hide their innermost thoughts behind deferential, dissembling, even stuttering masks."[37] Both Dyer and M'Graw had a sufficient investment in their slaves to warrant the costs of advertising and rewards; both masters were also unlikely to be duped completely by their slaves' nonverbal tactics. Rather, a diligent scrutiny of slaves' dependability was simply part of the cost of doing business.

Further south, references in eighteenth-century runaway advertisements suggest that slaves—a significant percentage of whom were new arrivals from Africa[38]—were less skilled in disarming tactics. Amid the hundreds of advertisements identifying other physical clues to a runaway slave's identity, Daniel Gardner's 1771 attribution of a "smiling Countenance" to an unnamed "Negro Man" is unusual in the *South-Carolina Gazette*, as is James Parker's 1787 use of identical language about Isaac in the *Gazette of the State of Georgia*.[39] Also rare are explicit acknowledgments of slave cunning. Philip Dell was distinctive in stating that his slave Sambo, although "very humble and smooth spoken," actually "pretends to be something complaisant."[40]

More typical in the Deep South were sketchy characterizations limited to slaves' downcast gaze. From James Jordan's 1737 remarks about Primus to Jacob Read's 1783 description of Mungo,[41] the Charleston gentry repeatedly cited a "down look" as one of the defining characteristics of their slaves without also mentioning a smiling countenance. The same trend also appeared in Savannah, from Jacob Waldburger's 1767 description of George to Samuel Stiles's 1788 remarks about Jack.[42] But in North Carolina where, like Georgia, Africans were marched for decades under British rule after disembarking in

Charleston,[43] advertisements during the early federal period suggest that better "seasoned" slaves had learned their lessons well. Many runaways were advertised simply as having a "down look,"[44] yet an equal number were said to display the smiling tactic.[45]

Aside from their possible clues to an increase in slave guile, early announcements of runaway slaves in the Deep South reflect the growth of a standard lexicon among newspaper editors. So many masters needed to advertise so many runaway slaves that editors developed a formula for these announcements that was both convenient and understandable. Conspicuous in that formula was the ingredient of a "down look" to identify troublesome slaves. In effect, Philip Dell preached to the choir when he advertised explicitly that Sambo was merely pretending to be complaisant. The gentry knew how to decipher a slave's downcast head: it was a diversion of eyes that was as likely to hide insolence as to show genuine deference.

Announcements of a "smiling countenance" were similarly formulaic and clearly understood, as illustrated by later advertisements in North Carolina. For example, Peter Wiss explained in 1803 that Bristol displayed "much cunning and artifice both by his language and smiles."[46] Seven years later and more piquantly, Elizabeth P. Dickinson announced that Frank had a "smiling artful countenance when spoken to, and is a very desperate bloodthirsty fellow."[47] Frequently linked to business concerns, this type of advertisement explicitly classified the smiling tactic as an exculpatory device: Payton generated "a quizzical smile" when he was "apprehensive of being detected in a fault"; Alford maintained "a sprightly appearance" when addressed and was not "apt to condemn himself unless carefully observed."[48]

Sparse evidence discourages firm conclusions about slaves' early use of disarming smiles in the Deep South, especially in view of contrary evidence in the Upper South. In Virginia and Maryland, for instance, eighteenth-century advertisements suggest that the gentry understood well the combined tactics of slaves to mask their insolence. In addition to curt attributions of a "down look" to runaways in Virginia who were variously named Tom or Jemima, Quash or Fox,[49] as well as Maryland slaves such as Caesar or Jacob, Harry or Scipio,[50] advertisers elaborated on this characteristic. In Virginia, for example, young Adam projected a "modest" attitude, thirty-five-year-old Joe appeared to be "very humble," and forty-year-old Kate seemed downright "sheepish" because of their downcast looks.[51] In Maryland, by contrast, Bob's "down-cast" scarcely disguised his "guilty" demeanor and his wily attempts "to talk very politely."[52] Many more runaways in both jurisdictions were advertised as having a "smiling" or "pleasant" countenance.[53] And others were identified as using a combination of tactics: "Abraham" displayed a "deceitful smile" as well as a "down look" in the opinion of James Donald, sheriff of Smithfield, Virginia; Boatswain responded with both a "down look" and a smile when addressed by Thomas Cockey of Baltimore County.[54]

Much to the slaves' dismay, tactics such as smiling soon became obvious ruses to the gentry. Virginians such as John Mayo and Peter Baker dismissed these behaviors as "deceitful" and "artful."[55] In the opinion of Marylanders such as Nathan Halley and Joshua Dorsey Jr., they were "dissembling" and "insinuating."[56] Stripped of basic masking devices, the slaves were found to be insolent more easily and more often. Indeed, the earliest statutes proscribing slave insolence were soon enacted.

Emblems of Disruptive Insolence

The specific emblems of work-related insolence included complaints or denials of guilt, assertions of independence or equality, and gross insults or threats. These effects were achieved through a combination of verbal and nonverbal cues usually addressed to an overseer. The narratives of both blacks and whites testify with remarkable consistency to the means and ends of this insolence.

Complaints or Denials

Nonverbal denials appear routinely in the lists of characteristics used to identify runaways. For example, Catesby Jones offered a hundred dollars plus costs for the return of young Billy even though this slave looked "very sullen when accused of any thing." Billy played the fiddle well and was a valuable house servant in Westmoreland County, Virginia.[57] The return of equally youthful Stephen was worth only twenty dollars to Peregrine Bond in St. Mary's County, Maryland. Stephen was not advertised as possessing any special skills or training, and he displayed "a remarkable surly down look when accused with having done amiss."[58] More than a generation later in North Carolina, Ann Ashworth described "her negro man, named Dick, about forty-five years of age" as typically "surly when interrogated."[59] Similarly W. D. Petway advertised that, "when interrogated," his mulatto slave Miles "generally frowns and looks down."[60] In these instances and many others, masters perceived a relationship between a downcast gaze and surliness or a sullen attitude—suggesting that a down look was not easily perfected to forestall white annoyance. Moreover, when used in combination with a frown instead of a smile, a down look meant resistance rather than deference.

Choosing from among the many labels used to identify unacceptable facial expressions, Thomas Lawson announced that the mulatto slave Billie adopted "a sour look when taxed with any thing amiss." Billie was a skillful "ship Carpenter" and played the violin, but his artistry failed him when he needed to obscure his resistance to correction on the job.[61] Worse yet, a mature slave named Caesar not only held "his head very high" but also adopted "a sour grim look."[62] Caesar emphasized his insolence by refusing to avert his gaze and made his denial so noteworthy that John Page described it as both "sour" and "grim."

Enslaved women faced the same problem of hiding their feelings when being criticized for their work, but they may also have enjoyed a nonverbal advantage based on their gender. In the case of Peg, a teenaged house servant in Essex County, Virginia, her master advertised that she had developed the habit of looking "greatly surprized" when corrected. In addition, Peg was "apt to cry."[63] Her tactics are distinctive among contemporaneous and later advertisements for runaways, and appear markedly superior to the sour looks that were readily perceived as insolent by masters. However, a look of surprise and shedding tears may well have brought as much unwelcome attention to a male slave as an unmasked denial.

Very young slaves enjoyed few exemptions from the typical punishment for nonverbal affronts. A former slave from Alabama recalled her beating for blacking her eyebrows in imitation of her mistress. "You black debbil," the woman screamed, "I'll show you to mock your betters." Abe McKlennan remembered a similar instance when he escaped punishment only because his master's son intervened: "The overseer cotch me by de shirt tail one day an' gwine whip me good fer makin' faces be'hin' hissen' back." More poignantly, youthful slaves might be punished simply for venting natural emotions during the abuse of their parents. For example, Henry L. McGaffey cried when he witnessed the whipping and salting of his mother. In response, his master declared "iffen I didn't shut up he wud beat me."[64]

Nonverbal resistance flourished among recently enslaved workers who lacked minimal language skills. In a 1658 Maryland case, *Attorney General v. Overzee*, Hannah Littleworth testified that the slave Antonio "instead of goeing to work . . . layd himself downe & would not stirre, Whereupon mr Overzee beate him with some Peare Tree wands or twiggs." This beating continued "till the negro was dead" because Antonio "remayned in his stubberness & feyned himselfe in fitts, as hee used att former times to doe."[65] Additional testimony by Job Chandler revealed that Antonio had no "speech or language . . . only an ugly yelling Brute beast like."[66] Speechless in the sense of commanding no English, Antonio developed a routine of simulating fits that would excuse him from laboring in Overzee's fields. At the time of his killing, Antonio doggedly resorted to his standard tactic. His inflexible response to a new stimulus—a vicious flogging—illustrates the severe limits of nonverbal denials and other speechless forms of resisting work. The basic ambiguity of these cues led to varied interpretations by the gentry, as illustrated in the several meanings attached to downcast looks in early-nineteenth-century North Carolina, South Carolina, and Georgia. Nonverbal resistance lacked the extra measure of precise meaning that could be achieved when deeds were allied with words.

Verbal denials could be relatively mild or intense. Occasionally, this speech might benefit a slave, as illustrated in the recollections of Jacob Branch. When "Uncle Charley" retorted to a threat of whipping by saying "What for you whip me, I doin' every bit what old Massa done tell me," he escaped punishment."[67] However, both mild and intense denials were usually declarations against a slave's interest. B. R. Bailey was not complimenting his middle-aged slave Phillis when he advertised her as "quick spoken when attacked by any person."[68] Fifty years earlier in Baltimore, Robert Moore more precisely revealed his slave's language "when charged with any thing:" Bob typically responded "No indeed!" If his master was accurate in identifying Bob as "an artful smooth-spoken Fellow," then this slave had consciously decided that his verbal denial would not be offensive.[69] However, it was distinctive enough to be perceived as useful in identifying a runaway. Earlier yet, Thomson Mason identified his mulatto slave Peter Deadfoot as "smooth tongued" but "apt to speak quick, swear and with dreadful curses upon himself, in defence of his innocence, if taxed with a fault, even when guilty." This slave's verbal denials were comparatively intense and his master understandably characterized him as having "a great share of pride." Yet, as a business investment, Peter Deadfoot had to be recaptured. He was also "a good butcher, ploughman, and carter; and excellent sawyer, and waterman." In fact, his master advertised him as "one of the best scythemen, either with or without a cradle, in America."[70] From mild to intense, slave denials struck masters as distinctive discourse.

For the gentry, complaints or denials were less than ideal from a purely business perspective. Even mild language was interpreted as a blow to efficient operation of the plantation. For example, when questioned "Where's the key to the corn-house?" by his new master, Christopher Nichols replied simply "I don't know, Sir." And when questioned next about whether the horse had enough to eat, Nichols restated his simple denial. His language earned him a threatened beating with a fence rail. Similarly, Eli Johnson witnessed a new overseer immediately kick out a slave woman's eye when she answered "No, Sir" to a question she did not understand.[71] Both of these former slaves had toiled in Virginia. "Very few Virginia ladies," observed the mistress of one plantation in 1843, "are brought up in a way calculated to make them what we call *good managers*." As part of her advice to remedy this shortcoming, she recommended: "Never let a servant say to you, 'I forgot it.' That sentence, so often used, is no excuse at all."[72] Managerial skill was also on the mind of a planter who wrote in favor of "moderate chastisement" for resistant slaves. But there are exceptions to every rule, and this planter said that "a slight punishment will only make matters worse" in the case of slaves who are "stubborn or impertinent."[73]

Slave denials amounted to business problems in the minds of overseers and masters. As one slaveowner remarked in frustration to his slave, "You so mean, I got to sell you. You all time complaining about you don't like your white folks."[74] After one of his travels through the South, Frederick Law Olmsted reported a relevant instance in which, for the first time, he saw a "writhing, groveling, and screaming" (and nameless) slave woman being flogged. She had left her work gang and was hiding in a gully when spotted by the overseer. When questioned about her conduct, she failed to reply, gave an "unintelligible" answer, and then offered an explanation that the overseer dismissed as a lie. Olmsted then reported her punishment as "thirty or forty blows" with a "tough, flexible, 'raw-hide' whip." Despite the lingering sounds of her "choking, sobbing, spasmodic groans," the overseer laughed as he quipped: "She meant to cheat me out of a day's work—and she has done it, too." The overseer later laughed again when replying to Olmsted's question about the necessity for flogging the slave so severely. "Oh yes, sir," he remarked, "If I hadn't punished her so hard she would have done the same thing again to-morrow, and half the people on the plantation would have followed her example."[75] Olmsted criticized the business decision to punish simple denials harshly in far broader terms, insisting that these severe penalties resulted from "the frenzy which often seizes whole communities." Yet masters and overseers had repeatedly told him their specific motive: to avoid a loss of managerial control and, worst of all, a reduction in the value of their business property.[76]

Of course, Olmsted was not entirely wrong in attributing slave abuse to factors other than business decisions. Roger, for example, had been a lifelong "cripple, being hardly able to walk & use[d] his knees more than his feet." Yet, when he was tardy in returning from oystering on a cold day in February, 1849—depriving his master, J. H. Sandiford, of the marsh grass which Roger was also responsible for cutting that day—Sandiford tortured the slave to death. Asked why he was tardy, Roger had replied that "the wind was too high." To Sandiford, this reply was *"impertinace."* After whipping Roger, Sandiford confined him "in an open outhouse—the wind blowing through a hundred cracks—his clothes wet to his waist—without a single blanket & in freezing weather." Sandiford also placed "shackels on his wrists & chained to a bolt in the floor and a *chain* around his *neck.*" A jury of Sandiford's peers found that "Roger came to his death by choking by a chain put around his neck—*having sliped from the position in which he* was placed."[77] Perhaps Sandiford had been merely negligent about protecting his investment in Roger, but the malicious torture of the slave branded the master as a violent bully rather than a poor businessman.

Lacking protection from violent bullies, many slaves repressed even their mildest denials and sought consolation in religion. Jacob Stroyer recalled being beaten three times by his master for no apparent reason and then consulting his father. "Mr. Young is whipping me too much now," the young slave complained, "I shall not stand it, I shall fight him." After warning his son that resisting the master would also endanger the young slave's parents, the father advised: "You must do as I told you, my son: do your work the best you can, and do not say anything." Finding his son unsatisfied by this advice, the father exclaimed that he could "do nothing more than to pray to the Lord to hasten the time" when their bondage would end.[78] As customary, the father first advised silence. Then, seeing his son's continued anguish at tangible oppression, he referred him to the intangible consolation of religion. This sublimation, based on the hope of an imminent millennium, "provided a way to survive the trauma of enslavement."[79]

Though profoundly disguised, this resort to religion could also be considered insolence because slaves would adopt the New Testament ideal of the "suffering servant" and actually feel superior to their oppressors.[80] As recalled by a South Carolina slave born in 1845, her mother had a religious experience in which a "pure white and shining" Jesus appeared to her. She complained to him about being separated from her husband, "with five little chillun and not a morsel of bread." But after hearing the apparition's disparaging comparison between her plight and his crucifixion, she found peace of mind: "After dat, everything just flow along, just as easy."[81] Similarly, his master's unfounded charge of pilfering became tolerable for William Grimes when he recalled a relevant biblical parable: "When I considered him accusing me of stealing, when I was so innocent . . . I then said to myself, if this thing is done in a green tree what must be done in a dry?" The slave then silently forgave his master "and prayed to God to forgive him and turn his heart."[82] Breaking his silence would have exposed William Grimes to the same penalties imposed on slaves who denied their culpability. Silently forgiving a master, who would be outraged if he realized what was happening, was less perilous and possibly more satisfying for a pious slave.

Slaves who failed to remain silent, whether tactically or unreflectively, clearly recalled the outcomes of their denials. In *The Fugitive Blacksmith*, a slave narrative prominent in abolitionist literature, the author described how his father, Bazil, responded to his master's criticism for not returning to work after the weekend. The master's words and deeds enact a claim to dual ownership of his slave's speech and labor. "I am always at my post," retorted the slave, "Monday morning never finds me off the plantation." For this and other perceived insolence by Bazil, his master whipped the slave "with most savage cruelty, and inflicted fifteen or twenty severe stripes with all his strength." Swearing, Bazil's master then declared: "I will make you know that I am master of you tongue as well as of your time." Despite having dutifully attended to his work and remaining silent, Bazil's son also endured a savage caning. Resting his back after shoeing a horse, the young slave straightened up and accidentally faced his master. This eye contact was offensive to the master. "What are you rolling your white eyes at me for, you lazy rascal?" he shouted, and then delivered "a dozen severe blows" to the hapless slave.[83] While not resisting his master's ownership of his speech and his labor, Bazil's son unwittingly displayed a nonverbal cue that was offensive.

More typical was Harriet Miller's testimony to the antebellum experience of her Uncle Levi with a cruel overseer. When this brutal Mr. Adams scolded Uncle Levi for the slow pace of his hoeing, the slave responded that he "was hoeing es fast as dis dull hoe will low me." Enraged by the slave's complaint, the overseer declared that the hoe was "sharp nouf" and struck the slave's head with it.[84] In one of the more successful episodes, Edward Hicks resisted his overseer's command to bite off the head of a worm he had bypassed when working in a tobacco field. "I told him I shouldn't bite the worm's head off," Hicks recalled, "[because] it was a thing I had never done, and I wasn't used to it, and wouldn't do it." After the overseer whipped him several times, Hicks managed to escape from the plantation. Moreover, upon being informed of the affair, Hicks's master levied a fine on the overseer of one dollar for each day the slave was absent because the overseer "had no business to make that disturbance among the people."[85] In this instance, Edward Hicks not only escaped severe punishment but also gained the satisfaction of seeing his tormentor suffer financial loss. This satisfying feeling is a prominent goal of insolence in the classical tradition of rhetoric. In addition, the intermediate role of the overseer in Hicks's narrative illuminates the significant influence played by these midlevel managers in establishing the meaning of insolence for the gentry.

Mattie Griffith Browne chronicled altruistic variations of slave denial in her 1857 autobiography. If it were not so consistent with other self-reports,[86] her narrative would be formally deficient in the present analysis because it relates events in New York rather than the American South. More substantively, her autobiography supplements literature that is now widely assumed to be abolitionist propaganda. On one occasion, Browne wrote, an older slave called Aunt Polly defended her against charges that she had untruthfully denied knowledge of another slave's escape route. Her master was already upset about her denial and "this unexpected boldness in one of the most humble and timid of his slaves, enraged him still farther, and he dealt [Aunt Polly] such a blow." On another occasion, an acquaintance of Browne was tied up and slashed for criticizing the beating of his wife.[87] These narratives emphasize the severe reprisals for relatively mild resistance. A subsequent tale in her autobiography reinforces Browne's point: she herself began to defend another slave, Amy, who was being beaten and, for her insolence, received "such a blow across the face, that [she] was blinded for full five minutes." Upon scolding Browne for daring to speak out, her tormentor exclaimed, "There, take that! you impudent hussy."[88] These altruistic denials could be perceived as especially insolent because they identified the victimized slaves as acting more gallantly than their white tormentors.

Elsewhere in her narrative, Browne returned to the basic theme of slave denial. She described another vicious beating of Amy for denying that she had stolen silverware.[89] On a more personal note, Browne reported a head wound that she had incurred by responding to her mistress "perhaps not so obsequiously as she thought it should be." Browne recorded her response to criticism for being lost in thought as the simple question "What have I done,

Miss Jane?" In return, her mistress roared "How dare you, Miss, speak *to me* in that tone?"[90] And again, Browne described a facial cut she had received for a "hasty reply" to Miss Jane.[91] Because of extenuating circumstances—Miss Jane had accused the slave of having sex with her husband—the reader might expect that Browne would receive an unusually severe punishment. However, her abuse was tempered because diplomatic responses of plantation mistresses to their husbands' rapes of slave women were commonplace. In this instance, perceived insolence in the slave's denial arguably elicited as much rage as the underlying accusation. Other, more socially prominent, mistresses disciplined their slaves with the enhanced skill and emotional restraint that sustained these women's standing in the community. Rosalie Calvert, for instance, punished her gardener for his insolence by sending him back to field work. She did not indulge herself by venting her disgust or rage, but she also did not compromise her steely determination to keep the upper hand. Although her gardener returned three times "begging [her] to take him back," the mistress of Riversdale refused.[92]

Variations on the theme of slave denials are curious and tragic. For example, Frederick Douglass told the story of one slave who unwittingly complained to his master and suffered the consequences. According to this tale a Colonel Lloyd owned many slaves, met one of them on the highway, and asked him about his owner. Not recognizing his master any more than his master recognized him, the slave replied that he was the property of Colonel Lloyd. Moreover, in response to additional questions, the slave replied that his master did not treat him well and worked him too hard. Two or three weeks later, Colonel Lloyd sold the slave to a Georgia trader as punishment for complaining.[93] In another unusual instance, a black overseer beat another slave for his insolence. William S. Pettigrew had elevated Moses to a supervisory post on his North Carolina plantation, and Moses wrote to his master about a "fracus" between himself and his "cousin Jerry." According to this 1858 letter, "Jerry was whipping" another slave. When ordered to stop by Moses, Jerry "did not and gave words."[94] Frederick Douglass's earlier tale illustrates that, as far as planters were concerned, a slave's intent was superfluous in judging workplace insolence. Equally disheartening for slaves was Moses's letter. On some plantations, at least, slaves could be punished for talking back to other slaves.

Simple complaints or denials, though perceived as insolent, were not likely to prompt legal process beyond plantation justice. But an analogous case of assault with intent to kill, *Bob v. State*,[95] illustrates the general impact of slave denials on the gentry. In this case the son of Bob's master suffered gunshot injuries to the left side of his head, and measurements of tracks left by the perpetrator that night matched exactly Bob's feet. Moreover, Bob remained silent when confronted with this evidence on the following day. Later, however, he admitted his crime on several occasions and received whippings. Legal errors in admitting most of this evidence resulted initially in a mistrial but, in a second trial, Bob was convicted and sentenced to death. The Alabama Supreme Court eventually reversed Bob's conviction, ruling that all of his tacit and explicit confessions were inadmissible. More to the point, Bob appeared to have caused his own indictment and prosecution by denying his guilt shortly after his final admission. A jailer had previously counseled the slave that admitting his guilt would persuade his master to sell him rather than let him be hung—a reasonable business decision. Yet, in the end, Bob "denied that he was guilty of the crime." His contrariness was noted as "insolence" in the law report.

An unlikely issue at the heart of litigation, a slave's denial could nonetheless provide relevant evidence in determining criminal guilt. In *Jeff v. State*, Mississippi's high court reversed a guilty verdict against a slave for assault and battery with intent to kill. Writing for the court, Justice Harris held that the judge's conduct of the trial and his instruction to the jury on "intent" were flawed. In essence, the judge barred Jeff from offering evidence rebutting the legal presumption of criminal intent in "the natural and probable consequences" of his conscious acts. The jury had only the testimony of John Ballentine, the victim, that Jeff had replied "he had done nothing to be whipped for" when confronted "where he was at work." After a brief fight, in which Ballentine struck Jeff "with a walking cane. . . . a good sized stick," the slave reached in his pocket for a "jack-knife"—a "deadly weapon," according to the testimony. Discouraged momentarily by Ballentine's counter-move of drawing his pistol, Jeff eventually "inflicted two slight wounds" on his foe.[96] In general, the jury would have little trouble believing that Jeff harbored criminal intent. In this specific case, jurors had no trouble at all after hearing that Jeff had spoken insolently to Ballentine.

The gentry's assumption of cunning and lying among their human chattel explains to a large extent their remarkably strong reaction to slave complaints and denials. If left unpunished, these utterances could prompt a belief among slaves that they were able to outwit their overseers or masters, that they could briefly become superior, that they could get away with insolence. The white policy—and black custom—of maintaining silence in the workplace further explains the rare occurrences of these utterances. The gentry had grown sensitive to insolence before many slaves had mastered the English language. Once slaves were linguistically proficient, their verbal denials exacerbated the already punishing outcome of their nonverbal cues.

Assertions of Independence or Equality

When slaves were "uppity" in word or deed, they damaged the gentry's presumption of black subordination. Landon Carter referred to this potential damage in describing his slave General in 1784. A "tailor by trade," General irritated his master because he spoke "readily, and without restraint, seeming to aim at a stile above that used generally by slaves, though something corrupt." General's personal deportment exacerbated "his ingratitude, and want of pretence" in depriving Carter of his skilled services—prompting Carter to authorize severe chastisement of the slave when he was recaptured. But the situation was yet more complex. General was "very remarkable as a runaway" because both his legs had been amputated "near the knees, which being defended by leather, serve him instead of feet."[97] Unwilling to compound his hobbled condition with fawning behavior, General elevated himself through his speech. He did not perfect his manner of address—it was "something corrupt"—but it was nonetheless deeply annoying to his master. More intensely than mere complaints or denials, slaves' assertions of independence impressed the gentry as emblems of insolence because they were perceived as explicit claims to equality.

The language of these assertions bears close scrutiny for its representation of slaves' resistance to the identity imposed on them by their masters. Caesar, for example, offended his Maryland master by boasting "much of his family in his own country, it being a common saying with him, that he is no common negro." Ironically, Caesar shared to a lesser degree the physically reduced condition of General: Caesar had "short pinched up feet" from wearing inadequate shoes and "was a little lamed thereby."[98] Despite his hobbled status, Caesar declined to follow the great majority of his peers in maintaining an abject silence. About the same time in South Carolina, Limus offended his master with his "audacity." Limus declared that "he will be free, that he will serve no Man, and that he will be conquered or governed by no Man." Moreover, although this slave suffered from having "the Ends of three of his Fingers cut off," he was "well known in Charles-Town from his saucy and impudent Tongue."[99] Young, healthy slaves also declared their independence, as illustrated by John Fisher's advertisement for Quamina. Asserting that he could "go when he pleases" and that his master could "do nothing to him," seventeen-year-old Quamina made good on his claim by running away from his duties as "a carver and chair maker." Perhaps emboldened by his value as a skilled worker, he had previously become "well known in and about Charlestown by his impudent behaviour."[100] Young or old, hobbled or hearty, these slaves uttered assertions that clashed sharply with their masters' presumptions about blacks and became alternative clues to their identity.

Claims to independence could be relatively mild. John Holmes, a former slave interviewed in Canada, recalled the time when he simply replied "not to-day" to his master's demand that he submit to a whipping. The master then threatened to shoot, but the slave merely opened his shirt and said "shoot away." Finally, the master ordered "Stand your ground," to which Holmes retorted matter of factly "I've got no ground to stand on." Mild outside their context, Holmes's words eventually prompted his master to shoot him.[101] Another Canadian resident told the same interviewer an anecdote about equally mild language of resistance. John Little had been tied to a tree for leaving the plantation without permission. His master taunted him: "Well, sir, I suppose you think you are a great gentleman . . . you think you can come and go whenever you please." Little responded simply that he "wanted to see [his] mother very bad," but received 500 lashes in punishment.[102] Mild or not, this language represented a challenge in the workplace and drew severe sanctions.

The fates of Samuel and Summer at the hands of Louisiana overseers illustrate clearly the risks faced by slaves in asserting independence and equality. Initially resisting a slave driver's orders to submit to a whipping, Samuel "swore he would not be whipped." The driver then threatened to get the overseer, to which Samuel replied that "he might get who he choose." Ultimately confronted by the overseer, Samuel admitted that he had resisted the driver and declared that he was "not going to be whipped by anybody, black or white." Indeed, the slave continued to resist submission to whipping, swearing "God damn him if he would," and ultimately raised his hoe in defense when the overseer pulled his pistol. The outcome was predictable. A "postmortem examination revealed that Samuel had been shot in the back, the bullet lodging near his spine."[103] Twenty years earlier, Summer had the audacity to assert equality with an overseer. According to the overseer, Summer stated that "I had abused his wife & that he was not going to put up with it & that I was an unjust man, and that I might go get my gun kill him & bury him but that he was not going to put up with any other punishment of himself or family." Shortly afterward, Summer ran away with another slave that the overseer had caned for "some impudence." But the overseer assured the plantation mistress that these episodes were "trifleing misfortunes" and that "the business progresses as it has heretofore."[104] Business interests were prominent in the decisions made by planters and their overseers about dealing with slave insolence. However, overseers' decisions that resulted in the death or loss of a slave diminished the value of planters' assets and required extraordinary justifications. These justifications rested most securely on evidence of continued business success.

The difficulty of justifying harm to slave assets prompted the most skillful overseers to develop enlightened tactics—notwithstanding the continued presence of men such as "Mr. Simmons," who "wouldn't take no talk or foolishness."[105] As Daniel Coleman wrote in the *Southern Cultivator*, overseers in Alabama must shun flogging and "acquire a moral influence" because "the hands are shrewd and cunning, and, under an incompetent overseer, they soon learn to disregard all reasonable restraints." Conversely, coping with the unremitting conflict between slave resistance and planters' demands was just as likely to disgust overseers. Again writing in the *Southern Cultivator*, a Georgia overseer decried the job as "mean and contemptible." He further expressed his determination to quit as soon as he could find "a better business."[106] The difficulty of finding work better suited to their social and professional status ensured that most overseers stayed on the job—demonstrably venting their frustrations on the victims least able to resist.

Given the likelihood of reprisals, slaves rarely made explicit claims to equality. In fact, a late antebellum report by Garnett Andrews in South Carolina suggests that only those slaves who shared labor with their impoverished masters in small business enterprises may have routinely asserted their independence. Colonel Andrews had stayed overnight on a small farm along with two other travelers and noticed an unusual delay in getting his breakfast. The mistress of the farm called for Charles to serve the meal but, after a surprisingly long delay, Charles appeared and "instead of being the husband, or some male relative . . . he turned out to be a big, very black negro." When scolded by his mistress, Charles "answered, that he would take his time, let gentlemen wait, no more gentlemen than he." Andrews was shocked by this event and admitted that it was "rather an extreme case."[107] Charles could not take pride in a special skill but he did exploit his unusual status in his owner's small enterprise. The gentry, in turn, were offended by an outburst that they perceived as insolent in the larger scheme of things. As for the mistress, her "class and race gave [her] a license to interpret any sign of independence as impudence, impertinence, obstinacy."[108]

Slaves themselves recalled painfully the times at which they spoke out in defense of their status in the planting business. Isaac Mason claimed to have suffered beating and shooting in Maryland for enhancing a simple denial of his master's accusations: when ordered to a cellar for punishment, the slave retorted "I will not do it!"[109] More commonplace, however, were slave retorts to overseers about their lack of authority.

Jacob Stroyer executed the carpenter's duties assigned by his mistress and resisted an overseer's subsequent order to work in the fields. "Did I not order ye into the field?" the overseer challenged him. "Yes, sir" the slave replied. "Well, why did ye not go?" the overseer then asked. After the slave explained that his mistress had instead authorized him "to learn the [carpenter's] trade," the overseer bellowed "I will give you ye trade" and whipped Stroyer.[110] Slaves like Stroyer repeatedly demonstrated their sensitivity to the chain of command on large plantations, invoking their master's superior authority in his or her absence as grounds for resisting an overseer's contradictory command—insolence to the overseer, but deference to the master.

Insolence and its punishment remained problems in the exceptional cases where slaves had been entrusted with an overseer's duties. John Hartwell Cocke, for example, elevated the slave George Skipwith to this type of supervisory position on plantations in Virginia during the 1830s and early 1840s. Later in Alabama, however, one of Cocke's white overseers—Elam Tanner—made it his business to investigate George Skipwith's conduct. Tanner discovered that a slave from a neighboring plantation was visiting

George Skipwith without permission. Tanner attempted to correct the visiting slave and became enraged when his black counterpart "abruptly spoke." Skipwith warned Tanner that he "had better be studdying about something that would profit him," and that Tanner "was not his master & had nothing to do there with him." The slave turned overseer was "well lashed" for his insolence on this occasion. In fact, Tanner probably had been looking for an excuse to whip this otherwise lowly slave who "does just as he pleases & stand with his arms hugged up & look at me plane hard all day."[111]

At the same time, Skipwith himself tolerated little verbal resistance from the slaves under his control. He wrote his master in 1847 that he had taken offense at the slave Robert's retort, "he knoed when he worked," when scolded for laziness. "I told him to shut his lips," the black overseer explained, "and if he spoke a nother worde I would whip him right of[f] but he spoke again the second time saying that he was not afraid of being whiped by no man." Matters became worse when Robert eventually swore that "he had as live die as to live."[112] In this complex hierarchy on an Alabama plantation, a black overseer had to report insolence from another slave to a master who could not rely on third-party reports from his white overseer. The only consistent factor remained slaves' disinclination to address their masters insolently.

Even if Jacob Stroyer's tale and George Skipwith's letter can be discounted, collateral testimony elicited in the 1930s Federal Writers Project illustrates the tactic of gaining equality with the overseer by pitting him against the plantation owner. For example, the former slave William recalled his resistance to an overseer's orders because they would have caused the slave to neglect his master's initial work assignment. As the overseer prepared to lash William for his resistance, the slave "straightened up and told the overseer that he would have to prove the better man if the whipping took place." Similarly, Hattie Douglas recalled when her mother refused an overseer's order to wash some socks. Her master was away, and she questioned the legitimacy of the overseer's command. He "struck her and knocked her out."[113] In William's case, his explicit challenge to the overseer underscored his claim to equality. Hattie Douglas's mother claimed her independence less belligerently but suffered a beating because the overseer perceived insolence in her subtlety.

More subtle yet, slaves might be punished for the status offense of simply having business skills as a blacksmith or carpenter. Again in Jacob Stroyer's autobiography, a particularly devious overseer is described as picking fights with slaves for their inchoate, unexpressed claims to equality with whites. "Oh, ye think yourself as good as ye master," this overseer would taunt. And when the slaves did not answer, he would exclaim "ye so big ye can't speak to me." Before administering punishment for their assumed insolence, the overseer would explain: "Ye think because ye have a trade ye are as good as ye master . . . but I will show ye that ye are nothing but a nigger."[114] This assumption of insolent intent also extended to slave children too young to qualify legally as capable of such an intent. Willis Cozart recalled a relevant episode when, as a four- or five-year-old, he received a suitably "little whupping" for telling other slave children not to perform their chores. His master had assigned the children "to work pulling up weeds around the house," but young Cozart persuaded them "Let's don't work none."[115] Rube Montgomery avoided the same fate, due to his mistress's intercession, when he refused to bring water to his "old boss" as ordered.[116]

Only slightly more offensive than simple denials, assertions of independence or equality were only slightly more likely to prompt formal legal process. The facts of *White v. Chambers*, a precedent-setting 1796 case, included perceived insolence by a slave who refused to allow a white passerby to use the fishing canoe he was guarding. The slave claimed to be following higher authority, "his master's orders." Offended by this slave's tactical invocation of his master's authority, the white passerby administered a severe beating. The master's recovery of five pounds sterling for injuries to his slave and court costs was affirmed, in part, because the appellate court preferred that punishment of slave insolence be administered only after "cool deliberation" by third parties rather than "by a freeman's putting himself upon a footing with a negro and taking satisfaction with his own arm."[117] This reference to equal status is striking. Affirming the original verdict, the high court acknowledged the tactical effect of slaves' invoking their master's authority against other whites. Moreover, at least in this late eighteenth-century opinion, personally taking vengeance on an insolent slave also lowered whites to the brute level of slaves.

As illustrated in an 1853 Alabama case, *Dave v. State*, assertions of independence were taken seriously because they were perceived to signify a rebellious if not murderous slave. Dave had ultimately used a "pocket knife" to cut his employer's overseer "in about twenty-six places" after being threatened with a whipping. Events preceding this knifing included the overseer's challenge to Dave for not dutifully feeding livestock on a previous evening, and Dave's assertion that he had been called away by higher authority. He asserted that "his master, Franklin Morgan, had sent word to him that one of his dogs had run mad and that he wished him, Dave, to help him kill" the dog. In curt language the overseer correctly insisted that, since Dave had been hired out, he was bound to obey his overseer and not his master. Ordered to submit to punishment by dropping his pantaloons, Dave replied "that he had done nothing to be whipped for, and that he would not do it." Dave's conviction for assault with intent to kill was set aside by the appellate court because the trial judge had disallowed testimony to his general character "as a peaceable and obedient boy."[118] Even if these character witnesses had been accurate in their testimony, Dave's insolence might have been found relevant to convict him upon retrial. He had taken what was for him an unusual step and crossed the line into unprofitable resistance on the job. More specifically, he had betrayed the unforgivable flaw of being an independent thinker.

A contemporaneous Arkansas case, *Brunson v. Martin*, more tragically illustrates a slave's assertion of independence to an overseer. James Martin was drinking his lunch "at a store in the neighborhood of the plantation" when he was overheard saying that he "had a rough and saucy set of hands to manage" for Robert A. Brunson. Later that afternoon, Martin took up his whip and strode "into the field where the hands were picking cotton." Things quickly got out of hand. Nathan, the first slave that Martin approached, asserted that he "had pulled off his shirt to the last overseer." Martin then pulled his revolver but Nathan exclaimed "*shoot and be damned.*" Nathan died from three shots in his left side. Although Martin testified that the slave had also charged frontally into him, the location of Nathan's mortal wounds suggested otherwise. Thus the appellate court affirmed the original jury verdict allowing Brunson to deduct Nathan's value, fifteen hundred dollars, from Martin's wages.[119] The overseer was a drinking man. He was brutal. In the court's mind, he might also have appeared cowardly. However, the court did not declare that slaves could with impunity assert their equality with overseers. The Arkansas legislature had provided that James Martin could not be indicted for a crime; rather, he had exercised poor business judgment and negligently decreased the value of Robert A Brunson's property.

Insults or Threats

The most intense type of work-related insolence transformed self-references by slaves into direct affronts to whites. Not merely denying their culpability or asserting their independence, slaves committed this type of insolence when they deprecated or intimidated their masters or overseers. Insults and threats share verbal and nonverbal features with the words and deeds of revolt, and distinguishing the two discursive realms can be difficult. Only the immediate context offers an interpretive guide.

The scholarship on slave resistance is substantial enough to resist a review here, but an episode in late eighteenth-century Virginia which has been counted among cases of servile insurrection may more meaningfully illustrate work-related insults and threats. The discourse attributed to a runaway slave in this episode is embedded in working conditions on one plantation rather than in large-scale revolution. Admittedly, the Virginia gentry had become alarmed for their own safety after the Santo Domingo slave revolt of 1791, and the condition of refugees pouring into Norfolk heightened the tension. Reports of organized slave violence in Albemarle County tended to confirm rumors of a plot against Richmond in 1793. However, when a runaway slave brandished "a reap Hook" in his master's face and declared "he would not serve him unless he was allowed certain privileges,"[120] the immediate context identified the slave's insolence as work related. The slave had already returned to the plantation. Furthermore, he expressed an intent to continue laboring if his master granted him special privileges.

Slaveowners faced a variety of insults from their chattel despite the plentiful discipline meted out to slaves, "making them cautious about saying anything uncomplimentary about their masters." Abuse of their family, for example, occasionally prompted slaves to speak insultingly. J. T. Tims remembered the time that his master remarked to Tims's father that he looked "mighty glum," hearing in reply "You'd be lookin' glum too if your wife and child had done been beat up for nothin.'" Confederate reverses also prompted slaves to lash out verbally. While being whipped by her master, Mingo White's mother retorted "Lay it on . . . 'cause I'm goin' to tell de Yankees when dey come." Even potential masters were fair game for insults. Delicia Patterson once discouraged "old Judge Miller" from buying her at auction: "I would not live on your plantation. I will take a knife and cut my own throat from ear to ear before I would be onded by you."[121]

Overseers apparently perceived as unavoidable their duties in regard to punishing intense types of insolence. Frederick Law Olmsted, for example, reported that a slave "insulted and threatened" an overseer while being punished. For his trouble, the slave earned "six buck-shot into his hips." Questioned about his attitude toward dealing harshly with slaves, the overseer remarked that "it's my business, and I think nothing of it."[122] His actions signified that slave insolence seriously troubled the overseer, but his remarks indicated that severely punishing it bothered him little.

The mistresses of plantations became targets of insults about their performance of gender roles. Analogous to the experiences of overseers, these women were reproached tactically for lacking real power. They knew, as did their slaves, "that the master embodied the ultimate authority in the household" and that "the shadow of the master brooded over all."[123] Moreover, these mistresses were held accountable for lives that reflected various ideals—ladylike nobility and moral excellence, as well as strict obedience to their spouses.[124] In their ongoing pursuit of these ideals, these women were especially susceptible to related jibes from their slaves—including the youngest. A former slave recalled, for example, that she and her sister had laughed aloud when their mistress had called them into the manor house to view their deceased master in his coffin.[125]

Helping to manage her parents' Maryland estate in the 1840s, Susanna Warfield engaged in a running battle with the slave Elisa. By her young mistress's own account, this slave was aware of which barbs would especially irk Susanna Warfield. In addition, Elisa usually escaped punishment regardless of the provocation, whether errors in hanging drapes or accidents in stoking a fire. The following entry in Susanna Warfield's diary recounts a particularly pointed incident. "Elisa has been in the tantrums this morning," the young mistress recorded, "and has told me that I am no lady—that Miss Annal and Miss Lucretia Van Bibber are ladies, but I am no lady."[126] A decade earlier in South Carolina, other slaves had similarly taunted their mistress: "You no holy. We holy. You no in state o' salvation."[127] Verbal assaults on their nobility or piety were precisely attuned to these women's greatest fears about their reputations. In fact, these insults could be so devastating that punishing their authors was at least momentarily forgotten. Here the analogy to overseers breaks down.

Journal entries by Sarah Gayle in antebellum Alabama poignantly illustrate the strained working relations between plantation mistresses and their slaves. She observed that the obedience of her slaves was scarcely satisfying because it was "accompanied by murmuring, sour looks & often surly language, that almost put me beside myself." One slave in particular, Hampton, displayed an "insolence and contrary disposition" for years. She finally threatened to sell him but he responded "with the utmost contempt." With mockery and laughter, Hampton stated that Sarah Gayle "was the only mistress he ever failed to please" and that "he could not be worsted" if he were sold to another.[128] The insulting language used by Hampton could just as well have been addressed to an overseer, but Hampton had good reason to expect a different effect.

One of the gender roles played by plantation mistresses—their pursuit of moral excellence—often restrained them from administering brutal punishments. As Keziah Brevard prayed in her antebellum South Carolina diary, "Lord . . . help me to feel a deeper interest in everything that *my master* commands I should—Oh make me thine—wholy thine, *Oh my God.*" More specifically, this mistress of two hundred slaves meditated on her related religious duties. "Lord . . . make us *all & every one*, bond and free, to love thee & do thy will as good servants," she reflected, "*we* are *all* thy servants."[129] Other mistresses simply responded to their slaves' invocation of morality. As a former slave recalled her related experience, she escaped a more severe whipping by exhorting her mistress: "Old Miss, if I were you and you were me, I wouldn't beat you this way."[130] Shouldering heavy responsibilities for plantation management, but conflicted over their working relationship with slaves, mistresses uniquely felt the pangs of slave insults.

In related letters from a Louisiana plantation, Tryphena Fox illustrated a dynamic interaction among the presence of the master, her gender roles, and working relations with slaves. This mistress, a Northerner, wrote frequently about her slave Susan who had been purchased in 1858. Susan was "good three or four weeks," Fox observed, "and then so ugly and contrary that an angel could hardly keep mild and pleasant."[131] Concerned about her own character as less than angelic, Fox also had to reckon with the plantation's chain of authority. By 1859 Susan had become the "greatest annoyance." On a particularly memorable day, Susan subjected her mistress to "unheard of impudence" at which Fox "told her [Fox] must tell her master as soon as he came from town."[132] Only at this point did the slave run away. Invoking the master's authority signified that serious punishment was likely, as opposed to Fox's mere agonizing over her harshly worded criticisms of the slave. As 1860 drew to a close, Fox exclaimed that the recaptured "Susan is worrying me again, beyond endurance." Particularly worrisome was the slave's "impudent" speech despite all that had been previously done about it.[133]

Mistresses may well have earned many of the insults they received as their slaves "found themselves the butt of the mistress's impatience, dissatisfaction, and frequently of her unevenly applied standards."[134] Mary Prince related in her *Narrative* that her "mistress was always abusing and fretting" her, "scolding and rating" her with "ill language." No longer able to tolerate this situation, the slave finally retorted that her mistress "ought not to use me so;—that when I was ill I might have lain and died for what she cared; and no one would then come near me to nurse me, because they were afraid." Her criticism "was a great affront" to her mistress and almost caused Prince to be sold.[135] Perhaps not aspiring to a reputation of being ladylike or pious, Prince's mistress would at least want to be known for having good business sense. It made no sense to destroy assets as valuable as houseslaves.

Insults or threats were not uttered lightly. They often capped an escalation of denials and assertions in a pointed exchange with masters or overseers. An early nineteenth-century episode in the North illustrates typical elements. James Mars's *Life* recounts that, as a teenaged slave in New York, he nearly suffered a whipping for threatening a master who was not known for drunken rages or brutal punishments. His master was not satisfied with the slave's work, but the slave countered that he "had done just what [his master] told me." Normally reticent, the slave angered his master enough that he began to whip him. "You had better not," Mars threatened and then ran off. From that day forward, according to the story, the master never directed "an unpleasant word or look" at the slave; for his part, the slave "was contented and happy."[136] The triumphalism in James Mars's narrative indicates its mixture of fiction with fact. Nonetheless, his tale illustrates the discursive escalation commonplace in threatening utterances.

In a more fully illustrative narrative, Solomon Northup related being sold into slavery despite his free status in Saratoga, New York. He was outraged, of course, and loudly protested his bondage: "I complained bitterly of the strange treatment I had received, and threatened, upon my liberation, to have satisfaction for the wrong." Meeting a blunt denial from his master, he renewed his complaint that he "was no man's slave" and deprecated his captors as "unmitigated villains." In a painful aftermath, he suffered beatings with a "paddle and cat-o'-ninetails."[137] Northup, according to the narrative, exhausted a slave's resources of work-related insolence by engaging in denial, assertion of independence, threat and insult. Equally significant was his subsequent account of adopting complete silence as a more salutary tactic.

Slave insults and threats in the workplace punctuate the fact settings of litigation. Several depositions in the 1780 investigation of William Selby for hanging a slave in Maryland forestalled a prosecution of Selby, and confirmed his defense that the slave Argil was "one of the most attrocious negro Villians." More specifically, according to Selby himself, Argil "Caused several Slaves to Leave their Masters & Join him in his thefts and Insolence." William Bell also stepped forward to swear that Argil told him "that [Argil] would not be Taken or molested by any person." In addition, Daniel Robins swore that, when he had questioned Argil as to his identity, "he Denyd & said he was a free man." The slave then refused to be led away by Robins, "got a fence stake & swore that if [Robins] Touched him that he would kill [Robins]."[138] Similar to legions of his fellow slaves, Argil used denial and an assertion of his independence before resorting to threats. But the closed nature of the system almost guaranteed escalation: milder insolence was punished and forgotten because business concerns were more pressing; a slave's subsequent resort to more intense forms of insolence was perceived as intolerable because of the losses associated with it. Even the milder forms of insolence were perceived as intolerable by white businessmen who foresaw a loss of profit in an unwieldy workforce.

Jacob v. State dramatically illustrates an escalation of insolence in Tennessee. Robert Bradford was upset with his slave Jacob for playing with another young slave when was supposed to be "pulling fodder." He "reproached Jacob for his idleness, and threatened to whip and sell him." Not to be outdone, "Jacob then told his master that he was as tired of him (Bradford) as he (Bradford) was of him." A struggle took place over the switch that Bradford was holding, and Jacob ran away. For the next several days, Bradford ordered Jacob to submit to a whipping every time the slave returned to the plantation, but Jacob would refuse and run off again. As this standoff continued, Bradford's brother Frederick eventually insisted that stronger measures should be taken and helped subdue Jacob when he once again returned to work. Initially, the same scenario was played out: Bradford threatened to whip Jacob and the slave resisted. However, when Jacob tried to fight free of Frederick's grasp, Frederick said, "You must not fool with me or I'll strike you." To which Jacob retorted, "Beat me then, and kill me if you please." Motivated by distaste for his brother's past clemency and the slave's present insolence, Frederick beat Jacob with a stick. Emboldened perhaps by his brother's conduct, Robert joined the fight and the three men struggled for supremacy. Finally—exclaiming "Damn it, clear the way"—Jacob mortally wounded Robert with a "butcher-knife" he had concealed. At trial, Jacob was convicted of murder rather than manslaughter after his deceased master's neighbors and other slaves testified that Robert Bradford was "an indulgent and kind master." On appeal, Nathan Green and his judicial colleagues affirmed the verdict because he found not "a single mitigating circumstance."[139]

Eight years later, in *Nelson v. State*, Justice Green referred to much of his reasoning in *Jacob v. State* as *dicta* and ordered a new trial in the case at hand. The slave Nelson had been convicted of second-degree murder in the killing of David Sellars at a "corn-husking." A planter, John Nesbitt, had asked Sellars, his son-in-law and former overseer, to supervise the activity. When Sellars used "a hickory stick as large as a chair post" to break up a quarrel among Nelson and other slaves, Nelson "spoke in an abrupt manner to Sellars, who then struck Nelson two or three blows." He retreated along with the other slaves but eventually returned at supper time. It was then that Sellars challenged him, "You have come back again, have you?" To which Nelson replied, "Yes, and if you will give a white man's chance, I will whip you like damnation." After the predictably severe beating then given him by Sellars, during which the slave incurred "one or two bad cuts on his head . . . and the blood was running down his face," Nelson killed Sellars with a knife that the slave normally used in his trade of basketmaking.[140]

Although Green claimed to "forbear any commentary" on the facts, he nevertheless distinguished these two cases by pointing out that—unlike Jacob—Nelson did not kill a master or an overseer but a white person who had no formal authority over him. In addition, Nelson had been beaten with a more deadly weapon than had Jacob. But the case was reversed and remanded, not on the facts in evidence, but because the trial judge had erroneously instructed jurors about provocation and available verdicts. Nelson might yet be convicted of unprovoked murder (there was no second degree of this offense available in the case of a slave). For Green, slave "insolence" lay at the heart of the case.[141] Nelson's killing of Sellars was not mitigated unless Sellars had beaten the slave illegally. If Sellars had beaten Nelson for just cause and within the approved limits of severity, then the beating was legal. If Sellars had beaten Nelson for an insolent threat, then just cause could be found in statutory law—despite Sellars's lack of formal authority. As Jacob and Nelson discovered, insults and threats were not taken lightly in the workplace. Indeed, as illustrated five years later in an Alabama case, *Nelson v. Bondurant*, a slave's "insolent and rebellious" response to a combination of between sixty and seventy lashes—administered by a total of four whites—might prompt a jury to suspect just cause for the beating.[142]

Other cases suggest that overseers, whether by incompetence or brutality, prompted the dynamic escalation of slave complaints into insults and threats. Brutality in particular tended to affirm for the gentry slaves' claims of equality with the class of whites from which overseers were typically drawn. Both overseer and slave were perceived as brutes. In *Brady v. Price*, Charles U. Brady accepted the job of overseeing Tempe Price's workforce of "ten or twelve man slaves" despite being told at the outset that "he might have some difficulty in managing them." Brady "thought he could manage them himself" but he was wrong. The overseer soon began having special problems with the slave Miles—difficulties that on one occasion resulted in "marks of blood" on Brady's throat. Miles "spoke up and said something impudent" on another occasion after Brady had issued orders to another slave; ordered "to hush and go about his business," Miles "again said something impudent in reply." A fight ensued but other slaves broke up the scuffle. Miles then left the scene to continue his "ploughing." The overseer waited an hour or two, loaded his shotgun, and pursued the slave. Not finding Miles, Brady tried again the next week when the slave once again was working. Miles ignored the overseer when first confronted, indicating that the slave did not find Brady to be particularly threatening; this time, however, Brady shot the slave in the back twice with birdshot. Finally cornered, Miles drew a pocket knife but put it away when Brady also drew his own knife and ordered the slave to submit. Following Miles back to the plantation house, Brady missed when he tried again to shoot the slave in the back. At trial, and affirmed on appeal, evidence that Miles "had been unable to work" since the shooting and "was of little or no value" persuaded the jury to award $516.67 to Tempe Price.[143]

Charles Brady was, at best, an ineffective overseer. He may also have been a cowardly brute. Despite enjoying formal authority over a slave like Miles, Brady was not taken seriously. Insolence toward Brady was as much an index of Miles's delight in belittling an impotent foe as his contempt in threatening a powerful oppressor.

The Georgia case of *Williams v. Fambro* illustrates the role of insolence in a similar interpersonal dynamic. In this instance a jury directed that Richard W. Williams compensate Allen G. Fambro in the amount of $1,200 despite the absence of eyewitness testimony that Williams mortally wounded Jim, one of the slaves he was overseeing for Fambro. Williams appealed the verdict and won a new trial because the trial court had barred him from using a former overseer's deposition about the deceased slave's character. Williams's predecessor, Robert D. Walker, stated that the slave Jim "was hard to manage and control" and had "a violent disposition." Moreover, the former overseer claimed that Fambro had told him "the negro was dangerous" and had cautioned him "to go armed, so as to defend himself." Three weeks later, when Walker tried to whip Jim for playing cards, the slave "swore he'd be damned if he should do it, and picked up a stick" to defend himself. The former overseer stayed on the job for four months "and whipped Jim three times."[144] In this case, a succession of inept or brutal overseers may have prompted a slave to choose threats when custom and his own experience would have argued against it.

A singular apologia for Southern overseers represents them as misunderstood professionals, attributing their "rapid turnover" not to their "incompetence" but to their "social disesteem" among planters, as well as a business policy of periodically "rotating" overseers. Nonetheless, in the same apologia, reviewing the evidence of flawed ability and malign attitudes among overseers prompts the apologist to conclude that "many who followed the calling . . . were conspicuously deficient" in the virtues sought by planters. Moreover, the policy of rotating overseers was strategic because slaves typically discerned their supervisors' "shortcomings" over time and then began to manipulate them.[145] Perceived accurately as insolence, this manipulation was often effective. Or, as an earlier study of overseers concluded, they were "not likely" to use their vast power over slaves "with enlightenment."[146]

Business concerns influenced the gentry's thought about slavery as clearly as their fear of servile insurrection—the ultimate rebuff to a presumption of subordination. Insolence in the workplace was perceived more immediately as a threat to profit margins than as a threat to white supremacy. The most persuasive explanation for the extent of injuries and deaths to masters and overseers at the hands of slaves was the primary focus on making a good crop. Pursuing a profit and not attending closely to the antagonisms they created by inept or brutal management, masters and overseers were slow to detect the violent backlash they incited among slaves who otherwise preferred to be outwardly submissive.

Managerial ineptitude may be excused to some degree by complex, hierarchical relationships in the planting business. Few humans could have deciphered clearly, much less mastered, the interpersonal dynamic that characterized relations between whites of various classes and between these whites and their black slaves. At law, for example, a casual white passerby of questionable character and social status could discipline slaves in the same manner as a master or overseer under certain conditions. In rare instances, black slaves themselves were elevated to the position of overseer (not to mention the other rare cases in which free blacks owned slaves) and similarly punished insolence from their subordinates. The gentry perceived insolence as a serious problem because it exacerbated the already difficult chore of coping with a complex business system.

Managerial brutality reflected a failure, very often by overseers, to come to terms with the business hierarchy. Ill prepared and poorly motivated in many cases, overseers predictably failed to satisfy expectations about their performance in the hierarchy, both from above and below. Their gritty resort to brutality, in turn, fostered work-related insolence from their subordinates as well as indignation from their superiors. Well aware of overseers' precarious status, slaves made them the principal targets of their resistance. Slaves might utter simple denials to masters and overseers alike, but more intense forms of insolence—assertions of independence and insults or threats—were often reserved exclusively for the overseers. Asserting equality with an overseer was far more plausible than addressing the same insolence to a master; insulting or threatening an overseer was less damaging to a slave's long-term interests than incurring the master's wrath—and did not make a slave immediately liable for sale down the river.

The mistress of a plantation drew insolence in a manner analogous to an overseer. Whether solely responsible for the business or the helpmate of a planter, she could be targeted for manipulation by slaves who sensed her susceptibility to insolent remarks about her authority. Though cast in the form of aspersions about her nobility or piety, these remarks fundamentally attacked her stature in the planting business as a woman, spouse, and helpmate.

Silence was not only favored by the gentry as a business policy, it also was the slaves' preferred choice in dealing with their oppression. Sublimation based on religious piety was another, less widespread, preference. Insolent responses were a last resort; alcohol abuse, for example, was less risky and more pleasurable. But slaves had to choose one or more of these tactics because running away was seldom practical. Denials were typically simple and direct: responding "No indeed" to accusations by a master was piquant but scarcely abhorrent; somewhat more irritating to the gentry was the slave tactic of asking, "What have I done?" The gentry understandably perceived assertions of independence and equality as more contemptible: when a slave declared that white visitors to his mistress's home were "no more gentlemen than he," he stunned his audience. Most intense of all, insults and threats usually brought swift punishment. However, exceptions to this rule can readily be seen when slaves denigrated a mistress's piety or nobility.

When slaves ultimately chose insolence, it appears to have been practiced in an escalating cycle of intensity for which the ineptitude or brutality of overseers was a driving force. An inept overseer might fail to resolve the problem of repeated slave denials and complaints or overreact viciously to this mild form of insolence, prompting a more intense degree of resistance. Available case law illustrates the many instances in which failures to manage the most intense insolence were preludes to violent resistance. This case law also confirms that slave indictments for murder or assault with intent to kill were commonly based on violence to supervisors other than the master.

4

The Polk Overseers

Overseers gained an unsavory reputation despite their key position in the planting business. A gossipy letter to James K. Polk about the related travails of Andrew Jackson illustrates the extent to which an overseer might be shunned while at the same time enjoying considerable influence. A slave had been killed, J. P. Erwin wrote, after he "had been guilty of some misconduct & was brought to the Gen. in chains." General Jackson prescribed ten lashes as punishment. The slave, "alarmed at the threat of the Gen. of giving him so many lashes," had fought Jackson's overseer when "the overseer started off with him to execute this order." The overseer, "probably in self defense," killed the slave. Upset about losing a valuable asset, Jackson threatened the overseer but "he in turn threatened the Gen. & said the investigation would injure him most and that he had been the cause." The delicious part of the gossip, wrote Erwin, was that the whole affair "was then hushed up."[1] Occasionally enjoying congenial relations with planters, overseers were more generally treated as pariahs who breached their employment contracts when they sought alternative friendships with slaves. Indeed, the more elaborate contracts with overseers banned selected forms of address to slaves.[2]

The work-related stress on overseers scarcely ameliorated their social isolation in the planting hierarchy. They were subject to supervision not only by their employer but also by legions of his or her business associates, relatives, friends, and neighbors. Keeping all of these supervisors happy was predictably difficult. Contacts with slaves were equally vexing. Exercising qualified and temporary authority, overseers became natural targets of slave insolence without having reliable and approved means of remedying the problem. As a result, they reacted in proportion to their personal resources of ingenuity and experience. Two centuries of slave beatings and killings testified to how meager these resources could be.

Overseers who toiled for James K. Polk encountered typical problems with slaves. During the 1830s and 1840s, including his terms as governor of Tennessee and president of the United States, Polk owned between twenty and thirty slaves who worked on plantations he owned individually or jointly in southwestern Tennessee and north central Mississippi. Sarah Polk inherited the family business upon her husband's death in 1849. The Polks were absentee planters who relied on reports from their relatives, agents, and neighboring planters, as well as from their overseers: Ephraim Beanland (late 1833 to December 1834), G. W. Mayo (January 1836 to October 1836), George W. Bratton (November 1836 to his death on July 2, 1839), John I. Garner (July

1839 to late 1840), Isaac H. Dismukes (late 1840 to December 1844), and John A. Mairs (January 1845 to 1858). Firsthand reports from these overseers and observations from others in the Polk business network illustrate the meaning of slave resistance—especially insolence—in the workplace.

A Meeting of the Minds

Planters' widespread dissatisfaction with overseers, resulting in a remarkable turnover, cannot be attributed solely to overseers' ineptitude or misconduct. Problems in this primary business relationship also arose from differing opinions about slave management as well as vacillation on both sides in applying these policies. Incidents in the Polks' working relationship with their overseers are representative.

Related friction between Polk and Ephraim Beanland began on the Fayette County plantation in Tennessee. On December 22, 1833, the overseer reported that the slaves Jack and Ben had run away during the prior month. Jack in particular had fled after being "corected" for burglarizing a grocery store and then "corected" again for "telling em 5 or 6 positif lyes" in his defense. Although Beanland adopted a deferential tone and disclaimed that he was "able to advise" Polk, the overseer nonetheless declared that he wanted both slaves "brought back" rather than sold: "If they aint the rest will leave me also." After reporting on the crops, Beanland again addressed the issue of slave discipline. "Your negroes has traded with white people," he advised Polk, "and bin let run at so loce rained that I must be verry cloce with them."[3] In essence, the slave Jack had uttered a denial and subsequently fled after he "was very badly whip'd indeed," including being "salted . . . four or five times during the whipping."[4] Sensing that his conduct needed justification, the overseer specifically appealed to Polk's pecuniary interest in slave assets and generally defended his treatment of Jack by citing the formerly loose rein given to Polk's slaves.

Beanland prevailed in the matter of Jack's recapture, although Polk incurred significant expenses in recovering the slave from the Arkansas Territory where he had fled. Next, the overseer also urged his employer to have Ben returned rather than permitting the slave to be employed at an iron works. "Ben ought to brought back," Beanland argued early in 1834, "for he is a grand scoundrel." Moreover, in a business sense, the overseer claimed that not returning Ben to the plantation would compromise discipline of the remaining slaves: "If I corect any of the others they ar shore to leave me . . . for they must be youmered to as well as ben."[5] In this instance Beanland took the extraordinary step of instructing his superior about the planting business. Arguing against any semblance of catering to the slaves, the overseer insisted that he could not otherwise maintain his control over them.

Later that same month, Beanland repeated his argument that other slaves "will run away" unless Ben was returned. He cited as proof his recent problems with the slaves Hardy, Jim and Wally—all of whom had abandoned their plowing and fled despite Beanland's claim that he had "not struck them a lick nor threeened to do it." More pointedly, he asserted that he "did [not] now that they was insulted any way."[6] Implicit in this latter denial is the type of friction that impaired the planter-overseer relationship: Beanland had clearly been instructed by Polk not to antagonize or "insult" the slaves—a remarkable turnabout in a business where slaves were routinely and brutally punished for their impudence toward overseers. And once again, as reported in a letter early the next month, the overseer prevailed.[7]

Having persuaded Polk to do things his way, Beanland exhausted his rhetorical reserves early in April when he reported another incident involving the slave Jack. Prefacing his letter with the claim that "I thinke that I am getting on tolerable well at this time," the overseer then abruptly reversed himself. "On munday last," he reported, "I took up Jacke to corect him and he curste me verry much and run alf before my face." The slave had learned how Beanland responded to simple denials; immediately after cursing the overseer, Jack fled. Beanland soon apprehended Jack, stabbed him twice, and placed him in chains, but not until the slave had broken a stick over Beanland's head. Continuing in an antithetical mode, Beanland expressed his resolve to "worke" Jack despite the slave's oath "that he will never stay with the Polk family any more."[8] After repeated disciplinary problems, runaway slaves were customarily sold to a broker in an effort to expunge their bad example for other slaves. In contrast, Beanland resisted custom and its practical appeal to Polk.

Six months later, Beanland was compelled to report that Jack had been true to his word, had continued to run away, and also successfully encouraged other slaves to join him. "I say sell the aolde scoundrel," Beanland now advised Polk, "tho if you wante him worked send him on and I will take good care of him and secure him." The double irony in his overseer's remarks could not have escaped Polk's attention: first, Beanland was now attributing to Polk a desire to keep Jack on the job; and second, the overseer was asserting his ability to manage a slave that had cursed him, beat him, and fled to Arkansas more than once. Worse yet, Beanland also asserted that Polk was in danger of breaching his duty to fellow planters. "I wante you to sell Jack and never let him come here no more," the overseer wrote, "for they is a greate meny of the neighbors is afraide for him to come hear."[9] Beanland's temerity in warning Polk about his obligations must have been particularly rankling in view of the overseer's prior insistence on retaining Jack. Yet, despite the friction, Polk did not dismiss Beanland. Indeed, he entrusted him with supervising a transfer of business operations to Yalobusha County, Mississippi.

Slave resistance, including specific acts of insolence, had strained their working relationship but Polk did not replace his overseer when he began developing a new plantation. Rather, it was Polk's brother-in-law and partner in the Mississippi enterprise, Silas M. Caldwell, who fired Ephraim Beanland at the end of 1835. The new overseer, G. W. Mayo, lasted less than a year. About the same time that Mayo was fired, Caldwell sold his share in the business to Polk and his younger brother, William. Caldwell's last act before leaving the wilds of Mississippi was to hire George W. Bratton as overseer. Bratton earned satisfactory marks until his death in July 1839. However, Bratton's replacement quickly became enmeshed in the familiar pattern of slave resistance and flight during his brief term of service.

John I. Garner, Bratton's successor, did not lack confidence. Although he responded deferentially to Polk's directing him "how to manage . . . business," the overseer also asserted his special talent. "When I came here," he wrote to Polk, "there was some three or fore [slaves] lying up without a cause though I have not been pestered cence." Garner attributed his success at remedying the slaves' complaints and malingering to his skill at understanding slave psychology: "It recuire a person to lern the disposition of a negrow to manage them."[10] Only two months later, however, Garner began to narrate events that called into question his mastery of slave psychology. "The Boy charls" ran away "witheout any cause whatever"; moreover, complained Garner, he was "pestered withe mareners conduct."[11] A familiar pattern had reappeared in which the overseer reported that a slave had run away without cause and that slave misconduct was annoying him.

After slightly more than one year on the job, Garner advised his employer that he "had the misfortune to loose the work of three of my negroes." A fourth slave had tried to run away but was shot "in the legs." Garner's choice of words illustrates the business perspective from which slave misconduct was being viewed: he had lost "the work" of the slaves. The trouble had started when the slave Henry "had become . . . indiferent about his duty." Garner tried "to corect him," Henry "resisted" and fought back, and other slaves "refused" to help the overseer. The overseer's harsh response to Henry's grudging labor had escalated into the slave's assertion of equality and other slaves' refusals to assist in his punishment. This episode is all the more noteworthy because Garner also reported that one of the runaways, Charles, had been insolent: "I lern that charls told to the negroes that he cold of made his escape before if he had bin a mind to."[12] Threatening speech by Charles completed the cycle of slave insolence. Garner's claim to be a slave psychologist proved to be false, and Polk soon dismissed him.

The next overseer, Isaac H. Dismukes, avoided many of the problems that bedeviled his predecessor. Ironically, he was ultimately fired for creating new ones. Dismukes initially advised Polk that "wea are all wel with the exception of some little complaining nouthing though very sereis."[13] Having encountered nothing more than the mildest form of slave insolence, "some little complaining" that did not bother him, the overseer reported "I have noe diffeculty with my boys."[14] However, Dismukes began to face the problem of runaway slaves nine months into his tenure. He restated the arguments that Ephraim Beanland had addressed to Polk, insisting that the offending slaves should not be sold "if you wish to brake them from running away." Elaborating further, the overseer claimed that slaves "had reather bea sould twise than to bea whip once." Also like Beanland, Dismukes acknowledged that Polk routinely instructed his overseers to avoid antagonizing the slaves. Arguing that the slave Gilbert should be returned rather than sold, Dismukes promised that he would not "inger him by whiping him." As Beanland had eventually been forced to deny insulting Polk's slaves, now Dismukes denied that he would rouse their anger.[15] Enjoying a longer tenure than any previous overseer employed by the Polk family, Dismukes ultimately lost his job for spending too much time on entertaining himself. On the other hand, arguing with his employer over management policies was a routine part of the job.

Polk's success in presidential politics ensured that he would devote less exacting attention to his next overseer, John A. Mairs. Moreover, by the time of Polk's death, Mairs had secured a lengthy tenure by becoming indispensable to Sarah Polk. Yet the overseer encountered, if not created, the same problems faced by unsuccessful predecessors such as Ephraim Beanland and Isaac Dismukes. Although he reported at the beginning of 1851 that the "servents are all well at present," he also advised Sarah Polk that "some of them have behaved vary badly."[16] Sustaining his antithetical style one month later, Mairs wrote that "the negros are nough working vary well" but that "Gilbert has ran away."[17] Within the next two months Gilbert had returned but fled again, and Pompey had also run away.[18] Matter of factly reporting these incidents without elaboration, Mairs did not defend his own conduct nor did he provide any narratives of the slaves' misconduct.

Only in subsequent years, after his tenure was secure, did Mairs adopt a defensive tenor and fill in the details of slave resistance as his predecessors had done. In 1853, for example, he reported that the slave Joe had run away—taking another slave with him—"without enny cause."[19] One month later, after further consideration, Mairs wrote that he had "not touched" Joe after the incident but that the slave's bad example had to be remedied.[20] Perhaps sensing that he was insulated against the fates of his predecessors, Mairs now freely aped their style of reporting on plantation affairs. Outright disclaimers of his provocation of slave flight and denials of his antagonizing slaves were prominent.

Conditions had not improved by early 1856. Mairs now identified Harbard, "a bad boy," as the most troublesome slave on the Yalobusha County plantation. Harbard had already run away "wons or twis but dyed not stay out long." Nonetheless, the overseer declared his resolution to "ceap him at home and make him attend to his bisniss."[21] Notwithstanding Beanland's experience with the slave Jack, Mairs pursued the rehabilitation of Harbard for several months. In September, however, Mairs reported that Harbard had persuaded two other slaves to join him in fleeing to Memphis. In addition, slaves told the overseer that Harbard "tryed to get 2 others along with him" by boasting that "he cold of got away before."[22] Harbard's insolent boasting, a close parallel to the pivotal event in John Garner's unsuccessful tenure as overseer, punctuated the cycle of slave resistance and flight that once again disrupted the Polk family business.

The friction between the Polks and their overseers was no different than that described a few years earlier by John Nevitt in Adams County. Although Nevitt resided on his Clermont plantation near Natchez, he was frequently absent—by his own account—to play cards and attend duels as well as the less colorful activities of fishing and shopping.[23] His chronicle of plantation affairs during 1827, identifying the brief tenures of five different overseers during that one year, underscores the influence of slave resistance.[24]

Nevitt did not explain his decisions to fire three overseers during the first six months, although he noted the flight, return, and inconsistent punishment of slaves during the period. Nevitt hired Miles Purvis on January 1 "to oversee the Plantation" at an annual salary of six hundred dollars but, on January 4, he "discharged Miles Purvis overseer as unfit for his Employment." Two weeks later Nevitt "ingaged G. D. Blackman overseer for one year" at a salary of five hundred dollars. However, when the slave Bill "ran away" ten days later, Blackman was fired. Two days later, at the same time that "Bill came home," Blackman was "reinstated"—only to be discharged again on March 31. The next overseer, Thomas B. Hazard, lasted three months. During his tenure the slaves Maria and John ran away: Nevitt "whiped Maria and put Iron on her leg" when she was recaptured; perhaps because John returned voluntarily Nevitt "forgave him and set him to work." Nevitt did not report whether the overseer agreed with his disparate treatments of the two runaway slaves. Instead, he recorded Hazard's repeated absences from the plantation "with out knowledge."

Having fired Hazard on July 5, Nevitt managed plantation affairs himself for the remainder of the growing season but he fared no better than his overseers in managing the slaves. During August John and Maria ran away again. John was once again forgiven after he returned voluntarily; Maria received "a light whiping" upon her recapture. On August 27 "Cinthia run away" and received "a light whiping" the day after she returned voluntarily. She may have been punished, rather than forgiven, because Nevitt had recently rewarded the slaves with a half-day "hollyday" and "a dance at night" for their good work "during the making and laying by the crop." Regardless, after John ran away again on September 14, Nevitt decided to try another overseer.

Norman McCleod was hired on September 18 with a month-to-month salary of twenty-five dollars. Before McLeod was "discharged from further service as overseer" on December 17, slave resistance increased dramatically. The slaves George, Bill, and Rubin ran away during the first two weeks of McLeod's tenure. Maria also continued to flee the plantation. Recaptured on October 2 and punished with "a severe whiping," she ran away again on October 8. The following day, a Tuesday, McLeod "went to town and got drunk." Nevitt enjoyed relative calm on the plantation for the next month, but he could not have been pleased with the turn of events following McLeod's hiring. He certainly did not appreciate the remainder of his overseer's tenure. When Maria was recaptured on November 8, Nevitt "had her whiped severely an Ironed with a shackle on Each leg connected with a chain." He also enhanced his punishment of John whether the slave returned voluntarily or not: on November 23 he "put big Iron on John." During the next two weeks, Dilly, Maria, and Rubin fled the plantation and all received "a light whiping" despite returning voluntarily. Nevitt then replaced McLeod on December 20 with an overseer named "Fordce."

John Nevitt experienced the same types of friction with his five overseers in one year that the Polk family would later experience with six overseers during twenty years. Slave discontent, expressed most emphatically in running away, was not easily remedied. A lack of solidarity between planter and overseer predictably hampered the design and execution of remedies, typically resulting in inconsistent or uneven discipline of an already discontented labor force. As a business decision, replacing middle management was reasonable. The Polk overseers may have enjoyed longer tenures than Nevitt's overseers simply because their employer lived at a distance. Yet the common means of resolving this lack of personal knowledge—relying on a network of local observers—created another major source of friction unrelated to overseers' ineptitude or misconduct.

A Web of Authority

Silas M. Caldwell was not only James K. Polk's business partner, he was also his brother-in-law. Along with his wife, Eliza, Caldwell regularly reported on plantation affairs and the performance of overseers. Two other brothers-in-law, A. O. Harris and James Walker, also consulted actively with Polk, as did his younger brother, William, who briefly owned a one-quarter share in the Yalobusha enterprise. In addition, business agents and neighboring planters freely voiced their opinions about the Polk overseers. George Moore, Albert F. McNeal, William Bobbit, John T. Leigh, and John W. Childress were prominent in this second category of consultants. As a result, when the Polk overseers needed to explain their conduct, they had to plead their cases within a complex business network.

Ephraim Beanland initially confronted a web of authority in resolving the dispute over how to discipline the runaway slaves Jack and Ben. In complaining to Polk about "a set of white people that lives cloce hear that would spoile any set of slaves,"[25] the overseer obliquely criticized A. O. Harris and Silas Caldwell for subverting his position and for relying on slave complaints rather than firsthand knowledge. Harris, for example, interviewed the runaway slaves because they sought refuge with him and advised Polk that Beanland "will not treat your negroes as you would wish." More specifically, Harris reported, the slaves claimed that Beanland was "very severe" and responded only with "curses" to their hard work.[26] Hiring out one of the slaves at a nearby foundry, Harris reluctantly sent the other back to Beanland with the hope that "[James] Walker, when he visits the District, will . . . go to your place and set all things right."[27] Caldwell, for his part, visited the plantation and reported to Polk that the "negroes here are very much dissatisfied. I believe I have got them quieted. Some others spoke of running away." Moreover, wrote Caldwell, Beanland lacked "stability." Referring guardedly to slave complaints, he observed that Beanland "likes his liquor." Finally, though admitting his lack of personal "observation," Caldwell opined that "if Beanland would be more mild with the negroes he would get along with them better."[28]

Taking the offensive against his critics, Beanland wrote Polk that "haris done rong" when he found work for one of the runaway slaves off the plantation.[29] Pleading his case to James Walker, Beanland rebutted slave complaints about harsh treatment. "I never corected him," the overseer explained his treatment of the slave Hardy, "tho I talked to him and it insulted him and he went off." But the web of authority was most vexing. Beanland added effusively: "I do not like in the first plase I must please Calwell and Mr. Haris as it apeares and then if I donte please everry negro on the place they rin away rite strate and then if I do not make a crop my imploier of ciorse will not like it and I would like to now how I can please them all and make a crop two."[30] Clearly upset by the notion that his treatment of slaves was ironically being adjudged as insolent and that the issue of profitable farming was being ignored, the overseer criticized Harris and Caldwell for undermining his authority on the plantation. Two months later, one of the slaves cursed Beanland to his face and beat him with a stick before the overseer could subdue the slave.

Beanland's successor, G. W. Mayo, was the target of criticism within the Polk business network long after his dismissal. Albert F. McNeal, a neighboring planter in Mississippi, compared Mayo unfavorably with his successor, George W. Bratton. According to McNeal, Bratton had "the negroes completely under his control" unlike the previous regime in which "they were no doubt spoiled by the inefficient and trifling" management by Mayo.[31] McNeal continued to figure prominently in the friction between Polk and his overseers. In 1839, for instance, he became the target of criticism by Bratton's successor, John I. Garner. Garner, the self-proclaimed slave psychologist, complained to his employer that McNeal was harming plantation management by offering "protection" to runaway slaves.[32] Overseers took risks when they criticized people higher in the planting hierarchy, but Garner evidently calculated that his position was secure.

Despite Garner's show of confidence, he had more than one consultant to pacify. Again based on slave testimony, Silas Caldwell questioned Garner's explanation of his problem with insolent slaves during October 1840— including the shooting of Perry. Countering the overseer's claim that "there was no difference in the world" between himself and the slaves,[33] Caldwell reported that in addition to Perry's injury "the Overseer had threatened to shoot [Henry] for nothing." As a result, Caldwell decided to offer refuge to Henry because "he says he is afraid to go back." Moreover, Caldwell expanded his scope of criticism to include the charge—based solely on Henry's testimony—that Garner had "not got a good crop of neither corn or cotton."[34] His business partner's linkage of slave mismanagement with poor crops prompted Polk to dismiss Garner.

Garner's replacement, Isaac H. Dismukes, became the object of even greater scrutiny in the Polk business network. One of Polk's business agents in Mississippi, William Bobbitt, inspected the Yalobusha County plantation and reported favorably on the overseer, calling him "an energetic businessman." Most importantly, in view of the recent trouble with Dismukes's predecessor, Bobbitt reported that the "negroes and he are getting along smoothly and so far as I can ascertain they are well satisfied with the overseer."[35] In this account, at least, the overseer was fitting comfortably into the planting hierarchy, but Bobbitt's report also confirms that Dismukes was subject to evaluation from above and below. More than a year later, he received another favorable evaluation from John T. Leigh that reported healthy slaves and a fine crop.[36] In the meantime, Silas Caldwell and his wife expressed contrary opinions of Dismukes's worth. Again reporting the testimony of a fugitive slave, Caldwell advised Polk that "the Overseer says he will kill [the slave] and is afraid to stay there."[37] Wounds on the slave's neck and arms convinced Caldwell that the fugitive was telling the truth. Shortly afterward, conveying "the negroes own tales," Eliza Caldwell mentioned additional criticisms of Dismukes in a letter to Sarah Polk. "From all accounts," Mrs. Caldwell observed, "the overseer drinks and manages badly."[38] Perhaps because his advisors submitted conflicting reports, Polk did not fire Dismukes for several more years.

Although he enjoyed a much longer tenure than Dismukes, John A. Mairs did not escape having to cope with the web of authority that surrounded him. In his particular case, this web featured several members of the extended Polk family. During 1845, for example, one of Sarah Polk's nieces interceded on behalf of a slave under Mairs's regime. Mary S. Jetton, representing her "Aunt Peggy," contested "the treatment of Caroline by your Overseer" and asked Sarah Polk to "get Uncle James to write to [Mairs] on the subject." The niece communicated fears that "the girl will be used bad at [Polk's] farm" and inquired about buying the slave in the near future.[39] In a remarkable turn of events three years later, Eliza Caldwell commended Mairs. Writing to her brother during his presidency, Mrs. Caldwell assured him that "the Overseer was very moderate with [the recaptured slave Addison]." To Eliza Caldwell's delight, Mairs "corrected him but not bad." Moreover, she reported that one of her neighbors—a man on whom Polk could "depend"—considered Mairs to be "a first rate man."[40] This overseer served the Polks for many years and became indispensable to Sarah after the death of her husband. Mairs's long tenure may be attributed, at least partially, to commendations of his work from unlikely references such as the Caldwells.

Just as dissension over policy between the Polk family and their overseers was not unique on Mississippi plantations, neither was their overseers' need to cope with a complex web of authority. While managing a plantation in Lowndes County for the Hamilton family of Williamsboro, North Carolina, Harlan Crenshaw was under the scrutiny of several family members as well as neighboring planters. Like his fellow overseers, Crenshaw filed reports on a fairly regular schedule. But on the same June day in 1841 that Crenshaw cautioned his employers not to expect a bumper crop due to "cold nights and Lice" and "want of rane,"[41] a neighboring planter named Thomas Bell wrote contrarily: "I was at your plantation yesterday all is well Crenshaw is getting on very well your crop are in good order the lice has injured your crop some you will make a fine crop."[42] Clearly, if the overseer failed to report regularly, then he might miss opportunities to confirm or deny contemporaneous assessments of his work in the Hamilton business network.

James A. Hamilton visited the plantation during the following February and advised his brother, Charles, that "no management skill or labour could have changed the result" of the poor 1841 crop foreseen by Crenshaw and disputed by Bell. Indeed, the visiting planter reported, Charles had "erroneously" blamed the overseer for the setback. "All our neighbors voluntarily concur in praising his industry, close attention, and general management of all matters concerning the plantation," James Hamilton elaborated, and "Bell made as small if not smaller crop." Nonetheless, Crenshaw was fired. On a hopeful note, James Hamilton wrote that he was "very much pleased" with a new overseer named "Herron."[43] In this instance, the rapid turnover in overseers appeared to benefit everyone, including Crenshaw.

Thomas Bell again reported to the Hamilton family during the following July, predicting good harvests of cotton and corn.[44] And again in June 1843, Bell advised Charles Hamilton to tell his brother that "Mr. Herron" was "doeing well."[45] Herron had succeeded but Crenshaw had also prospered. Yet another Hamilton brother, Robert, in reporting on the family holdings on Red Creek in southern Mississippi, recited recent achievements by the overseer James had dismissed. "The crops are better here than they have ever been known to be within the memory of the oldest settler," Robert wrote to Charles. Moreover, Robert asserted that Crenshaw "has, it is said, the finest crop on Red River and has got his name up."[46] Lacking additional testimonials, it remains moot whether Crenshaw prospered after he left the Hamiltons because he had improved his communication skills, or because he was no longer answerable to three brothers and their consultants. More certainly, his experience with the Hamilton family illustrates that overseers needed to cope with a web of higher authority.

The Polk overseers did not have to cope with slave insolence on a regular basis. Both the business policy of planters and the survival tactics of slaves ensured that insolence was unusual in the plantation routine. Moreover, the slave insolence that was addressed to the overseers was apparently never addressed to planters. Indeed, while Silas Caldwell owned a half interest in the Yalobusha County plantation, he routinely harbored fugitive slaves from his own work force. At the same time, the Polk overseers did not dine at their employer's table, much less enjoy anything approaching a social relationship with the Polks. Ephraim Beanland and his successors were caught in the middle of a planting hierarchy—equally liable for not being satisfactory to the slaves and not satisfying expectations of the planters. Seeking temporary relief, these overseers occasionally abandoned their duties, drank to excess, and breached their employment contracts in various other ways. They also lashed out at slaves when provoked by the milder forms of insolence.

Socially isolated and under pressure to produce good crops, overseers were tempted to react viscerally to slave resistance—much as the slaves themselves reacted to analogous oppression and stress. Slaves on the Polk plantations insolently addressed overseers with complaints, assertions of equality, and outright insults despite knowing the consequences. Like slaves, overseers knew better than to breach formal and informal rules but occasionally could not restrain themselves. Employment contracts such as those drafted by Plowden C. J. Weston banned overseers from directing "abusive language" to slaves; James K. Polk and his various consultants just as clearly banned overseers from insulting or angering the slaves. Of course, overseers could defend their offensive discourse under pain of being dismissed. For overseers this would be a monetary setback, but for slaves it would be a wrenching dislocation from family and friends.

Critical scrutiny from all sides may have been the final prompting event in overseers' vicious responses to slave resistance. As illustrated in the Polk business network, overseers were assessed by a variety of consultants. In some instances, these agents relied solely on slave testimony. Given prevailing attitudes toward slave resistance in the planting business, the overseer might well expect little or no disapproval for harshly punishing an insolent slave. If runaways could be kept to an acceptable minimum, then punishing insolence added nothing to the usual cost of doing business. Moreover, punishing slave insolence offered a satisfying outlet for the feelings of frustration and indignation aroused in an overseer as a result of being scrutinized and evaluated by a bewildering variety of men, women, and children. In these instances, self-persuasion replaced perception as the overseer convinced himself that he deserved satisfaction rather than spontaneously perceiving offensive slave behavior.

Part 3
The Social Perspective

5

"An Offence Which Consists of Inconsistency"

Compared with routine communications in the workplace, the ruling class had little need and less desire to interact socially with slaves. Indeed, slave insolence was a social problem. Members of the planter class despised threats to their social standing as much as they abhorred business reverses. Social classes had been established early. More particularly, as Europeans explored the Atlantic coasts, they may have debased Africans—as well as Indians and any other non-white people—because of color, religion, and custom.[1] As Tryphena Fox illustrated in an 1857 letter, this debasement was firmly established in the twilight of the planting culture. "I am a little timid," this Northerner confessed, "among such a rabble of negroes & Creoles as surround us & no decent white person within a mile."[2] Although clear social norms relevant to the plantation system had been established, grounding their speech in these norms might not insulate slaves from being perceived as insolent because of a double standard. Among whites, for example, speaking out of turn was discourteous. For blacks, it was anathema.

In articulating their legislative and business perspectives, the gentry also expressed basic norms of Southern society: men must be honorable and women must be virtuous. The prominence of duels and the axiomatic "cult of true womanhood" illustrated these basic norms.[3] Affronts to either norm prompted swift sanctions because, not only did violations offend personally held beliefs and values, they also attacked the corporate character of the society. Moreover, class distinctions justified a double standard in judging normative violations. The distinctions between classes of white people reflected varying degrees of wealth whereas the gulf between white and black reflected differences in kind rather than degree. Indeed, the gulf might be interpreted as a denial of any social standing to blacks. Consistent with either interpretation, the gap between white and black could never be bridged and it validated a double standard in assessing the slaves' adherence to social norms.

The social order was so compelling that whites had to monitor their form of address to slaves. For example, an observer advised Frederick Law Olmsted that "a young English fellow" had been run out of a Virginia town for talking to slaves "free like." The local gentry made no allowances for the recent immigrant's lack of acculturation because they feared that his egalitarian conduct would "make [slaves] think too much of themselves." More socially acceptable was the outlook of a Tennessee planter's wife who detested the thought of living among free blacks. "If they was to think themselves equal to we," she declared, "I don't think white folks could abide it—they're such vile saucy things."[4]

Only the most recently arrived Africans might not recognize the social order, but slaveowners nonetheless lectured their chattel about knowing their place. Sella Martin may have misinterpreted the relatively sophisticated atmosphere of New Orleans and was eventually sold by his master, John P. Cady, for remaining "saucy" despite advice to the contrary. In a noteworthy prompting event, the slave had quarreled with the commander of a boat on which he was working and received fair warning from Cady: "Your notions are too elevated for a slave, and if you are going on in this way insulting white people, some one of them will kill you, and be justified for doing it." Not especially altruistic in delivering this warning, the master feared that he might lose his slave "without hope of compensation."[5] In broader terms, however, the warning articulated white perceptions of the social order.

Distinctions were arguably less severe between the lower classes, but slaves nonetheless had to monitor their speech about white yeomen. James Bolton recalled that slaves "never hyard nuffin' 'bout no po' white trash in them days, an' effen we had hyard sumpin' lak that, we 'ud er knowed better'n to let Marster hyar us make such talk."[6] As an index of the social order's significance to planters, Bolton not only feared impudence to his master but also restrained himself from speaking critically of lower-class whites in his master's presence.

Remaining silent in the master's presence was more customary than deferring to poor whites. H. C. Bruce may have unwittingly suffered repeated whippings because he saw "this unfortunate class of Southern people" in Missouri as possessing "few more privileges than the slaves." Bruce had been sent on horseback to secure garden seed, and his master had cautioned him not to ride the horse too hard. Happily obeying because a more leisurely journey prolonged his respite from field work, Bruce was later charged by a poor white with riding the horse at a gallop. His master then threatened to whip him for disobedience. In error, Bruce actually secured this punishment by claiming that his accuser was lying. Soundly whipped according to his master for "disputing a white man's word," Bruce again denied his guilt and was whipped again. "Will you have the impudence," his master shouted, "to dispute a white man's word again?" To which the now enlightened slave replied, "No sir." Later in life, Bruce again violated the tenuous distinction between blacks and poor whites by impudently resisting punishment by a yeoman to whom he had been leased—"in language which he understood."[7] In essence, as Bruce learned painfully, maintenance of the social order required that slaves defer to all whites regardless of their relative social position.

Defining slave insolence in this social setting was difficult because a vocabulary reflecting white social norms could not easily be adapted to assess slave conduct. In *Ex Parte Boylston* Justice O'Neall struggled to identify a standard against which slave speech could be measured. He found no statutory law against slave insolence but admitted that "insolence beyond all doubt is a violation of duty, which the social condition of the slave imposes upon him."[8] Justice Wardlaw, author of the majority opinion in *Ex Parte Boylston*, found a common law against slave insolence in South Carolina—despite "its undefinable nature and various shades"—because society demanded sanctions for any "language and deportment of a slave towards a white person, which is inconsistent with the relation between them." He stated further that insolence was "multiform and incapable of definition," much like "ungentlemanly deportment" or any other "offence which consists of inconsistency between conduct and station."[9] For Justices O'Neall and Wardlaw, the rules of etiquette remained largely unwritten but sustaining them was nonetheless paramount.

Other judges sustained sanctions against slave insolence as desirable for discouraging more serious breaches of social conduct. Frederic Nash, author of *State v. Bill*, endorsed the delegation of extraordinary powers over slave misconduct to local magistrates in order to stave off "higher and worse offences" against "the domestic order of the State." This higher purpose of pre-emptive strikes against breaches of social etiquette obviated the need for legislative clarity in defining the offences. "Standing in the relative position which the white man and the slave occupy," Nash observed, "there are and must be a great variety of the acts of the latter which cannot and ought not to be suffered, and which could be highly calculated to exasperate."[10] Nash occasionally expressed a morose perspective on his life and times: his correspondence reveals gloomy meditations on a "treacherous treacherous world" that "entices us with forgetfulness of higher duties."[11] Combined with the unsavory and slanderous charges made by the slave Bill against a white woman in the case under review, Justice Nash's mindset ensured a decision against the slave's interest. This decision nonetheless rested on the judge's admission that "it is manifestly impossible to define" slave insolence.[12]

Technically difficult to define, offensive speech by slaves was readily abhorred as socially deviant. Simple, spontaneous perception of this deviance was doubtlessly common among white Southrons who genuinely believed in their superiority. However, as the issue of slave insolence migrated away from tangible business concerns toward abstract social norms, Southrons engaged just as commonly in self-persuasion when they decried offensive speech by slaves. At both levels, the gentry recognized slave insolence in drunken mutterings, complaints and insults, affronts to women, and a variety of nonverbal cues.

Drunk and Disorderly

Losing self-control by abusing alcohol was no excuse for violating the social order. Planters and slaves alike used liquor as a social lubricant and a means of relieving various types of pain, emotional as well as physical. But, while an intoxicated planter would be seen as merely discourteous unless his drinking led to violent conduct, a drunken slave was likely to be perceived as outrageously insolent. For example, Thomas Jefferson described Sandy as "insolent and disorderly" in 1769 when this slave had taken to "drink."[13] Jefferson also indicated that his slave would swear frequently under the influence of alcohol—an unusual vice for people who generally had not mastered English by this time. As Gustavus Vassa claimed sarcastically in 1814, Africans were unlike "more civilized people" and were "totally unacquainted with swearing." Indeed, the strongest language this slave could recall among his peers were expressions like "may you rot!" "may you swell!" or "may a beast take you!"[14]

Elsewhere in Virginia during the following decade, runaway slave advertisements echo Jefferson's complaint and illustrate the double standard used in assessing slaves' use of alcohol to obtain relief from various sorts of pain. Slaves were described as "very talkative" when drunk and "very bold."[15] Indeed, Robert Donald described his slave Prince as "quarrelsome" when drunk despite the slave's poor command of English.[16] Other slaves were perceived as "loud and pert" or "impertinent" when intoxicated.[17] Worse yet from a white viewpoint, when the slave Sam got drunk he tended "to ridicule the country in general."[18]

Maryland slaves were perceived similarly when they had been drinking heavily: "very talkative and quarrelsome," "very impudent," "saucy," and "impertinent."[19] Irritating to his owner, the slave Tom Salter "value[d] himself much of his manhood" when drinking.[20] In the following decades, Maryland slaveowners complained that their drunken chattel ceased to be "very civil" or became "very pert."[21] The slave Dan became especially unruly "when drunk." He would both sing and swear.[22] Quarrelsome slave conduct associated with drunkenness remained a problem,[23] especially the slave Harry who, according to Alexander Hamilton, quarreled "wildly and stupidly."[24] Punctuating his peers' complaints, George Trotman curtly described his slave Mary as "very insolent when drunk."[25] As a rhetorical index of their feelings about slave misconduct, these slaveowners commonly modified their descriptions of impudence and pertness with the adverb "very." For George Trotman and his peers, slave insolence was *very* antisocial. Intoxication was no excuse.

In North Carolina, slaveowners also emphasized the trouble they perceived in slave drunkenness and modified their complaints with intensive adverbs. Daniel's owner advertised that the slave "was fond of spirits, and a small quantity will make him noisy and troublesome."[26] Other slaves were described as "insolent and quarrelsome" or "broad and insulting" in their speech when intoxicated.[27] His owners complained that the slave Charles was "very forward and saucy" when intoxicated, and the slave Robin—despite being "a tolerable bright mulatto" and "a very good Tanner and Currier"—was perceived as "very outrageous" when drunk.[28] Further south in Georgia, slaveowners expressed equally intense feelings. The slave Sarah was "very talkative and quarrelsome" under the influence of alcohol; "under its influence" Dumba was "very noisy and troublesome."[29]

Whether in spontaneous perceptions or self-persuasion, alcohol-related insolence by male and female slaves offended their social superiors. Late in the period, for example, Tryphena Fox explained that her slave Mary had succumbed to "laziness & impudence" and that *the* reason" was a "jug of whiskey" hidden in the slave's room.[30] Underscoring her belief in the singular cause of her slave's deviance, Fox illustrated a widespread perception. Moreover, when slaves demonstrated their need for alcohol to escape the pain of slavery, they implied an indictment of the peculiar institution. As Frederick Law Olmsted observed, drunken insolence contrasted sharply with sober slaves' habit of maintaining silence around whites: "At Jackson, Mississippi . . . late at night, a number of servants had been conversing together in an animated manner. After some time, a white man joined them, and they immediately became quiet."[31] Whites perceived alcohol to erode self-imposed barriers by slaves against speaking frankly and critically in public. Tryphena Fox, for one, was convinced that her alcohol-dependent slave Mary grew "more impudent" despite decent treatment.[32] This drunken insolence grated on planters' nerves to the extent that it became a distinguishing characteristic in advertising for runaways.

Slaves' reluctance to acknowledge this phenomenon in their antebellum narratives may be related to the formally religious associations of the abolition movement. Abolition and temperance were twin planks in most platforms of social reform. In contrast, a similar lack of acknowledgement by former slaves who were interviewed in the 1930s more likely reflects a continuing reluctance to complain openly about social inequity. "We warn't allowed to sass nobody," Ann Parker mused in a 1930s interview, "and we old ones still knows that we is got to be polite."[33] Former slaves like Ann Parker still recalled clearly those instances in which drunken behavior was permissible for whites but sanctioned for blacks. The white overseer, James Martin, was not liable for criminal charges in Arkansas when, after drinking in town, he shot and killed the slave Nathan.[34] However, an intoxicated mulatto, Larue, was arrested and fined heavily in Louisiana after merely returning the jibes of a white passerby.[35]

Complaints and Insults

Unwilling to accept drunkenness as an excuse for slave insolence, planters scarcely tolerated sober instances of antisocial speech. As Temple Wilson recalled, a slave "back in dem days sho' knowed his manners an' how to be polite."[36] In extreme cases, minding one's manners could mean the difference between life and death. After James Redpath regaled a Virginia slave with an anecdote about a Northern black man ridiculing a white bully, the slave declared that "it wouldn't do to do dat here; dey would kill us right away."[37] At least some slaves "were beaten to death for . . . talking back to a white person."[38]

More likely than killings were beatings and prosecutions. A young Thomas Jones recalled his whipping for "giving saucy language" to a white youth, calling him "a poor, ignorant white servant boy." In the same social context, Jones narrated the story of another young slave named Ben. While carrying a basket of food for his owner, Ben had it overturned and its contents scattered on the ground by a young white tormentor. Ben was immediately whipped by a white passerby when he reacted to the prank by calling his tormentor "some hard name."[39] This initiative taken by a mere passerby to discipline Ben illustrates the degree to which the gentry saw a corporate duty to sustain their social order.

Adult confrontations were predictably more perilous. For example, Francis McKleduff scolded the slave John several times for walking through his yard but John continued to use McKleduff's yard as a short cut. Tired of being reprimanded, John retorted that "he would be god damd if he did not go where he pleased." A brawl ensued after which the slave was sentenced to one hundred lashes for his abuse of McKleduff.[40] A decade earlier, a quarrel between the slave Jarrott and a white teenager named Thomas Chatham resulted in the slave's conviction for murder. Jarrott accused Chatham of stealing his winnings from a card game, and reviled him by stating that "any white man who would steal a negro's money, was not too good to unbutton a sheep's collar" and that Chatham had been "raised and had lived on stolen sheep." The dispute ended only after the antagonists had fought each other with knives, fence rails, and hickory sticks.[41] These confrontations involved rights and privileges that whites reserved for themselves, illustrating the degree to which the members of the gentry persuaded themselves that slave insolence posed a threat to their dominance.

Members of the planter class did not have to rely on self-help in sanctioning slave insolence. They also had legal remedies. Mrs. Thomas readily had Amy Lapier fined "ten dollars and the costs of prosecution" after Amy had been convicted in a South Carolina magistrate's court of "having slandered and insulted" the white woman.[42] Analogously in Kentucky, a white named Williams was sued by the slandered party for uttering aloud that the "negro Jude said that Mrs. Greenwade was a drunken whore."[43] When challenged in the market by a black woman about his purchase of vegetables, a white man "turned round fiercely and asked what she meant by insulting him." He then prosecuted the woman for using "insolent and abusive language to him."[44] Similarly, Turner Turket gained a legal sanction against the slave Anthony for the "gross insult" he had addressed to Turket.[45] Like Turket, Southrons could eschew physical violence in defending their honor against slave speech because legal sanctions were readily accessible.

In at least two senses, then, slave complaints and insults were adjudged as abnormal. First, when slaves spoke insolently they were seen to violate social norms. Second, it did not happen routinely. As Frederick Law Olmsted stated, after acknowledging "complaints of growing insolence and insubordination among the negroes," he personally observed no evidence for these complaints—instead seeing "sullen, jocose, or fawning" behaviors by slaves.[46]

Black narratives underscore the rarity of socially intolerable speech by highlighting the severe consequences. Mattie G. Browne, for instance, recalled the time she criticized her master's plans for burying her close friend, Aunt Polly. "It's right dirty and greasy, Master," she remarked when he proposed burying the slave in an old box. Her master responded violently: "Who keres if 'tis? What right has you to speak, slut? Take that for yer impudence! [kicking her] Who tole you to put yer mouth in?"[47] Gustavus Vassa narrated two related incidents. In the first, a slave was "damned very heartily" by his master for complaining about the seizure of his boat by the island's governor. In the second instance, Vassa himself suffered a "volley of imprecations" and threats of whipping for complaining to the authorities about a theft of his fruit by whites.[48] For uttering these complaints, despite their grounding in social norms of honoring the dead and respecting private property, slaves encountered a white backlash.

Sanctions were no less immediate and severe for slave complaints that were committed to writing. A Georgia slave gained no sympathy when he sent a letter to a white preacher criticizing his neglect of a sizeable portion of his congregation. "I want you tell me the Reson," the slave wrote, "you allways preach to the white folks and keep your back to us." Speculating on the reason, the slave queried whether God had directed the preacher "to keep [his] face to the white folks constantly" or whether he did so "because they give [him] money?" In addition, according to the slave, the preacher discriminated against black members of the congregation in two other ways. First, he insisted that the Bible provided guidelines to salvation despite the slaves' inability to read: "This would do very well if wee could read I do not think there is one in fifty that can read." Second, the preacher made his services comfortable only for whites: "Did god tell you to have your meeting housis just largn enoughf to hold the white folks and let the black people stand in the sone and rain?"[49] Attendance at religious services was widely approved for slaves as long as the preacher was white, but complaints about their treatment at these meetings amounted to insolence. In effect, the Georgia slave complained about a double standard. Biblical principles approved by whites were being applied unevenly to blacks.

Artistic compositions by slaves might have cloaked their critical purpose in elegant form but they too drew the wrath of planters for threatening social stability. As early as 1774, Nicholas Cresswell complained that songs among Maryland slaves revealed "a very satirical stile and manner."[50] Although many of the songs were merely "rhythmic accompaniments to labor" or simple dance tunes, others expressed or implied criticism of the plantation system in general ("Run nigger, run, de pat-roller' ketch yo'") or masters and mistresses in particular ("My old missus promise me.... When she die she set me free.... She live so long her head git bald.... She give up de idea of dyin' a-tall").[51] A North Carolina slave, George Moses Horton, tried to raise money to buy his freedom in 1829 by publishing a book of his poems. Included in the collection was "On Liberty and Slavery," a lyrical indictment of black bondage:

> Bid Slavery hide her haggard face,
> And barbarism fly:
> I scorn to see the sad disgrace
> In which enslaved I lie.[52]

Similar in tenor to the other nine stanzas of the poem, this language was tolerable only to the handful of sympathetic whites who aided Horton's publishing efforts. Most whites were irritated to read a reminder that the peculiar institution was outdated ("haggard") and barbaric; they also did not appreciate being scorned by a slave, notwithstanding his erudition. Not surprisingly, Moses Horton did not gain his freedom until federal troops marched through the state in 1865.

More palatable were the sentiments expressed in another of Horton's poems, "The Slave's Complaint." Here the slave lyrically pleaded for ultimate relief from his bondage:

> Heaven! in whom can I confide?
> Canst thou not for all provide?
> Condescend to be my guide
> For ever:
> And when this transient life shall end,
> Oh, may some kind, eternal friend
> Bid me from servitude ascend,
> For ever![53]

Because of its grounding in biblical principles, Horton's lyrical complaint was arguably less insolent than directly castigating the institution of slavery and indirectly its adherents.

Slave songs that failed the test of patriotism were intolerable to members of the planter class. Susan Snow recalled a childhood experience in Mississippi when she voiced one of these songs in the presence of her mistress. In response to a song by white children that ridiculed Abraham Lincoln, Snow repeated verses she had heard being sung by other slaves:

> Ol' Gen'l Pope, he had a short gun,
> Fill it full of bum,

> Kill 'em as dey come.
> Call a Union band,
> Make de rebels understand
> To leave our land,
> Submit to Abraham.[54]

Snow's mistress did not appreciate being reminded, however lyrically, of Confederate military reverses and Abraham Lincoln's victories. She beat the young slave with a broom.

Earlier compositions, such as a parody of "Hail Columbia" that was sung by South Carolina slaves at clandestine meetings during the War of 1812, were more threatening. This song's lyrics include threats of violent revolt:

> Let *independence* be your aim,
> Ever mindful what 'tis worth,
> Pledge your bodies for the prize,
> Pile them even to the skies.

The song also urges slaves to place their trust in divine assistance—normally a palatable sentiment—but it impugned white virtue at the same time:

> Look to heaven with manly trust,
> And swear by Him that's always just
> That no white foe, with impious hand
> Shall slave your wives and daughters more,
> Or rob them of their virtue dear!

A concluding call to battle ensured white outrage at the song:

> Blow the clarion's warlike blast;
> Call every negro from his task;
> Wrest the scourge from Buckra's hand,
> And drive each tyrant from the land!

Crafted with choruses that urge "death or liberty,"[55] the parody illustrates one of the more intense communicative breaches of the social order. Ironically, a sentiment like "death or liberty" was thoroughly consistent with white norms that had arisen from revolutionary fervor.

Much of this insolent poetry affronted Southern patriotism, or at least the planters persuaded themselves of this effrontery. In effect, slaves were permitted no speech that devalued the institutions by which their lives were regulated. As illustrated in an earlier example, Sam's drunken speech was particularly annoying to his master because he tended "to ridicule the country in general."[56] Sam was not unique.

As a young slave, Joe Rollins had been disciplined like many of his peers not to say "Yankees Comin'."[57] Yet, in moments of distress, a slave might lapse into traitorous talk. Mingo White recalled this type of exceptional speech when his mother was being whipped: "Lay it on," she taunted her master, "'caise I'm goin' to tell de Yankees when dey come."[58] Mingo White's mother expressed her unpatriotic sentiment in relatively blunt language, but her words scarcely matched the intensity of a related outburst by Leonard Allen. This slave could not restrain himself from criticizing one of his master's sons for joining the Confederate forces. Initially "under his breath," Allen complained "Look at that goddam soldier. He fighting to keep us niggers from being free." Later, after his master asked "What you mumbling 'bout?" the slave boldly repeated aloud his criticism. The master quickly "shot a hole in Leonard's chest big as your fist."[59] Moreover, a slave's traitorous conduct was seen as final confirmation of a flawed character. Dr. James G. Carson found this confirmation when one of his slaves had "run off to the Yankees." Carson was quoted by his biographer as claiming that the slave "was the worst negro on the plantation, he was always in trouble with the others." Indeed, the slave "was constantly quarreling" with his wife. "I didn't know what to do with him," Carson confessed, "now he has settled the question. I am glad to get rid of him."[60]

Slave complaints and insults varied in intensity, yet torture and death appear as commonplace sanctions in both white and black narratives. The legendary ease with which Southrons perceived affronts to their honor seems too facile an explanation for this system of severe punishment. Then again, the normal remedy for insults—duels—were not appropriate because they were reserved for disputes between social equals.[61] When combined with an allegiance to the social order, a strict demarcation between white and black classes, and a heightened sensitivity to sectional interest in wartime, the likelihood only increased that slaves would suffer remarkably for their insolence.

Affronts to Women

Among other socially proscribed acts, male slaves drew sanctions for dishonoring white women. Recent scholarship has illustrated repeatedly the central roles played by sex and race in Southern culture,[62] but the additional fuel added to this volatile mix by slave insolence has not generally been examined.[63] This emblem of insolence was all the more striking because of its rarity. As Joel B. Fort, a judge in Robertson County, Tennessee, recalled about the late antebellum period: "Such a thing as an insult of a white woman by a negro was unheard of."[64] Exacerbated by this lack of context, affronts to women were perceived as deeply troubling.

Bill v. State illustrates the perceived significance of slave insolence in a case of assault on a white women. The slave Bill had been convicted of assault with intent to rape Mary Smith, a white woman, and Tennessee's William Turley painstakingly reviewed the evidence establishing that Bill was the perpetrator—"the only question upon which any doubt arises." Mrs. Smith and her own slave had testified that her attacker had "pulled her from her horse and threw her upon the ground, informing her what his designs were." In Justice Turley's opinion, the slave's "use of insolent language" prior to the assault corroborated his "nefarious design." Bill had answered Mrs. Smith's query about his identity with the ambiguous reply "one," and he had spoken insolently to her immediately before his attack.[65] Notwithstanding the witnesses' testimony about his actions, Bill's speech was sufficiently antisocial to illustrate his criminal intent. His death sentence was affirmed.

The following year in South Carolina, the slave Tom received twenty-five lashes for his "rude and insolent behavior" toward a white woman. He had accosted Mary Manus several times, including one time he exposed himself to her and "expressed a desire to have Intercourse with her Saying he would give her a dollar."[66] Unlike Mary Smith, Mary Manus was illiterate and scarcely represented upper-class norms. Nonetheless, Tom's insolence could not go unpunished because it violated the social order.

Slave speech about a white woman outside her presence might also be adjudged as insolent. Late at night, for example, the slave Bill "was discovered concealed under the bed of Thomas Thompson, with an intent to commit some felony or violence." Defending himself to his captors, Bill "impudently and insolently" made accusations that were "injurious to the character of a young lady living in the house." Tried before a magistrate, Bill was convicted not of housebreaking but false and "highly slanderous" speech.[67] More intolerable than the slave's violating his home, Thompson could not abide the interloper's verbal assault on the character of a young white woman in the household.

Consistent with a double standard, slaves were not entitled to defend the virtue of their own women. Slave marriages were generally not legal; proscribing slaves' retorts to attacks on their women rested on an equation between this form of insolence and antisocial behavior. As recounted in *State v. Tackett*, the slave Daniel was killed but his killer, Tackett, went free because of evidence that Daniel "was insolent and impudent to white people"—though not necessarily to Tackett. The complicated facts of this North Carolina case include a longstanding hostility between Daniel and Tackett based on the latter's affair with the slave's wife, Lotty, a free black. Daniel had been overheard complaining two or three weeks before his death that, although Lotty had betrayed him, "he had given [Tackett] a beating, and that if [Tackett] did not let his wife alone he wold kill him." During the two weeks before his death, Daniel had repeated his threat and had fought with Tackett. On the night of the killing, Daniel was sleeping outside the house where his wife lived, Tackett found him, and they quarreled. Tackett asked "who he was and what he was doing there." Impudent to the end, Daniel retorted "by asking who [Tackett] was and what he was doing there." Soon after this exchange, according to a witness, Tackett shot Daniel to death.[68] On appeal, Tackett's conviction was reversed because of Daniel's provocative behavior.

Two decades later in South Carolina, Charles temporarily abandoned a slave's typically deferential tactics toward whites in defense of his wife. His conduct was especially galling because of his reputation for hard drinking. On the day that Charles was sold to a new owner, he quarreled with his old master and accused him of "keeping his wife." Later, when Charles's wife was being whipped by a young neighbor of her master, she ran "crying and calling for her husband." At that point, Charles came to her rescue and was overheard to swear that "he would mash [her tormentor] to the earth."[69] Charles was more highly motivated to defend his wife than Daniel, but the gentry's perception of slave speech was identical in both cases. Despite acting in accord with the social norm of defending womanly virtue, both slaves were adjudged as insolent.

In a further irony, slaves learned white social norms as they became accustomed to their status in the South but they could not reliably predict white judgments of their social conduct despite its normative consistency. In fact, as an index of their social learning, slaves acknowledged their insolence on those occasions when they defended female virtue. However, they assumed that their speech was warranted. Interviewed in 1863, Isaac Throgmorton recalled a related incident in Louisiana for which a slave was whipped to death. His master "had taken his wife, and said he was saucy." Throgmorton, however, saw nothing unusual in the slave's reaction: "Of course he would be rather saucy, if [the master] had taken his wife."[70] The death of this slave illustrates that the motive for defending a black woman's virtue was irrelevant, even though this motive was consistent with the Southern code of honor.

In the melodramatic *Incidents in the Life of a Slave Girl*, published in 1861, the heroine relates feelings she associated with dishonor. For a long time the unwilling sexual partner of her master, Dr. Flint, she had found a man she wanted to marry. Carrying his child, she confronted her master and received a tongue-lashing from him: "I was lowered in my own estimation, and I had resolved to bear his abuse in silence. But when he spoke contemptuously of the lover who had always treated me honorably; when I remembered that but for *him* I might have been a virtuous, free, and happy wife, I lost my patience. 'I have sinned against God and myself,' I replied; 'but not against you.'" She acknowledged losing her patience and trading contempt for contempt, but she thought her speech was warranted. Later in her narrative, she recounted the time when her child, Ben, tried to shield her against her master's abuse: "This was too much for my enraged master. He caught him up and hurled him across the room."[71] This slave's self-disgust at her relations with her master was only heightened when her child nearly died in an effort to defend her.

Along with conduct in accord with other norms endorsed by the gentry, defending a woman's virtue was denied to slaves. Despite its grounding in the white belief system, this type of slave speech infuriated members of the planter class. Its irritating power appears starkly when measured against the likelihood that slaves might also be found insolent merely on the basis of involuntary nonverbal cues.

Unspoken Insolence

Frederick Douglass indicted plantation society for the scope of slave behaviors — "a mere look, word, or motion" — that could prompt vicious sanctions. "Does a slave look dissatisfied?" he asked rhetorically. "It is said, he has the devil in him, and it must be whipped out.... Does he forget to pull off his hat at the approach of a white person? Then he is wanting in reverence, and should be whipped for it."[72] Thomas Hedgbeth anecdotally confirmed Douglass's indictment by identifying the wide range of verbal and nonverbal norms to which slaves were subject in North Carolina society. Having reached the age of twenty-one, Hedgbeth tried to vote but was turned away. "I felt very badly about it," he recalled, "but I knew better than make an answer." Moreover, he recognized the customary gestures of submission: "Unless I took off my hat, and made a bow to a white man, when I met him, he would rip out an oath, — 'd__n you, you mulatto, ain't you got no politeness?'"[73]

The gentry shared a detailed knowledge of which slave behaviors were considered antisocial, but not all slaves were in a position to learn the bewildering regimen. In antebellum Maryland, as Isaac Mason recalled, he learned too late "the methods they took to teach negroes their manners." While walking along Pratt Street in Baltimore, he found himself behind two men standing and conversing on the sidewalk. "I could not very well pass around them," he explained, "and to proceed I had to go between them, which I attempted to do." The men beat him severely.[74]

Travel accounts from the antebellum period record nearly identical norms in Virginia. James Redpath expressed his progressive annoyance "at seeing an [black] old man or woman, as [he] approached them, getting off the sidewalk altogether" and tipping their hats to whites.[75] Frederick Law Olmsted also found noteworthy this regimen of deference. He once observed an incident in which a "Virginia gentleman lift[ed] his cane and push[ed] a woman aside with it" when this slave failed to notice his approach. Later that same day, Olmsted saw "three rowdies, arm in arm, taking the whole of the sidewalk." Coming upon a black man, they jostled him "giving him a blow as they passed that sent him staggering into the middle of the street."[76] Thus, not only were the restrictions on slaves' social conduct customary, they were occasionally used to reinforce slaves' recognition of the social hierarchy.

The deep meaning of pedestrian conduct for the gentry can also be appreciated by assessing its rhetorical value for Southrons who protested postbellum emancipation. Mocking the system in which blacks were supposed to hold social equality, a white newspaper editor adopted the persona of a freedman,

"Pluto Jumbo," and reported ironically that "a cupple ob de colored ladies pushed a white gal off de sidewalk, when de purpusperous white wench gib sass to dem."[77] In a world turned upside down, whites would be outraged if social changes were great enough to require their surrender of sidewalks to blacks.

Surrendering sidewalks to the gentry and doffing one's hat were not always sufficient displays of subservience. As James L. Smith recounted, a slave could excite "evil passions" among whites by dressing better than they.[78] Predictably, confrontations between black and white when there was a narrow class distinction made clothing all the more troubling. In Washington, D.C., for instance, Francis Henderson observed "frequent quarrels between the slaves and the poor white men." Particularly on Sundays the slaves, "many of them, being fond of dress, would appear nicely clad, which seemed to provoke the white men."[79] Critical white observers also noticed the provocative effects of clothing on city streets. James Redpath reported that lower-class troublemakers "take great pleasure, whenever they see a well-dressed colored person with his wife approaching, to walk as near the edge of the pavement as possible, in order to compel them to go into the street."[80] Most distressing for slaves, perhaps, was offensive behavior over which they could exercise little choice or control. It took considerable acculturation among whites for slaves to realize that kinesics such as their customary way of walking would be perceived as impudent, much less their facial expressions. Yet these normally spontaneous, involuntary cues affronted the gentry.

James Beadnall thought that his slave Clem's "swaggering Air . . . in his walk" was eye-catching enough to be included in advertisements for his recapture, and other eighteenth-century Maryland slaveowners had similar ideas: the slave Sam was described as having a "proud bold lofty carriage"; Eben had "a prodigal walk"; Moses had "a very swanky walk"; and, like his peers, Harry was "impertinent" in his "proud swaggering walk."[81] In nineteenth-century North Carolina, slaveowners were offended by gaits that suggested undue pride and an air of independence in their slaves: Bright Jernigan thought that Argil walked "quick and very proud for a slave"; Nero was an "impudent fellow" in the estimation of Henry Young partially because the slave was noteworthy for his "swaggering"; according to John P. Cook, there was a "bold independent air" in Jim's gait; for David Gill, Abraham displayed a "bold, impudent swaggering air, which will attract the attention of everyone."[82] In effect, Abraham had made the serious mistake of revealing his insolence in a manner that, by the gentry's standards, would attract everyone's attention. The slave thereby transcended any personal affront and raised his mannerisms to the level of a social problem.

Just as offensive to the gentry were facial expressions that did not feature the smile or downcast gaze that slaves routinely used in their social performance of subservience. Some members of the gentry could not specify the precise components of a "look" or "countenance" that troubled them, but they nonetheless expected their peers to recognize them as "impudent" or "impertinent."[83] In only slightly more precise variations on this theme, slaves' looks were advertised as "grum" or "grim,"[84] and "surly."[85] As indistinct as these descriptions were, slaveowners counted on them to identify runaway slaves in a society where these looks and countenances were abnormal.

To avoid sanctions, slaves had the daunting task of controlling their facial expressions in order to avoid being noticed. The slaves Cuffee and Essex, for example, drew unwanted attention to themselves by displaying respectively "a bold countenance" and "a discontented countenance" that was antisocial in early eighteenth-century Virginia. Thirty years later, the slave Josee also erred by revealing "a sour ill-natured countenance."[86] By advertising runaway slaves in this manner, the gentry expressed a perceived link between "bold" looks and "discontented" attitudes—ultimately judging as "ill-natured" the slaves who displayed these facial cues. As the slave Abraham may have learned to his dismay, it was not safe to display an "air, which will attract the attention of everyone."

The gentry attached a social meaning to slave insolence by interpreting a larger affront to plantation society in the personal insults they experienced. Slaves were seen to engage in antisocial behavior when their speech was discourteous. However, the gentry had considerable difficulty in defining the parameters of this antisocial speech. They knew it when they saw it—to paraphrase a twentieth-century judicial axiom about obscene speech—but they rarely could articulate its elements. Nonetheless, Southrons agreed that slaves could be offensive not only by their words but also by their looks and gestures.

Speaking critically of social and political institutions or quarreling with lower-class whites was not permissible for slaves in any social setting, including those occasions on which being drunk and disorderly offered whites an excuse for their discourteous behaviors. Of course, sober speech of this kind by slaves was at least as reprehensible from the planters' perspective. For example, whites readily discouraged slaves' adaptations of religious and patriotic sentiments to their songs of protest. This double standard for assessing white and black conduct became most clear to slaves after they had learned the social norms of the dominant class, especially the expectations that men should be honorable and women should be virtuous. Slaves discovered that their speech might be adjudged as antisocial regardless of its normative fidelity. A member of the gentry would be admired for asserting his manhood or defending his wife's honor while, for the same type of speech, a slave would run the risk of violating the social order. Speaking lasciviously to a white women, or merely speaking ill of her, made a slave liable to the most severe punishments.

Equally vexing for slaves was white annoyance at their costume and mannerisms, including involuntary nonverbal cues. Slaves might avoid dressing stylishly, surrender the right of way on a sidewalk, doff their hats, and display other deferential gestures when they encountered whites, but postures and facial expressions might still be perceived as insolent. Even if the gentry could have defined and classified these unspoken insults in their various ordinances—as were regulations about clothing and rights of way—slaves would have had a difficult time adjusting these typically involuntary behaviors. They would have needed to innovate styles of walking briskly that could not be mistaken for swaggering; they would have needed to display sad or tired countenances that could not be mistaken for surly or ill-natured looks.

To avoid insolence in social settings—a difficult task considering that whites were persuading themselves of this misbehavior when they did not spontaneously perceive it—slaves needed to escape the gentry's sense perceptions. A slave who was neither mute nor invisible could involuntarily violate social norms. Life on plantations, where masters expected slaves to break the rule of silence when interrogated and to be highly visible on the job, did not offer a training ground. In social interactions with the gentry and other whites, slaves needed a distinctive repertoire of communicative behaviors, a style of speech that muffled their voices and obscured their personalities.

6

The Reluctant Mistress

Frances Anne Kemble (1809–1893) played the role of plantation mistress with considerable misgivings, preferring the social whirl with which she had grown familiar at an early age.[1] She had grown up in a family of Shakespearean actors, becoming a popular leading lady by the age of twenty at London's Theatre Royal, Covent Garden. She had taken up acting because her father was in peril of losing the theatre to creditors and, in 1832, she joined her family in a two-year tour of the United States to revive the family's fortunes. In the process, Fanny Kemble established herself as a star on both sides of the Atlantic. Dynamic and attractive, she drew the attention of many men including Pierce Butler of Philadelphia, heir to two plantations and hundreds of slaves in Georgia. They married in 1834.

Her motives for marrying into the Butler family and not returning to England with her family remain a mystery: she decried American society and she deplored slavery. In 1835, despite her new husband's objections, she published a social critique. This record of her unflattering assessments of America during her theatrical tour drew blistering reviews on both sides of the Atlantic: American critics thought it ungrateful, British critics called it coarse, and most everyone was appalled by its unladylike candor. Kemble had originally planned to publish an antislavery tract together with her 1835 critique, but her husband dissuaded her. He also resisted her visiting the family plantations. However, when the longtime overseers resigned in 1838, he finally agreed to take his wife and their two young daughters on an inspection tour of the real and chattel property in Georgia. During the next four months, Kemble wrote a chronicle of her experiences in the literary style of thirty-one letters.[2] Many years later, after her divorce and fearing that England might ally with the Confederacy, she published her chronicle as the *Journal of a Residence on a Georgian Plantation*.[3]

Kemble endorsed a less democratic, more discriminating social order than what she perceived in the Northern cities of the United States. She also espoused a moderate abolitionist stance that she had learned from William Ellery Channing, the influential Unitarian minister. In the chronicle of her Georgia sojourn—a document that does not necessarily reflect a strict chronology of thought because of its emendations prior to publication—she voiced a distinctly critical perspective on the planting business and Southern norms, but she nonetheless affirmed that slaves were social deviants. Since she qualified her observations as more accurate and expert than those published by other European visitors to the South,[4] Fanny Kemble merits close scrutiny as a case study of the social perspective on slave insolence.

Personal Criticisms

Shortly after her marriage and two years following her introduction to Channing's Unitarian ministry, Kemble described slavery as a "sin against humanity."[5] In the first installment of her *Journal*—her refutation of a pro-slavery tract—she argued that denying slaves their freedom was reprehensible because it reduced them to the level of "beasts." In this initial letter, Kemble illustrated vividly the "realities" facing slaves before she even departed for Georgia, underscoring the paramount role of perception rather than experience in the public debate over slavery: "Scorn, derision, insult, menace—the handcuffs, the lash—the tearing away of children from parents, of husbands from wives—the weary trudging in droves along the common highways, the labor of body, the despair of mind, the sickness of heart—these are the realities which belong to the system, and form the rule, rather than the exception, in the slave's experience." Though totally inexperienced, Kemble identified whites' scorn, derision, insult, and menace as disturbing realities that confronted slaves. Ironically, these four threatening modes of communication also summarized the realities of slave insolence for planters. More expansively, Kemble argued that slavery violated "the elementary rights which God has granted to all men alike." Far from objective about her impending trip to the South, she gloried in her prejudice "against slavery" because to do otherwise would be "disgraceful" for a proper Englishwoman. Nonetheless, she announced her expectation of finding "many mitigations" in the plantation system.[6] To this extent, she acknowledged her personal ambivalence and conflict of interest as the spouse of a slaveowner.

Not surprisingly, in view of her acting career, Kemble attended to the centrality of speech in defining the social sin of slavery. For slaves, she observed confidently, "every action is controlled, every word noted." This same factor was significant in her comparison of North and South. In the Northern cities, with which she was familiar, Kemble observed "the tone of utter superiority assumed by even the gutter urchins over [free blacks]."[7] Regulation of their speech in the South was so severe that slaves could reasonably be compared with dumb animals; their stigma was sufficiently durable that it disadvantaged free blacks in the North.

The conditions surrounding Kemble's acting career may also have prompted her to identify vicariously with the human chattel she was going to inspect in Georgia. Acting may have impressed her as "a form of slavery" because it involved "the loss of freedom, submission to her parents, and the sacrifice of all she made to the demands of their creditors."[8] More certainly, she recalled the constant surveillance to which she was subjected as a young actress and the parental norms by which she was kept "silent and quiet and oppressed."[9] Again, the factor of speech was prominent. She could compare her acting experiences with the condition of slaves in the sense that every action was controlled and every word noted. Silence and related oppression were particularly troubling.

According to Kemble, slaves' power of speech offered clear evidence of their human potential. In the middle of her chronicle, she observed that the slave Isaac "*does* speak, and therefore I presume he is not an ape, orangoutang, chimpanzee, or gorilla." However, almost in the same literary breath, Kemble revealed her ambivalence toward slavery in the form of slaves she actually encountered as distinct from the ideal forms she had earlier envisioned. She remarked that Isaac's physical appearance otherwise marked him as bestial. "I could not . . . have conceived it possible," she confessed, "that the presence of articulate sounds, and the absence of an articulate tail, should make, externally at least, so completely the only appreciable difference between a man and a monkey." Yet "Isaac *speaks*," she once again emphasized, "and I am much comforted thereby."[10] Kemble joined most of her social peers in expressing wonderment at slaves' power of speech because it belied the bestial nature typically attributed to Africans. Then again, unlike most of her peers, she felt no shame or fear. Rather, her brief firsthand experience had been educational and she felt "much comforted."

Elaborating on this theme, Kemble used the argument a fortiori in observing that, if a mature slave like Isaac exhibited humanity by his speech, then it was even more striking when very young slaves did the same. For example, a youthful slave named Jack responded thoughtfully to a point made by Kemble's Irish maid, Margery. "Well, den, I do tink so," Jack exclaimed suddenly, "and dat's the speech of a man, whether bond or free." Struck by this exclamation—especially the phrase "speech of a *man*" which she underscored—Kemble ruminated on its larger significance. She concluded that this episode illustrated "an inherent element of manhood superior to the bitter accident of slavery," and that it demonstrated a "vital self respect" which could sustain slaves in their adversity. With dramatic flair, she further observed that their power of speech demonstrated slaves' potential to achieve "perfect freedom, in spite of the ignoble and cruel bondage of their bodies."[11] Less sublime but more relevant to the present analysis, Kemble's attention to the factor of speech emphasizes its complex influence on the gentry's perceptions: reassuring for some, troubling for most.

Although her trip to Georgia offered firsthand knowledge of the planting business, Kemble also learned the oddities and inequities of slave laws. Beyond technicalities such as statutory bars to slave testimony at trial, which she misunderstood to be absolute,[12] she was surprised to find that "a very large and handsome edifice" under construction in Charleston would become a jail for the fifty or sixty slaves who routinely violated the nightly curfew. Equally striking to her were the distinctive sources of alarm she noticed among Southrons. Nightly precautions in Charleston, she reported, reflected a dread not of "foreign invasion, but of domestic insurrection." Mocking the "manifold blessings of slavery" asserted by South Carolina's governor, Kemble observed that she would "prefer going to sleep without the apprehension" of having her throat cut by her servants.[13] Not yet having reached the Butler plantations, she had already seen evidence of the stress within planter society that explained its unique legislation. Although the men customarily denied their "habitual sense of danger," she wrote, "every Southern *woman*" to whom she spoke admitted her deeply felt insecurity.[14]

The inequities of slave laws impressed her on at least two occasions. Upon learning about the legal bar to slave testimony, Kemble pointed out the "inconsistency which might be said to border on effrontery" between keeping slaves so ignorant that they could not be presumed to understand "the obligations of an oath" but admitting them to church membership. Their admission into the churches presumed that slaves were "capable of assuming the highest Christian obligations," including "the duty of speaking the truth at all times."[15] This contradiction was one of several social patterns that dismayed her. Combined with a fear of servile revolt, Southrons' presumption of black subjugation rendered the legal system incomprehensible to a British observer.

As a postscript to her observations on the laws of slavery, Kemble recounted her reaction to the lack of legal sanctions when one member of the gentry killed another during an argument. The killer, Dr. Hazzard, shot his victim because of the man's insolence. But, as Kemble mused, "shooting down a man who had offended you was part of the morals and manners of the Southern gentry." Sanctions for the killing of insolent blacks were even less likely than for the killing of insolent whites.

Although sensitive to the legal climate of slavery, Kemble devoted substantially more of her editorializing to the planting business. In these observations slave insolence was prominent. The assumption of slave deceit, for example, was commonplace. In discussing the "credibility of any Negro assertion" with Pierce Butler, Dr. Tunno agreed that slaves should not be believed "on any occasion or any subject." Rare exceptions were acknowledged, but the two planters perceived them "as habitual liars, for they are slaves." Kemble herself decried the method for assessing slave deceit—"it is very seldom that any special investigation of the facts of any particular case is resorted to in their behalf"—but she did not explicitly deny the two planters' conclusion.[16] Indeed, she dismissed the slaves' "vehement professions of regard and affection" upon her arrival as self-serving tactics.[17] Later she observed that a glowing compliment paid to her by one of the slaves was "outrageous flattery," as commonplace among slaves as among "the low Irish." Both races, she asserted, were committed to "propitiating at all costs the fellow creature who is to them as a Providence—or rather, I should say, a fate—

for 'tis a heathen and no Christian relationship."[18] Although she criticized plantation justice as an all too convenient vehicle for enacting planters' biases toward slaves, she did not deny the truth in what planters perceived. However, her own perceptions of inherent deceitfulness among slaves were explicitly based on social class rather than race.

The business administration of slave complaints also troubled Kemble. When she visited the plantation infirmary shortly after arriving in Georgia, the slave Harriet complained that she could not tend properly to her sick child because of the exhausting work schedule. Naively, Kemble repeated this complaint to the overseer who "vehemently denied" it. The next morning, shortly before Kemble revisited the infirmary, the overseer horsewhipped Harriet. After hearing about this whipping from the infirm slaves, Kemble left "disgusted and indignant." Yet she did not pursue the matter with the overseer because it "could have produced no single good result."[19] Instead, before dinner that same night, she asked her skeptical husband to investigate the incident. Questioned at dinner, the overseer explained that Harriet had been punished not for what she had told her mistress but for speaking "impertinently" to him about her work assignment for the day. According to the overseer, Harriet had faked illness and retorted insolently when he challenged her. "Very well," she had chided the overseer, "I'll go, but I shall just come back again." To Kemble's further disgust, after the overseer had narrated this tale, he then admitted to lashing another slave at the same time "for some such impudence."[20]

Kemble reacted strongly to insolence-related whippings, punctuating her account with several incidents involving elderly, infirm female slaves. The slave Teresa, for example, suffered this fate and caused Kemble herself to feel "tortured." She felt a singular "misery" about the slave's treatment: "It is almost more than I can endure to hear these horrid stories of lashings inflicted because I have been invoked."[21] Her pain only increased when her husband perceived "neither hardship nor injustice" in the slaves' punishment but rather the application of "a regularly established law" that sustained the "system of discipline." Indeed, although Kemble argued cleverly that the "corporal chastisement" of female slaves was unmanly, Pierce Butler replied that he merely found it "*disagreeable.*"[22]

Referring to a related incident that had happened before her visit, Kemble recounted "a strange anecdote" related by her husband. Sinda had achieved a prophet's status among the other slaves and had caused a work stoppage by forecasting the imminent end of the world.[23] The clever overseer had sensed no advantage in using the whip against so powerful a force. Instead he waited for the day of doom that Sinda had predicted to arrive and, when nothing happened, he "tremendously flogged" her for the business loss she had caused. To Kemble's way of thinking, Sinda's punishment for "false prophecy" was less significant than her followers' renewed submission to the plantation regime: "The faith of her people of course reverted from her to the omnipotent lash again." After meeting the "hideous old" Sinda, Kemble tried to envision the difference it would have made to the slaves if they had gained freedom from their bondage not by death—the usual way—but by the second coming of Christ.[24]

As a rhetorical device, Kemble emphasized the suffering of old female slaves by recounting their own words. After visiting "a poor old creature called Nancy," Kemble reported her discourse. "I have worked every day through dew and damp, and sand and heat, and done good work," Nancy exclaimed in tears, "but oh, missus, me old and broken now; no tongue can tell how much I suffer." The irony in this slave's disclaimer emphasized her eloquence. More explicitly, Kemble reported her admiration for the "wonderfully striking and pathetic forms of speech" which slaves could utter.[25] The great tragedy she observed involved a clash between speech and silence as much as the tension between freedom and bondage. Slaves were perfectly capable of articulating what was evil in the planting business, but planters would not listen.

Kemble's most substantial meditation on this tragedy happened after "a most painful conversation" with her husband. He urged her to stop confronting him with slave complaints and "horrible stories of misery and oppression." In turn, she began to question the wisdom of continuing to act as the slaves' advocate. Although she felt "bitterness and indignation" upon observing the slaves' plight, she also supposed that her frequent advocacy had made Pierce Butler "weary of hearing what he has never heard before, the voice of passionate expostulation and importunate pleading against wrongs that he will not even acknowledge." More significant than her own pain in witnessing atrocities, she admitted the possibility of doing more harm than good by championing the slaves' cause. "When I am gone," she considered, "they will fall back into the desperate uncomplaining habit of suffering." Even more troubling to her husband was her potential rending of the social fabric. He feared the "contagion of freedom." More specifically, he resented her "way of speaking to the people, of treating them, or living with them." Pierce Butler was a planter first and husband second. He detested his wife's appeals to his slaves' "sense of truth, of duty, of self-respect."[26] In this social context, the slaves would suffer and their tragedy would increase if they broke their customary silence.

Fanny Kemble ultimately saw little benefit to herself or the slaves by criticizing the planting business. In the larger social context, the gentry did not perceive speech and freedom as consistent with the slaves' status. The silence and bondage enforced on plantations were analogously imposed on slaves in towns. Always a proper Englishwoman and ambivalent in her attitudes toward slaves, Kemble struggled to express even a moderately abolitionist stance. She bemoaned the tragedy of slaves' silence but she believed, along with other members of the gentry, that slaves were deceitful. More particularly, when she articulated her social perspective, she echoed planters' concerns about keeping up appearances.

Social Conventions

Kemble recorded her social judgments of slaves based on both their verbal and nonverbal communications. Her initial observations distressed her, despite never encountering drunken slaves or slaves who directly affronted her. At a stopover in Portsmouth, Virginia, she reported that the first slaves she had ever seen "looked horribly dirty, and had a lazy recklessness in their air and manner." Already annoyed by what she perceived generally as a lack of graciousness and hygiene in America, she recoiled at the slaves' appearance and behavior. These creatures, she concluded, did not fit among "rational humanity."[27] By comparison, the mulattoes she later observed in Philadelphia—"people descended from slaves, and in many cases born and bred themselves in slavery"—impressed her as "less insolent" than Irish servants and "less insubordinate" than white Americans. But these descendants of slaves also were "dirty and lazy."[28] Kemble was not unique among plantation mistresses in reacting critically to slaves' dirty appearance. Far away, along the Mississippi, Tryphena Fox linked the insolence of her slave Susan with a "filthy" appearance.[29] However, for Kemble, a dirty appearance clashed fundamentally with proper social conduct.

Kemble partitioned her annoyance at slave appearances from her equally negative appraisals of lower-class whites and the housing and furnishings in the South. She was content to judge the social standards and skills of slaves without reference to the context of their bondage and deprivation. Arriving at Charleston, she found nothing that changed her first impression. Amused by the classical Greek and Latin names given to slaves, she nonetheless was appalled by "the tribe of black-faced heathen divinities and classicalities" who waited on her. By her standards, they were "stupid, dirty, and inefficient." She was favorably impressed by the "colored woman" who ran a boarding house in the city but not this woman's slaves: "Their laziness, their filthiness, their inconceivable stupidity, and unconquerable good humor, are enough to drive one stark-staring mad."[30] These slaves' time-honored stratagems of smiling and laughing failed to disarm Kemble because she could not dismiss their lack of decorum. To her mind, their dirty and shiftless appearance meant social deviance.

Intellectual commitment to a moderate abolitionism did not insulate Kemble against feelings of disdain for individual slaves. Indeed, in her experience, only those members of the gentry who actively defended slavery interpreted the customary appearance and social stratagems of slaves as proof of their complacency. In Savannah, for instance, she endured the dinner-table conversation of "a tiresome worthy old gentleman" who urged her to interpret positively "the appearance of 'our blackies' (the Negroes)." Putting a rhetorical question to her about the slaves, this recent immigrant from Scotland argued "no want of cheerfulness, no despondency, or misery in their appearance, eh, madam?" She silently rebutted this argument on two grounds: the old man's relatively brief acquaintance with slavery and her own "small prejudices in favor of freedom and justice."[31]

To her credit, Kemble discounted standard pro-slavery appeals. In contrast to another artistically inclined visitor from the North, her interpretation of social appearances was critical. Traveling north from Savannah in 1854, Charles Ward wrote about his visit to a rice plantation near Washington, Georgia. This young artist and scion of a distinguished New York family reported that "the blacks seemed industrious & contented." Furthermore, he restated an overseer's quip that "them niggers were an amazin' sight happier" than the weary traveler himself.[32] Fanny Kemble was no less weary of her trip to the Butler plantations. She was, however, less susceptible to local justifications of the peculiar institution.

Kemble's ambivalent stance toward slavery, complicated by her annoyance at slaves' lack of decorum, survived her transition from familiar urban contexts to the plantation milieu. Writing about her initial explorations of Butler Island, she mocked Southerners' defense of slavery and restated her conviction that it was "sinful." But her attention was quickly drawn to the plantation slaves' dirty appearance. Her two young footmen, she complained, were "perfectly filthy in their persons and clothes—their faces, hands, and naked feet being literally encrusted with dirt." Her housemaid was similarly "offensive in her person." Yet Kemble rejected the argument of "the Southerners" that slaves were inherently filthy and had earned their subjugation. She pointed out that the scandalous intimacies between masters and their female slaves contradicted these same men's stated antipathy toward slave bodies, and she asserted that slaves' "peculiar ignorance of the laws of health and the habits of decent cleanliness" were the "real and only causes" of their debased appearance. Furthermore, she observed, the "stench" in European hovels was equal to that "in our Negro houses," as was the "filth and vermin" in clothing.[33] Not restricted only to slaves, a filthy lifestyle was characteristic of all oppressed people regardless of race. According to the reluctant mistress, inherent flaws were illusory. Instead it was an ignorance of better living conditions that kept slaves in a miserable state.

Kemble made this reasonable argument while coping with an irrational institution. Yet she also disclosed her underlying sense of superiority later in her report. Arguing that the "total absence of self-respect begets these hateful physical results," she revealed her assumption that the gentry was capable of bestowing self-respect on slaves. "Well-being, freedom, and industry," she contended, "induce self-respect, self-respect induces cleanliness and personal attention, so that slavery is answerable for all the evils that exhibit themselves where it exists." To her mind, once the gentry abolished slavery, slaves would take pride in themselves and their appearance. They would abide by the gentry's social norms as soon as the gentry permitted it. The only desirable social norms were white and, as always, whites retained the power to grant admission to their society. Until that time, the "majority" of slaves were incapable of escaping their social station—"from lying, thieving, and adultery, to dirty houses, ragged clothes, and foul smells."[34]

As an article of faith for Kemble, slaves' social performance was typically associated not only with dirt but also with stupidity. For example, she described one of her house slaves as "so stupid that he appears sullen from absolute darkness of intellect . . . scarcely a little higher than the brutes."[35] This slave's color and nonverbal communication signified "darkness" of mind as well as body, and stigmatized him as little better than an animal. On the other hand, exceptional slaves illustrated for Kemble the heights to which "these *inferior* creatures" could be raised by their masters. Sarcastically underscoring an "inferior" status for most slaves, she sang the praises of Frank—the head driver on the Butler Island plantation. Although she found him "as ignorant as the rest of the slaves," he impressed her with the "intelligence" he had "developed by intimate communion in the discharge of his duty with the former overseer." Because this overseer had entrusted Frank with responsibilities, the head driver had developed self-respect. Not accidentally, he was "always clean and tidy in his person, with a courteousness of demeanor far removed from servility."[36] Again, the nonverbal cues of a socially approved cleanliness and demeanor confirmed for Kemble a slave's progress toward reaching his full human potential.

Kemble's writings indicate nothing less than her genuine desire for slaves to achieve a full social communion. However, her assumptions that it was a white prerogative to define the terms of this communion, and that it could only be bestowed by enlightened whites rather than grasped by capable slaves, illustrate her conflicted thought on the nature of slaves. The slaves themselves contributed to her state of mind by giving contradictory testimony about their desire for freedom. Shortly after reaching the Butler plantations, Kemble's Irish maid questioned the slave Mary about her desire for freedom. In response to a query whether she thought slavery "will not always be so?" Mary enthusiastically said, "Me hope not."[37] But the slave Jack responded quite differently when asked the same question: "He stammered, hesitated, became excessively confused, and at length replied, 'Free, missis! what for me wish to be free? Oh no, missis, me no wish to be free, if massa only let we keep pig.'" Kemble perceived Jack as highly intelligent and concluded that he was lying about his disdain for freedom in order to avoid "offending by uttering that forbidden wish." Yet upon further questioning, Jack simply repeated: "No, missis, me no want to be free; me work till me die for missis and massa." Jack's performance impressed Kemble as a "sad spectacle" and she dismissed it as a defensive mechanism,[38] but the contradictory testimony on freedom had nonetheless taken its toll on her estimate of slaves' readiness for social communion.

She adjusted her assessment of slaves yet again after reflecting on the songs they sang in the rice fields of the Georgia sea islands. For one thing, slave songs had never impressed her as making much sense. After hearing one song that featured a single lyric, "Oh! my massa told me, there's no grass in Georgia," she learned that it might recite the complaint of slave transported from Virginia or Carolina after being deceived by his master about the relative ease of clearing fields in Georgia. Another song whose initial lyrics were "very pretty and pathetic" disappointed Kemble when it lapsed into "nonsense verses about gentlemen in the parlor drinking wine and cordial, and ladies in the drawing room drinking tea and coffee." Her criticisms ignored the likelihood that both songs lamented the lot of slaves in comparison with the good life enjoyed by their masters and mistresses. However, she acknowledged that "many of the masters and overseers on these plantations prohibit melancholy tunes or words, and encourage nothing but cheerful music and senseless words." Moreover, she agreed with the prohibition. "I think it a judicious precaution enough," she wrote, because "these poor slaves are just the sort of people over whom a popular musical appeal to their feelings and passions would have an immense power."[39] Susceptible to the "melancholy" lyrics in popular music, slaves would scarcely profit from full social communion with a white population full of hustlers who would exploit the slaves' susceptibility to manipulation.

Flaws in the nature of slaves troubled Kemble but related flaws in their masters persuaded her that social communion was a faint hope. She complained that Southerners were fond of exhibiting "the degree of license to which they capriciously permit their favorite slaves occasionally to carry their familiarity." This license included a tolerance of insolence. Prompted by a local slaveowners' amusement rather than anger when his slave pestered him for his coat, Kemble saw "the profoundest contempt and injustice" in the incident. By showing favoritism in this case, the master had degraded the slave by treating him as a pet and had retarded general progress toward instilling self-respect in slaves. But the analogy to animals with which Kemble validated her objection betrayed a low estimate of slaves. She argued that this master's vain effort to explain his conduct as proof of his general kindness to slaves was "as good a proof of it as the maudlin tenderness of a fine lady to her lapdog is of her humane treatment of animals in general."[40] Kemble could not escape her base perception of slaves as so dirty and stupid as to be little better than animals. And yet slaves could speak and disrupt the social order with their insolence.

As far as exercising control over the disorder caused by impudent inferiors, Southern masters impressed Kemble as no more effective than other

"American heads of houses." In the North, these men were "impatient of system, of order, of necessary and legitimate control." Like slaves in the South, Northern children were "allowed to be at once familiar and rude" toward their fathers. She judged that these men's "manners to their servants" were "far from good," making them personally liable for "the disorder, discomfort, and insubordination of their households."[41] In the larger community of planters, Kemble assigned a similar liability. Promoting insolence by tolerating it among favorite slaves and by punishing it unevenly, planters themselves were often at fault for that portion of social disorder attributable to slave speech.

Scarcely a model of constancy herself, Kemble seldom discouraged slave speech that most of the gentry would have punished swiftly and savagely. Criticizing three teenaged slaves for wasting time playing instead of cleaning their hut—a "spectacle of filthy disorder"—she admonished them that "it was shame for any woman to live in so dirty a place and so beastly a condition." But the young slaves rejected Kemble's critique of their filth and brutishness: "They said they had seen buckree (white) womens' houses just as dirty, and they could not be expected to be cleaner than white women." No sanction was forthcoming. Instead, Kemble responded simply that "it was more disgraceful" for white women to keep a dirty house because they "were generally better informed."[42] Her response to the unspoken insolence of dirty, disorderly appearances and an insulting comparison with white women was merely to display annoyance. By her own standards, she should have instead corrected the three for speech that would have enraged most of her social peers.

In a related incident, she explicitly confessed that a slave retort had "silenced and abashed" her. Again annoyed at the lack of personal hygiene among the slaves, she scolded an old nurse in the infirmary for not washing two slave children. The old slave replied: "Missis no b'lieve me wash um pickaninny! and yet she tress me wid all um niggar when 'em sick."[43] This time Kemble made no response at all. Her chronicle does not explain whether her silence arose from shock at being insulted by a slave or from agreement with the slave's argument. She merely observed that, despite the exchange, the two children showed no signs of ever having been bathed.

Kemble was not alone among Georgia plantation mistresses in expressing frustration at slaves' apparent inability or unwillingness to accept the gentry's social norms. Both before and after Kemble's 1839 visit to Georgia, counterparts related similar experiences. In an 1831 letter to her husband, Sarah Alexander recounted conditions in Wilkes County. "I hope the time will come," she complained, "when we shall be free the troubles of a black family." The slaves irritated her "by their frequent indispositions" and she had lost patience as a result of "their carelessness and disobedience." She expressed deep resentment at the "vexations attendant on the care of 80 who have no characters they care to support."[44] Alexander perceived a lack of character among her eighty slaves rather than the passive aggression which they were more likely displaying.

In an 1852 letter to her son, Anna King reported similar feelings about her slaves on St. Simon Island. "I do believe if I stay here," she wrote, "I must sink under my nervous state." Part of the reason for her exasperation was the intransigence of the slaves: "The negros are disposed to give all the trouble they well can—as is always the case when they see a chance to improve." Ultimately, she confessed who had gained the upper hand in the contest. "I have never suffered so severely by being a slaveholder," she complained, "that I would even sell out at a sacrifice."[45] King perceived that slaves actively resisted personal and social improvement and, like Sarah Alexander, she failed to consider that their resistance was strategic.

Perceiving a deeply flawed nature in slaves, reluctant mistresses like Fanny Kemble became discouraged or morose. Of course, an alternative course of action was to treat the slaves haughtily as social inferiors. To Kemble's "dismay," her older daughter chose this course while visiting the Butler plantations. In one instance, the child "said something about a swing" and several slaves quickly built one for her. Analyzing this incident, Kemble expressed misgivings about "learning to rule despotically your fellow creatures before the first lesson of self-government has been well spelled over!"[46] Conflicted to the end, she decried her daughter's despotism while pontificating herself over the slaves' lack of social graces.

Kemble failed to win the freedom of any slaves before or after leaving the Butler plantations in 1839. Her own marital problems took precedence and she eventually abandoned husband and daughters for Europe in 1846. Not having secured emancipation for slaves, she took no delight in Pierce Butler's financial need to sell more than half of his seven hundred slaves in 1849—the same year he and Fanny negotiated their divorce.[47]

Kemble paid special attention to slaves' power of speech in determining their place in the social order. Unlike dumb animals, slaves merited humane treatment because they could articulate their needs and defend their methods of satisfying these needs. Nevertheless, Kemble ultimately doubted that slaves would ever occupy their rightful position in American society because, to her mind, they continually fell short of achieving the human potential otherwise promised by their power of speech. They were often judged unfairly, but they contributed to their own degraded status by lying and by failing to exploit the few advantages offered to them. She was no apologist for the plantation system, but she was also no publicist for African Americans.

In particular, Kemble's disgust at what she perceived as slaves' indifference to filth and disorder prompted her to discount their readiness for social communion with whites. That she indicted European peasants for the same failing suggests a bias resting on class rather than race. Nonetheless, she never expressed an appreciation for the conditions of bondage and deprivation with which slaves had to cope. She complained of her need to transport soap and other commodities to Georgia for own personal hygiene, yet she failed to acknowledge the slaves' lack of access to goods which they saw as niceties but which she considered necessities. This nonverbal evidence of slave deviance was powerfully persuasive.

Kemble also revealed an ambivalent stance toward slaves' verbal insolence and its punishment. She never suffered drunken utterances or direct affronts from slaves but she routinely encountered complaints. Responding herself merely with reasoned discourse to complaints that would have enraged her social peers, she nevertheless criticized other members of the gentry for not disciplining their slaves for the same insulting behaviors.

Fanny Kemble's ambivalence cannot be ignored but should not be condemned out of hand. Her gender and status as a planter's wife, much less the full biographical details of her life, offer explanations if not justifications for her judgments. However, she also provides a compelling illustration of how slave insolence was perceived in the social realm. Visiting the American South from a nation that had outlawed the peculiar institution and acting on a personal antagonism toward it, she nonetheless confirmed fundamental aspects of the gentry's perceptions.

Part 4
The Moral Perspective

7

"The Crowning Glory of This Age"

In addition to the legal, economic, and social meanings of slave insolence, the gentry perceived a moral dimension. As adherents to a Scottish philosophy that embraced "common sense" doctrine and an innate "moral sense" in mankind,[1] the Southern gentry could be expected to embrace this dimension of meaning. Although sporadic,[2] their efforts to control the slave population through religious training and exercises implicitly reflected many planters' views that slave insolence, along with other resistance, was immoral.

Religious indoctrination was required because slaves were commonly believed to take little interest in "moral improvement."[3] Exceptions to this rule demanded attention. For example, a planter's journal "Devoted to Subjects Moral, Speculative, & Commonplace" emphasized a devoted slave's virtue in his obituary. The author had inherited "Jack, aged about 65 years," from his mother—he had "stood high in her regard"—and was himself thoroughly satisfied with the slave. Jack "set a moral & industrious example. . . . He was not a professing Christian. Yet no man white or black . . . was more exemplary in his conduct."[4] Slaves who were admirably moral by the gentry's standards were rare and attracted special attention. The great majority of slaves were perceived far differently.

Planters who perceived their relationships with slaves as patriarchal saw impudence as "a transgression of the Fifth Commandment—Honor thy father and thy mother."[5] They were encouraged in this perception by ministers such as Alexander Glennie of South Carolina who preached to slaves against "the sins of the tongue."[6] The emblems of paternalism may have "deflected attention further from the ruthlessly manipulative and repressive system" in which slavery flourished,[7] but the moral dimension deserves close scrutiny as the fourth facet of slave insolence. To maintain a properly critical stance, critics should recognize that the paternalism articulated by partisans such as Thomas R. R. Cobb was a one-way street,[8] a myth by which members of the gentry persuaded themselves of their dominant yet benign status. In fact, for both slaves and some plantation mistresses, the "beneficent paternalism of the father was ever shadowed by the power of the master, just as the power of the master was tempered by the beneficent paternalism of the father."[9]

After her antebellum tour of the South, Harriet Martineau observed that slaveholders behaved paternally only if their slaves remained "ignorant, docile, and contented."[10] If Martineau had taken into account another aspect of paternalism, the literal status of some slaves as members of their master's extended family,[11] she might have modified her judgment. The offspring of masters typically enjoyed special privileges while remaining enslaved. Nonetheless, in both types of conditions, slaves had no choice in the arrangement. Rather, planters wished to believe that they promoted contentment among slaves through several patriarchal behaviors. Prominent among these were the provision of food, clothing, and lodging, and the exercise of power over the naming and punishing of slaves.

Providing slaves with food, clothing, and lodging constituted the most readily observable evidence sustaining the myth of paternalism. The weekly distribution of food demonstrated a planter's power over his chattel,[12] and the semi-annual distribution of clothing ritualistically confirmed this power,[13] but planters argued that they were also enacting higher motives. Although they acknowledged their self-interest in maintaining a dependable labor force, they also claimed intangible rewards. John Taylor illustrated these blended claims to pragmatism and idealism in his *Arator*. "The addition of comfort to mere necessaries," he explained, "is a price paid by the master, for the advantages he will derive from binding his slave to his service, by a ligament stronger than chains, far beneath their value in a pecuniary point of view." He then continued that the master "will moreover gain a stream of agreeable reflections throughout life, which will cost him nothing."[14]

Taylor would have predicted Catherine Carson's "agreeable reflections" on her special gifts of food to slaves. She felt that her beneficence primarily fulfilled a moral duty; in turn, her slaves satisfied their duty of showing affection. "I have the gratification of giving them apples, or some other little rarity," she explained to her father, "which they consider a great '*treat*.'" She also provided her slaves with "flour and molasses" every Saturday, reporting that "this little kindness they have not known for a long time and I assure you they can appreciate it." More dramatically yet, she wrote, the slaves celebrated their master's goodness on Christmas. "The men and women all collected at our door with a parcel of the rudest instruments of music I expect you ever heard, and commenced playing and singing." In an apparently jubilant display of affection, the slaves then "marched round the house several times with great form, and called for their Master and Mistress." At that point, she recalled, her husband "went out, they seized him, seated him in a chair and carried him round the house several times." Unlike Fanny Kemble, Catherine Carson perceived no self-interested survival strategy in her slaves' fawning behavior. Rather, she saw only the mutual performance of a moral contract. "Far from being afraid" of her slaves, she contended, "I feel they would be a protection."[15]

If the Carsons' biographer was accurate, then Mrs. Carson "felt her responsibility for the spiritual and material welfare of the servants." In addition, her husband "was cultivating among the planters an interest in the religious instruction of the negroes." Mr. Carson "saw slavery as God's will & said there was some divine purpose to it."[16] For the Carsons, a paternal attitude toward the two hundred humans they kept in bondage was righteous; they perceived divine approval of their slaveowning as long as a moral contract was maintained. The Carsons tried to live up to their contractual commitments. However, their slaves lacked bargaining power altogether and would doubtlessly be condemned as immoral if they expressed resentment at their lot.

The power to name slaves constituted a commonplace but less overt form of paternalism. Exercising control over the formal identity of a slave implied power over the person. For example, less bizarre names were given to slaves who exhibited greater levels of acculturation.[17] Moreover, this power could be extended to anyone in the master's (white) family, including his children. One slaveowner, for instance, customarily included a naming ceremony in the event surrounding new slaves' arrival at his plantation: "The young people of the family would select names from novels they had read and other sources, and sew these names into the clothes of each [new slave]."[18] Having his children name the slaves might convince a master that he was promoting a familial relationship, but this practice would readily illustrate for slaves their relative powerlessness.

Combined with the imposition of organized religion, the moral implications of naming slaves were unmistakable—as illustrated by a remarkable incident in the 1850s at St. John's Plantation Church. "Many Negro babies were baptized on the day of the consecration of the church," wrote Janie Polk. But one of the slave mothers lisped badly and, when she asked that her baby be christened "Lucy, sir," the minister thought she was asking that "Lucifer" become her child's Christian name. "No proper name for a Christian child," he scolded, replacing it with the name "John" during the ceremony. "Thus," Polk concluded, "little Lucy was named John."[19] By controlling the process of formal identification, planters confirmed for themselves their more substantial control over slaves. In the case of St. John's Plantation, even gender identities were perceived as susceptible to this control.

Perhaps the least convincing forms of paternalism were the "rituals of punishment."[20] Planters' ability to discipline slaves for unacceptable behavior confirmed their status as dependents but these punishments also revealed paternalism as a myth. In these acts the master performed the role of judge as well as father, and the slaves scarcely portrayed themselves as loving children. An ideal relationship based on mutual affection lapsed into the real relationship based on power.

Expounding a morally satisfying relationship with their slaves, masters tried to convince themselves and others that future generations would fondly recall the peculiar institution. In response to a 1920s survey, for instance, Joel Fort reported that the "affection between master and slave . . . was beautiful" and that "the confidence [of] the one in the other was faultless."[21] Nonetheless, white and black narratives routinely described the punishment of slaves, from kicking and slapping, to whipping and salting, or worse. Faced with contradictory experiential evidence, planters found it difficult to sustain the myth of paternalism. In fact, complaints arose during both the eighteenth and nineteenth centuries about the drawbacks of paternal behavior toward slaves. The owners of runaway slaves in particular were accused of having "too much indulged" their slaves or treated them "more like a free person than a slave."[22] This casual indictment was reconstituted formally in selected lawsuits.[23] Southern evangelicals like James Henley Thornwell and Moses Waddel who owned slaves and treated them humanely "were regarded by other slaveholders as too lenient.[24] In terms of institutional impact, an overly indulgent master was no better than a cruel master.

The moral meaning of slave insolence derived from the myth of paternalism and was no less abstruse. Interpreted as a sign of ingratitude for their sustenance, a sign of resistance to their identity and discipline, impudent speech meant that slaves were sinning against a divine agent, disrupting a family, or betraying a friend. In fact, these three facets of meaning were commonly interspersed in narratives from the period. Unlike other meanings of slave insolence, its immoral manifestation was very private and—according to generations of planters—personally hurtful.

Divine Agency

Although never confirmed by slaves, many planters claimed divine agency in their mastery.[25] This argument in their internal persuasion gave birth to several types of appeals to exterior audiences. Ultimately, as partisans of the Old South faced a war for survival, the argument lost most of its genuine cogency as self-persuasion and became a topos of sectional rhetoric.

John Taylor's *Arator* again provides a succinct declaration of the principle of divine agency: "Religion assails [the slaveowner] both with her blandishments and terrors. It indissolubly binds his, and his slave's happiness or misery together."[26] Appointed to fulfill God's design, masters enjoyed supreme authority but they also faced dire consequences if they failed in their mission. William Byrd II had acknowledged these consequences during the winter of 1710–1711 when he interpreted the high rate of illness and death among his slaves as divine punishment for his sins.[27] Typically guilt ridden, this self-proclaimed descendant of biblical "Patriarchs" had no reason not to make an honest confession in a diary that was encoded and never intended for public inspection. More commonplace was the 1859 injunction of a Tennessee minister that the "first duty of masters is to study the duties of masters." Failure to study the duties attached to divine agency was a moral lapse: "The master who ignores them, and proceeds upon brute principles, will vex his own soul."[28] The problem for slaves in responding to divine agency was the certainty of being adjudged immoral if they sassed God's agent.

Because Africans, free or enslaved, were customarily treated as pagans, identifying Christian doctrine that mandated their deferential speech and behavior was ironic. As early as 1638, for example, the General Assembly of Maryland "excepted" slaves from "persons being Christian."[29] Thereafter in the South, "to be Christian was to be civilized rather than barbarous, English rather than African, white rather than black."[30] Yet the heathen status of slaves made it easier for masters to claim quasi-religious authority, including the power to pontificate over informal slave marriages. Addressing newly arrived slaves, Emmaline Eve's brother-in-law made it a practice to "arrange the men in one row and the women in another and make signs to them to choose each man a wife and would read the marriage service to them."[31] If a master could visualize himself as performing a priestly role for his slaves, then he certainly could convince himself that their insolence was an affront to the Almighty.

For their part, slaves were lectured about their moral duty not to speak insolently to their master. Thomas Bacon, for example, delivered a sermon on this topic to Maryland slaves in the mid–eighteenth century. "Poor creatures!" he admonished the congregation, "when you are *saucy* and *impudent* . . . what faults you are guilty of towards your masters and mistresses, are faults done against God himself." The reason was simple. According to Bacon, God "hath set your masters and mistresses over you in His own stead, and expects that you will do for them just as you would do for Him."[32] Rev. Bacon, rector of All Saints parish, also collected and published the laws of Maryland.[33] More likely than not he saw a strong correlation between sacred and secular authority, and had little trouble envisioning an affront to God in slaves' insolence to their "masters and mistresses."

Related indoctrination of the slaves continued throughout the antebellum period, as illustrated in the mid–nineteenth-century preaching of Alexander Glennie in South Carolina. His congregation of slaves was instructed that obedience to their masters was "the will of God," and that resistance was not only an offense against their masters but also a "sin against God."[34] Charles C. Jones concurred. He exhorted masters to correct their slaves "for sins against God as well as against [themselves]." Indeed, God commanded their attention to this duty: "The Christian world outside look to us to do our duty, and, more than that, *God our Saviour looks to us to do our duty.*"[35] Several biblical passages could be interpreted to sustain the doctrine that "the Lord is greatly offended when [slaves] are saucy, impudent, stubborn, or sullen,"[36] and white preachers were quick to cite these texts for authority. Pauline epistles were especially fruitful: the first letter to Timothy (1 Tim. 6: 1–5.) was cited for its command "Let as many servants as are under the yoke count their masters worthy of all honor, that the name of God and his doctrine be not blasphemed"; similarly, the letter to the Ephesians was cited for its order "servants be obedient to them that are your masters according to the flesh with fear and trembling, in singleness of your heart, as unto

Christ."[37] Despite its apparent biblical authority,[38] the practical effect of this preaching is questionable. Only rarely did slaves themselves acknowledge that they could not be "unfaithful to [their] Earthly Master, and faithful to God."[39]

By the late antebellum period, the doctrine of divine agency was fully canonized. A Tennessee minister opined that the "Southern plantation is *imperium in imperio*. . . . the master is armed with magisterial power, by the laws alike of God and man."[40] Slaves were not mere hirelings, declared Charles C. Jones, "but servants belonging to us in law and gospel."[41] On the other side of the pulpit, Keziah Brevard meditated in her diary on her God-given duties as an owner of two-hundred slaves in South Carolina. Despising John Brown for failing to act "as one of Christ's Apostles" and instead attempting to foment a "preposterous" slave revolt, Brevard found relief in biblical doctrine. "Did God set the children of Israel to cutting their masters' throats to flee [free] them from bondage," she quizzed herself rhetorically. Answering enthusiastically in the negative, she recalled that God "brought them out of Egypt in his own peculiar way & he can send Africa's sons & daughters back when he knows they are ready for their exode." She confessed that slavery was "a dirty subject" but that "had I not thought of those cruel abolitionists who wish to free such people in our midst I would not have spoken this truth here." Ultimately, Brevard decided that she would dispense with her slaves if only she could. But great forces resisted her. "Could I for a misdemeanor now & then cast them off without a rebuke from my Heavenly father?" she queried. "While I believe I am an accountable being," she concluded, "I cannot do it."[42] A correlation of moral and legal authority pervaded both clerical and lay arguments about slavery, ensuring the publication of related doctrine in judicial opinions.

As sectional tensions mounted late in the antebellum period, high priests of the law affirmed the doctrine of the slaveowner's divine agency. The most striking of these affirmations, a portion of Eugenius A. Nisbet's opinion in *Neal v. Farmer*, features oratorical *dictum*.[43] A Georgia jury had ordered William Neal to pay eight-hundred twenty-five dollars to Nancy Farmer because Neal had killed her slave; Neal appealed this verdict on the grounds that he had not first been convicted of a crime as a basis for Farmer's civil suit. Writing for the supreme court of Georgia, Justice Nisbet affirmed the judgment in favor of Farmer.

In addition to his legal analysis, Nisbet recited a history of slavery and then articulated the moral ground of his decision. "The curse of the Patriarch," he said, "rests still upon the descendants of Ham. The negro and his master are but fulfilling a divine appointment." According to the judge, "Christ came not to remove the curse." Rather, he asserted, "recognizing the relation of master and servant, [Christ] prescribed the rules which govern, and the obligations which grow out of it, and thus ordained it an *institution of christianity*." His explicit reference to a "divine appointment" and his grounding of the institution of slavery in Christian doctrine locates Justice Nisbet's thought at the high-water mark of antebellum paternalism. If he had stopped his argument at this point the judge might have saved his rhetoric from sounding disingenuous, but he continued in a self-consciously apologetic style.

The remainder of the judicial homily explained why Nancy Farmer did not need to rely on a criminal statute about the murder of slaves in order to gain satisfaction from William Neal. "It is the crowning glory of this age and of this land," Nisbet orated, "that our legislation has responded to the requirements of the New Testament in great part, and if let alone, the time is not distant when we the slaveholders, will come fully up to the measure of our obligations as such, under the christian dispensation." Having warmed to his purpose of addressing an audience far removed from Georgia, he insisted further that the "laws of Georgia, at this moment, recognize the negro as a man, whilst they hold him property—whilst they enforce obedience in the slave, they require justice and moderation in the master." More specifically, according to the judge, Georgia laws protected the slave's "life from homicide, his limbs from mutilation, and his body from cruel and unnecessary scourging." These same laws also articulated the slave's "right to food and raiment, to kind attentions when sick, and to maintenance in old age." Finally, "in conformity with indispensable legal restraints," public sentiment in Georgia ensured that slaves were entitled to "the benefits and blessings of our Holy Religion." Clearly addressing abolitionists and Northern sympathizers, the judge wrote an apology for slavery that elaborated on John Taylor's *Arator*. In this apology, the principle of divine agency was subsumed by references to the practice of secular humanism.

Conceding that there were "violations occasionally on the part of the master, of the obligations of humanity," Justice Nisbet nevertheless contended "that the relation of master and slave in Georgia, is an institution subject to the law of kindness to as great an extent as any institution springing out of the relation of employer and employed, any where existing amongst men." In this peroration of his *dictum*, the judge explicitly lapsed into an attack on opponents of slavery. Appeals to the moral underpinning of slavery in the South were transformed into a veiled criticism of wage slavery in the North. No longer was belief in the principle of divine agency expressed artlessly as self-disclosure; it now became a well-crafted count in an indictment.

Nisbet's private and public attainments confirm his rhetorical stance in *Neal v. Farmer*. From early manhood he was an elder in the Presbyterian Church and played "a prominent part in its councils, in its presbyteries, synods, and general assembles," prompting one biographer to claim that his "religious faith has given a beautiful symmetry and completeness to his life."[44] As a United States representative from Georgia, he co-authored an 1840 *Address* to constituents in which abolition was decried as emblematic "of official infidelity, of commercial suffering, and constitutional infraction." Moreover, it was consonant with relaxation in "the tone of public morality."[45] Later in his career, as chair of the committee appointed to draft Ordinances of Secession, he would deliver these resolutions in the state convention.[46]

He resigned from the House of Representatives in 1841 after "a violent altercation" during the tariff debate that threatened "injury to [his] Christian character."[47] Two years later, in a lecture to the Georgia Historical Society, Nisbet endorsed the literary and educational merits of "the Bible, the Catechism, the Sunday School tract." More expansively, he also declared that "Christianity comes with her commission from God, and adding humans means to her divine power, asserts her empire over the heart and will." Within this Christian empire of antebellum Georgia—comparable to biblical "Canaan, with slight modification"—Nisbet asserted that "Knowledge of God, alone inspires a just sympathy for our fellow creatures. We weigh them in the scales of immortality and learn their value."[48] If he had acted at home in accord with his lecture, Justice Nisbet invoked a divine agency over his slaves Auston, Pearman, Lucinda, and Frank.[49]

Discounting completely the chatty revelations of a Catherine Carson or the beliefs expressed in a century-long sermonic tradition is problematic unless the scope of this criticism is restricted to the externally persuasive quality of this discourse rather than its self-interested or fraudulent character. Carson had little incentive to lie willfully to her father, and the preachers believed in a much greater wrath if they consciously deceived congregations. As self-persuasion these messages arguably expressed commonplace perceptions and moral interpretations of slave conduct: speaking insolently to a divine agent affronted the divinity. However, when the principle of divine agency was ultimately applied to sectional propaganda, its persuasive quality suffered. In effect, the gentry risked much when they ascribed to this principle and suffered great losses—including credibility—when they tried to impose this article of faith on others.

Family Happiness

Consistent with their religious convictions, planters perceived that slave insolence disrupted an idealized family atmosphere on plantations. Of course, the definition of "family" differed from conventional thought; slaves occupied merely a quasi-intimate relationship with their owners. Otherwise, as legislators had complained almost since the 1619 arrival of Africans,[50] miscegenation would be more rampant than it actually was. As Fox-Genovese has observed, the common phrase of "my family, white and black" referred principally to "the perspective and preeminence of the white slaveholder."[51] He defined the familial roles and he controlled their functions.

The family atmosphere perceived as an ideal of plantation life was a climate in which the slave should adopt "the attitude of a minor toward his parent."

In this setting, as a Virginia planter argued in 1837, allowing a slave "to cultivate an insubordinate temper" actually impaired "the happiness of a negro."[52] The gentry relied on widely shared experiences in which impudent if not rebellious youngsters ultimately ruined their own lives if they were not reminded of the abiding happiness afforded by a stable family life. Moreover, one could reasonably assume that only miscreants worked against their own happiness. As a planter declared in 1853, "all living on the plantation, whether colored or not, are members of the same family."[53] But reason alone did not sustain the gentry's perspective on the plantation family. Religious conviction was equally compelling. Slaves were taught that their spiritual salvation rested on their assuming "the simplicity and willingness of a little child."[54] They were left to calculate for themselves how much of their physical salvation also depended on childlike obedience.

The entries made by John Walker in his Virginia plantation journals during the 1820s and 1830s illustrate the development of a blended viewpoint, sacred and secular, that also characterized arguments about divine agency. Walker initially made dispassionate references to his slaves, calling them "hands" between 1824 and early 1827. On his forty-second birthday, he began annual reports that bespoke a change of heart. His August 15, 1827, entry expressed humble thanks to his "blessed Master" for preserving his life and pledged to continue "striving for heaven." Closing this birthday entry, he asked for divine blessing on himself and his "Servants." By 1831 he gave thanks "to Almighty God for sparing my life and all my family" and pledged continued efforts to achieve heavenly union by himself "and all my dear family."[55] Subsequent entries confirm that by 1831 Walker was thinking of his slaves as family members who were entitled to divine protection.

On August 9, 1832, he acknowledged receiving a letter about the death of a slave named Lewis whom he had hired out to "John Barr a Colier" in Richmond. He expressed his "humble hope and trust" that Lewis's "soul rests in Heaven." Next, in his birthday entry for 1832, Walker reported that "the blessed Lord has taken from us this year three of my family viz our dear daughter Sarah in Octo^r last a little coloured child named Sam in May last son of Melinda & a coloured man this 4th of Aug^s named Lewis died in Richmond at the coal pits."[56] In the same literary breath, Walker identified two of his slaves in the same way that he referred to his daughter as a dearly departed member of his family. He maintained this form of address throughout the remainder of his annual reports.

"The Lord has taken from us one our family a coloured Boy Henry," Walker wrote in his 1833 report. He had noted in March, on the day of the slave's death "from the Lock Jaw," that "Henry was a favorite little boy and was beloved by all on the place." Another member of the plantation "family," Eliza, died in 1834. During the following year, four of Walker's "coloured family" died in a reminder that "The Lord giveth and he taketh." Happily,

Walker could report on his birthday in 1836 that "none of our family (died) the past year though some severe afflictions."[57] John Walker was not guilt ridden over the deaths of his slaves because of his belief in eternal reward. He was clearly convinced that his slaves were eligible for the same salvation as himself and that they belonged to his plantation family. At the same time he explicitly distinguished these family members as "coloured" and dependent, thereby acknowledging their peculiar status and their moral duty to treat him deferentially.

Intermixing the same moral and familial themes, plantation mistresses added their voices to the chorus of paternalism. References to house slaves in particular as family members abound in these women's antebellum diaries and correspondence, attesting to the scope of their self-persuasion. Rachel O'Connor, for instance, managed 77 slaves on her Louisiana plantation but reserved special mention for young slaves like Isaac. "I have sixteen little Negroes a raising," she wrote to her sister in 1836, "all very healthy children, excepting my little favorite *Isaac*. . . . I wish I did not love him, as I do, *but it is so*, and I cannot help it." Several years later, she justified her maternal stance: "I am not afraid to love the little black children. Christ suffered on the cross for us all and it is my duty to take care of all that he has seen proper to place under my charge, for his sake" (consistent with this family atmosphere on her plantation, O'Connor also appointed two of her slaves, Leven and Arthur, as overseers.)[58] Similarly, Mary Bethell found it necessary to distinguish between her "Negroes" and her "white family" when reporting the degree of sickness on her plantation; Anna King eulogized her slave Hannah in terms of extended family: "As servant, daughter . . . she had not her equal."[59] Although plantation mistresses expressed their familial attachment to slaves with more linguistic intensity than did masters, the difference was in degree rather than in kind. The underlying notion of plantation "family" remained the same.

Yet slaves themselves did not appear to be moved by the gentry's self-persuasion about family happiness. The religious instruction that provided apparent authority remained suspect: adult slaves found the principle unpalatable, and the catechizing of young slaves coincided with the antebellum increase in sectional tensions.[60] Moreover, slaves' acknowledgments of a master's "fatherly" concern were as rare as their admissions of divine agency.[61] In practical terms, they expressed their skepticism insolently. Although Keziah Brevard professed a deep moral attachment to her slaves ("they are as our own family & would today have been a happy people if Northern fanaticism had not warred against us"),[62] she was troubled because her slaves shocked her with their insolence. Sylvia derided a recently deceased physician as "*no body, no how,*" and Rosanna declared that "she wished she could leave [Brevard] & never look behind"; Brevard exclaimed that "no one could believe the impudence I have taken from *Mack & Maria*"; even Jim and his four daughters turned on her, being "just as impudent as they desired."[63] Indeed, the constant insolence caused Brevard to question "God's ways" in placing her among so many slaves. "I have taken gross impudence hundreds of times," she complained about her slaves, even though she was "constantly administering to their comforts."[64] Scarcely the behavior to be expected from dutiful children, these slaves' speech indicated their disdain for the sort of family happiness sought by their mistress on her plantation.

The gentry countered skepticism about the efficacy of familial relationships between masters and slaves in practical terms. A Georgia physician declared that profitable plantations featured management in which the "*pater-familias*, or head of the family, should, in one sense, be the father of the whole concern, negroes and all."[65] Louisiana legislators renewed a traditional assertion that a slave owed "to his master, and to all his family, a respect without bounds."[66] However, once again sustaining a blend of sacred and secular authority, the most strident defenses of familial happiness were uttered in judicial opinions.

John B. O'Neall, in *Tennent v. Dendy*, articulated a relevant principle that affirmed the trial court's award of damages to Martha Tennent for Charles Dendy's beating of her slave before the hour at which he and other patrollers were authorized to discipline wayward slaves. Dendy had appealed on the grounds that, since Tennent had hired out her slave at the time, only the hirer had a cause of action. O'Neall dismissed Dendy's argument by fulminating on the special relationship between South Carolina masters and slaves, in which "the dependence of the latter on the former alone . . . cannot be too much encouraged." For O'Neall, slaves should believe that their masters offer "a perfect security." This belief would foster a relationship "little short of that of parent and child—it commences in the weakness of the one and the strength of the other." Moreover, it would "produce the corresponding consequences of deep and abiding grateful attachment from the slave to the master."[67] In this case, the judge opined that slaves should accept a quasi-familial relationship with their masters. Moreover, as later case law would decree, slaves did not have this special relationship with anyone else.

Richmond M. Pearson, in *State v. Caesar*, decided that North Carolina slaves might kill whites other than their master, and be found guilty of manslaughter rather than murder, if they were sufficiently provoked. The slave Caesar assaulted one white man and killed another, both of whom were drunk and disorderly, after they had beaten Caesar and his companion Dick. Justice Pearson, however, made it equally clear that slaves should not be found guilty of any crime less than murder, regardless of provocation, if they killed their master. The difference arose from the special type of relationship between master and slave, analogous to "the other relations of life" including "parent and child."[68] Thus, in exchange for enjoying the "perfect security" offered by masters, slaves should incur the most severe penalties at law if they harmed their fatherly masters.

Ebenezer A. Starnes, in *Jim v. State*, articulated this same notion as dispositive in Georgia cases. The slave Jim killed his overseer after being threatened but not harmed. Indeed, the deceased overseer, "a youth weighing about 100 lbs.," had run away and begged for mercy when Jim, "a stout man," resisted him. In this case, as the master's agent, the overseer deserved the same degree of "implicit obedience" as the master. According to Justice Starnes, this right was "similar to that which exists in the father over his children." Conversely, under Georgia law, a master could be punished for administering unreasonably brutal correction to his slave just as he could be prosecuted "if he committed murder or mayhem upon a free white citizen—even his child." In any event, "the slave must submit, as the child submits to the correction of its parent, and trust to the law for his vindication."[69] Unwilling or unable to articulate a mindset different from Justices O'Neall or Pearson, Starnes found the familial analogy sufficient for his legal argument.

The opinion in *Jim v. State* also illustrates a change in perspective. By 1854, the familial analogy had become politically necessary as well as legally sufficient. Nowhere in their opinions written in the 1830s and 1840s had O'Neall and Pearson commented explicitly on sectional strife. However, Starnes included a passage within his opinion that betrayed political self-consciousness. He acknowledged a debate over "the morality of slavery—of the responsibilities of those who established, or those who continue it—of how it shall be dealt with, and what shall be its destiny." But he declared that "this is not the place nor the occasion for such discussion."[70] Perhaps because of his relatively brief supreme court tenure of two years,[71] Justice Starnes never revisited this issue.

No longer exclusively a process of self-persuasion by the time Justice Starnes authored *Jim v. State*, articulating a familial perspective on slavery had become an artifice. As a result, notwithstanding their different contexts and purposes, the tenor of Starnes's writing lacks the simple, unaffected quality of John Walker's plantation journals.

Bonds of Friendship

Unlike the relationships between divine agents and their acolytes, or between parents and their children, friendship is characterized by free choice and equality between the parties. Nonetheless, either naively or artfully obscuring the elements of choice and equality, the gentry argued that slaves betrayed a friend when they spoke insolently to their master. This dimension of slave insolence, as conceptually difficult as finding proof of paternalism in rituals of slave punishment, was articulated less frequently and more self-consciously than other moral sentiments. Bearing these hallmarks of insincerity, appeals to the bonds of friendship merit close scrutiny of their premises and conclusions.

Patently idealistic appeals offer insight into arguably genuine articulations by the gentry. Expounding a related application of Christian doctrine, the Reverend A. T. Holmes wrote that "the master should be the *friend* of his servant, and that the servant should know it." Defining friendship as "good will, kindness, a desire for the welfare of him for whom it is entertained," Holmes contended that masters could befriend their slaves with "no compromise of authority, no undue familiarity." The slave, in turn, could take comfort in knowing that "he is not held in subjection by an unfeeling tyrant, nor driven to work by a heartless oppressor." Again, there was no danger of "improper familiarity" in the relationship because, due to "the relative positions" held by master and slave, both understand that "the *friend* becomes not the *companion*." In the "sunny South" perceived by Holmes, the slave basks in "the happy consciousness that his *master is his friend*." Holmes's essay bespeaks his good faith, despite his stereotypical reference to the sunny South. Yet he assumed readers' agreement that his invocation of "good will" was consistent with involuntary servitude. Brushing aside the scope of this intuitive leap, Holmes concluded that following his advice would prevent slave insolence. Motivated by friendly ties to imitate his master's model of "kind word" and "pleasant look," the slave would choose freely to avoid less righteous speech.[72]

Holmes then rounded out his advice by identifying the other role of "protector" that slaves should acknowledge in their master. The friends' "mutual confidence" in this arrangement dispensed with any problems created by their unequal status of "superior and inferior." The slave could "confidently look to his master for that protection" and, for the master, it was "both '*just* and *equal*'" because "it will advance the master's interest."[73] Having accounted for both free choice and equality, Holmes might have genuinely persuaded himself that slave insolence betrayed a trust between friends. In any event, his sentiments reflected an antebellum tradition of idealistic pronouncements on the master-slave relationship.

A Virginia planter insisted in 1837 that a master should gain recognition as their "protector" from his slaves. Having accomplished this goal, he would transform them into "honest, useful, and affectionate creatures." One year later a South Carolina planter wrote that if slaves recognized their master as their "protector" then they would become "much more true to his interest" than otherwise. Self-interest aside, one sympathetic Northern observer contended, many of the gentry were motivated by "a chivalric feeling" to protect slaves—much as one friend would serve as the champion for a weaker friend "who cannot return insult for insult and blow for blow."[74] However, this traveler's account stands out as a singular, perhaps gushing, endorsement of planter society. More representative, and contemporaneous with the Reverend Holmes's advice, a planter asserted that the effective management of slaves required the master to gain the position of both "protector and friend." Unlike his predecessors merely assumed in the 1830s, however, he stated explicitly that friendship did not mean equality: a slave must acknowledge that his master was "so far above him as never to be approached save in the most respectful manner."[75] Unlike Holmes's discounting of a clash with choice and equality, this planter's calculations came up short in accounting for a two-way street in the master-slave friendship.

As with planters' claims about divine agency and family happiness, slaves rarely indicated agreement with the notion of a mutually binding friendship with their masters. Moreover, even these unusual messages can be discounted as self-interested formalities. Kate S. Carney might have been delighted upon her return home to be greeted by a large group of slaves "from Aunt Beck Snell, down to Idella, the little darkey, our cook's youngest, Rosay, Helen, Jennie, not mentioning old & young, little & big,"[76] but even strangers to the South such as Fanny Kemble recognized the more likely self-serving motive behind these affectionate displays. More convincing is the sentiment expressed by a Virginia slave, Hannah, in a letter to her daughter. Several slaves had been transplanted in Richmond during David Campbell's tenure as governor, and Hannah instructed them on how to behave themselves. She specifically asked that her husband, Michael, remind the slaves "to take Good care of their Master and Mistress Knowing they are the Best Friends they have in this world." In a similar vein, the slave Lethe wrote to her young mistress, Virginia Campbell, of her "feelings of the utmost respect and esteem." More intensely yet, she exclaimed: "Oh Master! Oh Mistress! Oh Miss Virginia I want to see you all . . . my heart is large enough to hold you all."[77] On their face, these sentiments were persuasive: nothing could be more natural than to long for the company of "Best Friends."

In North Carolina, William S. Pettigrew's slave overseers, Moses and Henry, expressed the same sentiment more concisely. They concluded letters to their master with the phrase "your Servant and your friend."[78] Although self-interest may have motivated expressions of affection by Hannah, Lethe, Moses, and Henry, their letters bear sufficient elaboration to suggest that the slaves might have recognized bonds of friendship. At least acknowledging that addressing their masters less than fondly and respectfully would be perceived as betrayal, the slaves dictated sentiments consistent with the gentry's principles—not including divine agency or familial duty.

Extending the blend of sacred and secular authority for a moral view of slave management and, more specifically, enacting the spokesperson's role played by Southern judges, John B. O'Neall delivered an 1846 speech that emphasized the mutual bonds between masters and slaves. Justice O'Neall was midway through his long tenure on South Carolina's high court, but the audience of state agricultural society members was more interested in his credential as an innovative planter at "Springfield." He proposed that South Carolina would become "less a planting and more a farming State." In the meantime, the "one peculiar difficulty" at present could be remedied by fulfilling planters' duties toward "our slaves." Identifying his slaveholding interest with that of his audience, the judge then explained that slaves needed practical instruction as well as food and clothing—all of the provisions that an amicable as well as productive master provides. "Make them contented," he lectured, "and then

'Massa' will be as he ought to be, the whole world to them."[79] Fulfilling their duties as both friend and protector, masters would satisfy a grand design in planter society and become the slaves' "whole world."

O'Neall relied on credentials other than his planting innovations in his public speaking. As recounted in his autobiography, he gave up liquor and tobacco during 1832 and 1833. More formally, he ascended to prominent positions in both state and national temperance societies as well as serving as president of the Baptist State Convention's Bible Board.[80] With this impeccable identity, he was able to lecture other planters on the practical benefits of treating slaves amicably while at the same time adopting a moral tenor in addressing his listeners' duties toward their slaves. Not only this message but also the social prominence of its author bolstered the hope, if not the belief, that planters could cope with the "peculiar difficulty" facing their continued dominance in the South. Moreover, planters' agreement on rewarding respectful speech and punishing slave insolence bolstered the perceived righteousness of their dominance.

The moral meaning of slave insolence, the most abstract and difficult to explain of related meanings, relied for its cogency on the myth of paternalism but also sustained it. This notion relied on a strained analogy between the types of material support and discipline provided by masters to their slaves and that supplied by parents to their children. The strain in the analogy could be relieved only by assigning genuinely paternal (and maternal) motives to masters. In this sense, a moral perspective on slave deference located righteous motives in slaveowners. From this perspective, slaves did not merely enjoy the surrogate parenthood of their owners but also could relate to their masters and mistresses as divine agents and friends.

The doctrine of divine agency, a belief never embraced by slaves, identified planters as mediators of the sacred and the secular. This doctrine, in turn, held that slaves sinned against God when they insulted their masters. From the private meditations of William Byrd II to the judicial preaching of Eugenius A. Nisbet, planters were invested with special powers because of their divine agency—including an absolute right to slave deference—but special responsibilities as well. If they failed to reign morally over their slaves, then they might lose their immortal souls. This doctrine held religious or at least quasi-religious significance for generations of planters, as reflected in their private writings. However, when addressed to Northern opponents of slavery, belief in divine agency lost its authenticity as self-persuasion. It became a specious argument for abolitionists who, like slaves, found it incredible.

Similarly grounded in a moral perspective, the gentry also wanted to believe that slaves felt a familial attachment to their masters. Family happiness was supposed to brighten the often brutal and dreary routines of plantation life. Frequent references to slaves as family members in planters' journals and correspondence reinforced the notion that slave insolence violated the commandment to honor father and mother. Slaves rejected this notion as soundly as divine agency, but their masters and mistresses found it convenient and relevant for criticizing a lack of respect in their slaves' speech. By extension, high court judges relied on familial themes in reviewing crimes by slaves as well as crimes against slaves. Nonetheless, like the doctrine of divine agency, the familial perspective on slavery ultimately lost its credibility when it was retooled as an argument against abolition.

The perception that masters and slaves could be mutually bound in friendship relied solely on a secular morality. Unencumbered by supernatural overtones, this notion could be readily embraced so long as the slaves' lack of choice and equal bargaining power in the social contract could be discounted. And that is precisely what apologists for slavery tried to achieve. As friends, they argued, both masters and slaves could pursue the same planting interest: slaves were bound to work hard and treat their masters deferentially, while masters were bound to protect their slaves against need and harm. Unlike their conspicuous lack of agreement with the principles of divine agency and family happiness, some slaves appeared to embrace the doctrine of a mutually binding friendship with their masters. However, the language in occasional correspondence with owners and with other slaves can also be interpreted as a medium of tactical deference that most slaves used as a survival skill. Less ambiguous is John B. O'Neall's message to fellow planters that amicable relations with slaves were practical and profitable while the plantation system survived.

Southern judges like O'Neall were uniquely positioned to add legal, business, and social validity to the moral perspective on slave insolence. Their legal credentials were self-evident; they were large and small slaveholders; and judicial status often provided access to the upper class when it was not bestowed at birth. From their sanctuaries—most often a dusty hotel room on the circuit—these judges were able to blend sacred and secular themes in their opinions. As a result, their articulations of the immorality of slave insolence confirmed what many Southrons wanted to believe.

8
The Judge and Patriarch

Joseph Henry Lumpkin (1799–1867) embarked on crusades as zealously as he pursued his career. In effect, he concurred in his wife's advice to their daughter, Callie, that "happiness does not consist of great riches—nor honors, but in Godliness with contentment."[1] Attracting public attention primarily for his application of moral principles to his various campaigns for reform in Georgia and elsewhere, he applied these same principles to his judicial career. In the person of Judge Lumpkin," an enthusiastic biographer wrote, "religion has never suffered."[2] This perspective dominated his adjudication of cases involving slavery.

After graduating with honors from Princeton, Lumpkin practiced law from 1820 to 1844. A brief foray into state politics in the 1820s gave him less satisfaction than a judicial internship in the 1830s.[3] Thus, he relished his election by the Georgia legislature to the state's newly formed supreme court in 1845, and retained this judicial post until his death.[4] During his high court tenure, Chief Justice Lumpkin wrote over 500 opinions on slavery.[5] Assessed as "virulent" and "polemical,"[6] his later judicial opinions articulate a growing ardor to found his legal decisions upon reasons drawn from moral principle as well as other sources.[7]

Throughout his public life, he embraced Presbyterian doctrine with enthusiasm. "I now have a ruling sense of my helpless and condemned state," he meditated in 1827. "But the great mystery is—have I accepted my salvation? Do I rejoice with joy unspeakable of the thought that my sins were nailed to the Cross on Calvary and my pardon purchased there?"[8] In this spirit, he freely lent his skills at oral and written advocacy to several crusades. During 1847 he helped the Total Abstinence Society of Augusta organize a celebration of temperance and, upon a request from the President of Andover Theological Seminary, he agreed to review a manual on temperance.[9] His admission to the "Sons of Temperance" society the following year and his election as president of the state's Temperance Society in 1853 were predictable.[10]

Four years later, on behalf of the managers of the American Bible Society, he affixed his signature to formal requests of "distinguished public men" to endorse the "value of the Bible" in a pamphlet to be distributed nationwide.[11] In the cause of Christian education, he advocated "that system, which, while it dispels the darkness of the mind, warms and softens the moral winter of the heart."[12] His dedication to a certain type of religious education was demonstrably sincere and long-lived. Teachers and students dedicated a "Memorial" to him after he had served for sixteen years as superintendent of the sabbath school in Lexington.[13] Indeed, he castigated a faculty member after being invited to deliver Yale's Anniversary Address in 1854. "If I had as many sons as old Priam," Lumpkin wrote, "I would prefer them to be raised in ignorance of the alphabet—rather than send them to that institution."[14]

He acknowledged the complications attached to his melding of crusades and career but, perceiving his cause as righteous, he forged ahead. His campaigning for temperance, for instance, had to be divorced from its customary association with abolition. In a well-documented exchange of letters during 1849 with Father Theobald Mathew, a famous Irish advocate of temperance, Lumpkin challenged the priest to disavow his earlier attack on slavery as a "foul blot" on America. Father Mathew declined and Lumpkin ultimately counted him among "enemies in waging an unprovoked and most relentless warfare upon our hearths and homes, our peace and prosperity."[15]

Lumpkin's religious zeal complicated his staunch defense of slavery. In an 1854 letter, he lambasted the Roman Catholic doctrine of "transubstantiation" among other errors, but he simultaneously "feared that one of the evils of the present political agitation would be to silence the Pulpit—Ministers would be afraid to denounce the errors & abominations of Romanism lest they should be considered as party."[16] Lumpkin frequently addressed state and national questions in his correspondence, including the issues of whether Kansas should be admitted as a free or slave state and the repeal of the Fugitive Slave law.[17] In this correspondence, he never abandoned his double-edged partisanship in religion and politics.

His public statements on education contained the same message. Most noteworthy, perhaps, was his 1837 speech at the dedication of Oglethorpe University. After decrying the low number of Georgians in college, he urged his listeners to reflect on the "large proportion" of "foreigners and Northern men" among the state's "Lawyers, Physicians, Merchants, Mechanics and Ministers." Quickly turning to political trends, he forecast a need for well educated Georgians to defend the morality of slavery: "Who is so blind as not to see, that severe conflicts await us, resulting from our local interests. We want men thoroughly disciplined, to vindicate our peculiar institutions in our State, and Federal councils, and ecclesiastical judicatories; men who, should a separation be forced upon us in Church or State, by our misguided assailants, which we deprecate as the greatest of all evils, would be able to appeal successfully to the judgment of mankind, as well as the searcher of hearts, to show that we were blameless."[18] He endorsed a liberal arts training with which properly disposed graduates could argue the Southern cause. Never one to back away from a confrontation with the forces of evil, Lumpkin pursued educational ideals with the same fervor he articulated social reform and religious instruction.

Lumpkin saw himself as a public figure with clearly defined duties. Whether lecturing to the members of a Cliosophic Society or a Thalian Society, writing and speaking on behalf of his favorite crusades, or delivering opinions as chief justice, he dutifully urged a moral perspective on resolving problems. Owning merely a handful of slaves, he nonetheless confidently extended his moral perspective to matters involving the human chattel owned by major planters. His sense of moral duty required no less.

The Patriarchal Judge

Shortly after Lumpkin's death, the supreme court of Georgia commissioned a memorial which recited that in "private and social relations" the deceased chief justice adopted behaviors of "the patriarchal type."[19] Hardly critical, this eulogy affirmed the righteousness of paternalism. Lumpkin had consistently demonstrated that both his religious beliefs and his mundane experiences convinced him to treat slaves accordingly. More specifically, slave responses that lacked suitable deference, if not affection, shocked him as ill omens of a crumbling system.

Given the significance of slavery for Lumpkin, breaches of protocol were particularly disturbing. He poignantly expressed his anguish over slave insolence in a letter reporting events at a wedding reception to his daughter. "We are falling upon hard times," he surmised from speech patterns among the "some three hundred guests—white and black." In particular, he observed with considerable indignation that "no negro now calls their own master or mistress—or themselves—by their owner's name." More specifically, "daddy and mamma, are obsolete words in their vocabulary." The advent of a world without subservient slaves who referred to their owners as parents dismayed him. "What is to be next?" he asked rhetorically.[20] Having presaged the answer thirty years earlier in reflections on Gibbon's *Decline and Fall of the Roman Empire*, Lumpkin underscored that "the human race is most prosperous and happy when governed by absolute power under the guidance of wisdom and virtue."[21] As illustrated by the fall of Rome, if slave insolence eroded masters' absolute power, then the prosperity and happiness of plantation society would surely decline.

Rhetorical flourishes, but not the underlying rulings, in a trilogy of his appellate opinions during 1853, 1854, and 1855 illustrate the strength of Lumpkin's faith in a familial exchange of deference and duty between master and slave. In *Latimer v. Alexander*,[22] for example, Lumpkin led the court in reversing a verdict that compelled Henry B. Latimer to pay for his slave's medical treatment, although Latimer had approved neither the treatment nor the physician, Dr. James F. Alexander. Without violating his personal code of paternalism, Chief Justice Lumpkin obeyed "the principles of Law." He acknowledged that Latimer had hired out the slave for $91 to work as a waiter in Joseph Thompson's Atlanta hotel, that the slave contracted smallpox from one of the hotel's guests, and that Thompson called upon Dr. Alexander to treat the slave without notifying Latimer. Under these conditions, there was "no privity of contract between Dr. Alexander and Mr. Latimer" and consequently the physician must collect his fee of $100 from the hotelier. Moreover, according to Lumpkin, "the Law . . . will not permit a slave, hired as this was, for general and common service, to be employed in any hazardous business, without the consent of the owner." Of course, the timely provision of medical treatment to the slave made the result morally palatable.

Despite his reverence for the law, the chief justice initially expressed misgivings about its application under different fact settings. He applauded a South Carolina precedent by which an abusive master was compelled to pay for the unauthorized medical treatment of his slave. In that case, he declared, the "court considered, as every enlightened tribunal would do, that the master was bound by the most solemn obligation, to protect and preserve the life of his slave." Indeed, the master "could no more divest himself of this obligation, than could the husband and father the duty of supporting and maintaining a wife or child." Not only legally grounded but also morally enlightened, this result was fair because "the slave lives for his master's service alone." Not satisfied with his citation of this South Carolina case—"But I will go further"—Lumpkin also recited circumstances in which the more typical master would be financially liable for unauthorized medical treatment of his slave. But, in the end, the chief justice could not bring himself to ignore the rule of law regardless of its potential to discourage or delay emergency medical treatment for slaves—part of a master's "solemn obligation."

His belief in a familial exchange of deference and duty between master and slave did not permit Lumpkin to disobey the rule of law in *Latimer v. Alexander*, but he interjected all the exceptions he could envision to limit future applications of the court's decision. And his analogous reference to family obligation did not stop with the customary depiction of slaves as children of the master; he also compared this obligation with a husband's duty to his wife. Shockingly effusive, perhaps, Lumpkin's analogy reminded his contemporaries as well as later generations of sexual exploitation in many master-slave relationships. More relevant to the present analysis, the chief justice disclosed an intense reaction to failures in a paternalistic system, a system that he wanted to succeed.

He publicly declared related moral indignation during the next judicial session in *Cleland v. Waters*,[23] a case involving testamentary manumission of slaves. Again, his rhetoric and not his ruling reflects the moral perspective he shared with his Georgia constituents. Thomas J. Waters mentioned almost fifty slaves by name in his will, and included language that seemed to provide for the emancipations of his "body servant, William," as well as "the future issue and increase of the females," who were mentioned by name. Alternatively, if Georgia law prohibited this act, Waters declared that William and the nascent slaves were to be transported out of the state to enjoy their freedom. As for the remaining slaves, including "a large number of negroes not mentioned" in his will, Waters directed his son and two daughters to distribute them equally but "divide the said negroes in families, so that the principles of humanity may be observed." Upon Waters's death, his executors failed to persuade Judge Jackson of the Gwinnett Superior Court to void the emancipations. On appeal, Chief Justice Lumpkin decided that the lower court was wrong to rely solely on a "verbal, grammatical interpretation" of the will and ruled that emancipation "was not the intention of the testator."

It was morally unlikely, Lumpkin decided, that Thomas Waters—who had ordered his heirs to preserve slave families—had intended to free all children born in the future of his female slaves without also freeing the mothers. "Can it be consistent with this idea," Lumpkin asked rhetorically, "that the testator should have intended to have the tender infants . . . torn from their parents immediately upon their birth, and if refused an abiding place here, transported to some distant land?" In answer, Lumpkin fulminated that to sustain this intention would be "to disregard every principle of humanity—to outrage the holiest feelings of our nature." But the chief justice was not satisfied. In a sarcastic tenor, he disputed Waters's intention to emancipate William, the bodyservant. Otherwise, Lumpkin argued, William likewise "must be separated from his aged wife and their numerous offspring . . . and be sent off, 'solitary and alone,' to enjoy the fatal boon of liberty." The testator had ordered all other slave families to be preserved. Why would he reward William's faithful service, Lumpkin asked, by tearing him away from his family?

Far from an immoral institution, the chief justice argued in *Cleland v. Waters*, slavery was preferable to living free but isolated and alone. In this instance, at least, moral principles prompted the court to rule against liberty—an intriguing outcome but fully consonant with the perspective shared among the gentry. The reason was familial. Destroying slave families was no less immoral than disrupting the larger plantation family. However, to buttress his conclusion, the judge constructed a rhetorical device. Yet the sarcasm he used was more characteristic of a dissenting opinion than the text of a unanimous decision. In this case, the chief justice needed to voice a presumption against liberty that dissented from American revolutionary ideals and constitutional doctrine. Equally significant was his invocation of "the holiest feelings of our nature" to determine testamentary intent. This language marked a rhetorical shift from his more neutral reference to a merely "enlightened" stance in *Latimer v. Alexander* and prepared the ground for his openly sermonic style in the final installment of the trilogy.

In *Moran v. Davis*,[24] Lumpkin formally declared his belief in the master's role as divine agent for his slaves. Augustus B. Moran had sued Gardner Davis for $1200, the value of a young slave named Stephen. Acting as trustee for the slaveowner, Mariana Moran, the plaintiff had leased Stephen during 1852 to the defendant. Stephen ran away. Tracked down by a slavecatcher and his dogs, Stephen drowned while trying to avoid capture. The trial judge had instructed the jury that overseers and hirers of slaves were liable for damages only if they tracked slaves with dogs that might "materially injure" their quarry by lacerating or otherwise wounding them. Fearing a verdict against him because Stephen had drowned rather than dying from a dog attack, Moran appealed this instruction to Georgia's high court. Citing "general principles" as well as statutory authority and the current statistics on runaway slaves, Lumpkin affirmed the trial judge's instruction.

Having paid suitable regard to rule of law, the chief justice then turned to Holy Writ in order to illustrate that slavery was ordained to survive, "if the Apocalypse be inspired, until the end of time." At the end of the world, amid a biblically prophesied earthquake, solar eclipse, bleeding moon and falling stars, "every *bondman* (doulos, slave or servant) and every *freeman*" would hide themselves in hope of escaping God's final judgment. Notwithstanding the divine verdict, sacred scripture confirmed that the disparate roles of master and slave would endure forever. For Justice Lumpkin, the divine authority for slavery was compelling and suggested the "paternalistic goodness of masters."[25] As foretold in the scriptures, slavery was timeless and both slave and master were answerable for their respective satisfaction of allied duties.

Lumpkin spelled out the nature of these duties in an 1859 letter to his daughter. Among several other observations, he described the morally desirable attitude taken by one of the governor's slaves, Old Ben. "He seems to have no personal sense of the future," Lumpkin wrote approvingly. The slave acknowledged words of praise for his work such as "well done faithful old negro," but he was more concerned that "his real master will say the same hereafter." Lumpkin thought that Ben expressed "a capital creed for a servant" when he referred to God as his real master. Implicit in this creed was a prohibition against blasphemy at the highest level and insolence to the divine master's earthly agent. Uttering his hope that "God in his goodness will deal very kindly" with slaves like Ben in the final judgment, Lumpkin articulated the doctrine of a slaveowner's divine agency.[26] Masters were placed on earth for their slaves' benefit and, in this divine order, both classes of humans had moral duties to fulfill. Under ideal conditions, "servants" would be seen dutifully "tumbling over [one] another & calling for Mas William" when this elderly member of the gentry lay dying.[27] In return for deferential words and deeds, members of the gentry like Lumpkin would express shock over any ill treatment of slaves.[28]

In fairness to his legacy, Lumpkin's paternalistic stance toward working-class whites must be noted alongside his attitude toward blacks. When he urged the "Industrial Regeneration of the South," for example, he classified white workers as "poor, degraded . . . and ignorant" and insisted that they could only benefit "under the oversight of employers, who will inspire them with self-respect by taking an interest in their welfare."[29] His reference to a degraded folk who needed oversight illustrates the true scope of his paternalism and his exhortation to employers confirms his sense of moral duty toward subordinates—white and black.

The consistency with which he endorsed a moral perspective on solving problems, whether these were legal disputes or industrial developments, seems to imbue his pronouncements with authenticity. But his close attention to sectional politics is equally clear. He adopted a strongly pro-slavery stance in the 1850s and the degree to which his public declarations reflected perception, self-persuasion, or propaganda can be assessed only with collateral reference to his private communications.

The Judicial Patriarch

According to Lumpkin, his ownership of slaves was an intensely personal and meaningful experience. In one instance, "the death of old man Tom" caused him to meditate on his past and future. Tom was the last to die of four slaves that Lumpkin had inherited, "the last link that bound him to the estate of [his] father." Moreover, Tom's death made Lumpkin's own demise "appear very near—a present reality." Prompted to take stock of his future, he wrote of "a troubled dream" from which "we awake & find ourselves in eternity."[30] Yet slaves also provided a comparative measure by which Lumpkin assessed his present circumstances. In another letter to his daughter, addressed paternally as "My beloved baby," he explained how he had developed an understanding of slaves. "I never knew under what discouragements a negro works," he claimed, until he pursued his judicial career: "The more you do, the more you have to do." But then he indulged in hyperbole that marked his explanation as rhetorical. "I am so glad I am not negro," he wrote, "But then I am the next thing to it, Judge of the Supreme Court."[31] And so, even in his rhetorical flourishes, he illustrated the significance of slavery in shaping his perceptions. More prosaically, he saw his slaveownership as a meaningful point of contact with his past and future.

Crafting Lumpkin's public image in 1851, a biographer described "servants who yield him a willing obedience" primarily because he disdained "to address a servant harshly."[32] Yet during the following year he did not hesitate to sell a runaway slave, Emily, and he did not agonize over his decision. In fact, he declared himself "very well satisfied."[33] The nature of Lumpkin's personal relationship with his slaves was as complex as his sense of personal morality. Extra-judicial comments on *Bryan v. Walton* (1853) provide a touchstone for unraveling this relationship. He did not minimize his difficulty when this "hard case" involving "the status or condition of a free negro in this State" came before him for review. He also did not hesitate to resolve the case by denying to free Negroes "the social civil or political priviledges of citizenship."[34]

The underlying facts of *Bryan v. Walton* challenge lay appreciation.[35] Simply stated, the case involved a second-generation free black named Joseph Nunez who attempted to make a gift of slaves to the white guardian whom he was required to have under state law. This guardian, Alexander M. Urquhart, then attempted to hire out the slaves. A dispute arose over ownership of the slaves, based on Urquhart's denial of his guardianship, and Lumpkin delivered the court's opinion voiding the gift. Although Nunez was permitted by a statutory loophole to own slaves he had inherited, the chief justice opined, he could not validly transfer them to Urquhart without a written order from his guardian. Free blacks in Georgia—burdened with "the taint of blood" as "descendants of Ham in this country"—had "no civil, social, or political rights or capacity" except "freedom from the dominion of the master, and limited liberty of locomotion." In his role as Nunez's guardian, Urquhart alone could authorize gifts but he could not legally make a gift to himself. Moreover, the chief justice was prompted to comment extensively on the case: "I feel a strong inclination, I confess, to give my sentiments pretty fully upon this subject—to go beyond the usual limits of an opinion; and to speak in the style of argument rather than of authority." By these words, he alerted readers of what was to come next: a notable advocacy of the peculiar institution.

In his commentary, he expressed his "hearty and cordial approval" of the restrictions imposed on free blacks as emblems of the "unceasing vigilance and firmness, as well as uniform kindness, justice and humanity" required of the gentry. This roster of contrapuntal duties reflected his personal convictions about a "degraded race." Although the chief justice recited these convictions as "facts," they do not appear in the legal record: "In no part of this country, whether North or South, East or West, does the free negro stand erect and on a platform of equality with the white man. He does, and must necessarily feel this degradation. To him there is but little in prospect, but a life of poverty, of depression, of ignorance, and of decay. He lives among us without motive and without hope. His fancied freedom is all a delusion. All practical men must admit, that the slave who receives the care and protection of a tolerable master, is superior in comfort to the free negro." Through personal intuition and rhetorical invention, Lumpkin assessed the ill effects on runaway slaves of failing to recapture them. "Of one thing I am quite certain," he perorated, "in the United States, whether slaveholding or non-slaveholding, [freedom] is worse than slavery itself." Rather than citing facts, the chief justice clearly disclosed what he accepted as moral truths that guided his personal beliefs.

Among these convictions, Lumpkin affirmed the moral duty of all blacks to acknowledge their inherently subordinate status by behaving deferentially toward all whites. The freedom supposedly enjoyed by blacks such as Joseph Nunez or by fugitives in the North was illusory. Speaking or acting under the influence of this delusion was insolent. However, in return for absolute deference, their white masters provided care and protection. In "fact," even the care and protection provided by a merely "tolerable" master surpassed the quality of life endured by a free black. Although slaves were subject to their masters' "unceasing vigilance and firmness," they enjoyed the fruits of their masters' other moral duties: "uniform kindness, justice and humanity." For Lumpkin, a moral perspective on slavery mandated its dutiful exercise rather than its abolition.

The patriarch did not need to ponder at length the moral duty of slaves to speak and act respectfully to their masters. It was self-evident. Writing to his son-in-law, Porter King, Lumpkin expounded on the evils of misconduct by the slave "Jane." "The behavior of the hussy," he asserted, caused him great "mortification." He conceded delight in learning that Porter had consigned Jane to auction, musing that "next to a mean wife, I know of no greater nuisance than a worthless servant."[36] His comparison of an unruly slave with a troublesome wife underscored the paternal tenor of his letter. However, Lumpkin's son-in-law was well acquainted with a paternalistic master's moral duty to slaves, including naming their children and providing them with the necessities of life.[37] In turn, he expected displays of concern for the master's welfare and submission to flogging for sauciness.[38] Most probably the son-in-law anticipated Lumpkin's expression of embarrassment about Jane's misconduct—as well as his promise to make up the difference between her purchase price and the proceeds of her sale. By her insolence, Jane had broken the law, become a business liability, and offended the social order. Just as significantly, the saucy slave had violated a moral code endorsed not only by leading advocates of temperance and Bible study but also by ordinary subscribers to the dominant culture.

Lumpkin's distaste for the insolence shown by Jane was abiding and punctuated opinions he wrote in reviewing cases about negligently causing the deaths of slave hirelings. In *Scudder v. Woodbridge*, for example, the owner of a steamboat appealed a jury verdict ordering him to pay five hundred dollars for the death of a slave in his employ. Wylly Woodbrige had leased his slave Ned to work as a carpenter aboard Amos Scudder's *Ivanhoe*, but Ned drowned as a result of a black engineer's negligence. Restricting applications of the fellow-servant rule to cases in which the negligent co-worker was a free white, the chief justice argued that slaves were in no position to "see that every other person employed in the same service does his duty with the utmost care and vigilance." Indeed, he observed, "*They* dare not interfere with the business of others. They would be instantly chastised for their impertinence." Not content merely to state his opinion, he elaborated further on how "strange and extraordinary" it would be if liability for workplace negligence was applied equally to "slaves and free white citizens." Unlike white co-workers, slaves had no option other than to "silently serve out their appointed time, and take their lot in the mean while in submitting to whatever risks and dangers are incident to the employment."[39] For Lumpkin, the Neds and Janes of the South had a moral duty to behave deferentially if not silently in the presence of whites.

In another case, *Gorman v. Campbell,* Lumpkin underscored the corresponding duty of whites. Thomas B. Gorman (Lumpkin referred to him as James B. Gorman) had leased his slave London to work on Charles Campbell's steamboat, the *Sam Jones.* When the river was obstructed by logs, London volunteered to help clear a passage. Slaves were not usually permitted to do this type of work, but the riverboat captain allowed London to cut logs for half an hour before ordering him to step off one that was breaking free from the logjam. London refused and drowned when he slipped off this log as it floated downriver. At trial, a jury had found in favor of Campbell because the slave had undertaken freely a hazardous job despite the captain's warning. The chief justice reversed this verdict because the captain had initially permitted London to do dangerous work and ordered the slave to stop only when disaster was imminent. Justifying his reversal, Lumpkin appealed to the "humanity" of "all who employ slaves." These employers, he urged, should "watch over [slaves'] lives and safety. Their improvidence demands it."[40] No other finding would have been consistent with a paternalistic perspective on slavery; no other urging would have been consistent with Lumpkin's moral code.

Beyond a doubt, Joseph Henry Lumpkin was consistent. His commitment to several moral crusades was unwavering and his appellate career featured uniformly moral judgments about masters and slaves. Lumpkin, however, was not naive. Well educated and richly experienced, he reflected on his goals before speaking and artfully expressed his professional and personal opinions. A critical assessment of his moral perspective on slave insolence must therefore account for a potentially complex interweaving of honesty and guile.

As a young adult, Lumpkin genuinely embraced a moral code with which he thereafter measured human conduct. His generous investments in various reform movements, while advantageous to his public standing, cannot be discounted generally. Then again, he clearly recognized his problematic endorsement of movements such as temperance without also endorsing abolition, and he explicitly urged a system of higher education in Georgia so that slavery would not lack effective advocates in the state. In essence, he readily defended the political institution of slavery because it was consistent with a moral code in which he found the meaning of life.

Life in the South was meaningful for Lumpkin when slaves behaved in accord with what he considered a divinely ordained relationship between themselves and their masters. The solemn obligations of slaves included affirming the master's parental role, or more desirably, the master's divine agency. Within this relationship, failing to address master and mistress as father and mother was as much an insult as resisting their authority. Indeed, the ideal mentality for slaves inspired them to obey their earthly master as a sign of their devotion to their heavenly master. Lumpkin preached this doctrine from his judicial pulpit continuously during his tenure as chief justice, but his preaching coincided with the approach of war between North and South. Sorting out the elements of genuine perception and clever propaganda in his messages requires comparative analysis of his private and public communications.

In private, he confessed the fundamental significance to him of family slaves as tangible guides to his past, present, and future. Their lives and deaths demarcated grossly the more esoteric and refined developments within plantation society. Yet he never mentioned a personal affection for slaves themselves; they were wards rather than offspring. Lumpkin's public statements reinforced his paternal but distant relationship to slaves. He described slaves as hopeless, improvident creatures who needed fatherly masters in order to survive. Freedom was an illusion for them. Degraded and desperate, slaves fared best under the constant scrutiny of white superiors who in turn had a moral duty to care properly for their human chattel. In sum, Lumpkin's moral perspective was cold and calculated rather than warm and fuzzy: the paternalistic master was first and foremost a disciplinarian.

Joseph Henry Lumpkin was consistently honest. Not painting an especially attractive picture for abolitionists, Lumpkin starkly declared his beliefs rather than attempting to persuade opponents. Attempting to enact his ideals, he routinely combined the roles of judge and patriarch. Slave insolence was a moral problem not because masters should be loved but because they must be revered.

Conclusion

My narrow focus on slave insolence and several types of related narratives should not suggest that this lonstanding medium of resistance caused long-lived, widespread concerns among the gentry. It did not. Only during a few decades between the end of a revolutionary war and the beginning of a civil war did the gentry actively try to counteract this insolence through legislative and other measures. However, their concerns about insolent slaves illustrate the perceived fragility of the plantation system, the tenacity with which its defenders rallied behind it, and their extraordinary regard for the power of speech.

Slave insolence evoked dread that the social and moral fabric of the plantation system was less durable than leading authors and preachers cared to admit. This impudence clouded partisan depictions of a "sunny South" and countered clerical admonitions to obey cheerfully. If slave insolence had been commonplace, then it would have been attacked earlier and more relentlessly than it was. Its biting effect would have gradually been diffused as familiarity bred contempt, and it would not have pointedly called into question troubling dimensions of plantation society. Reviewing these dimensions, in order from the most abstract to the most tangible, highlights the degree of self-consciousness in the gentry's management of speech and race. This review also defines the driving force behind legislation against slave insolence.

The Moral Perspective

Pronouncements of the moral perspective reveal the full range of unreflective, self-persuasive, and propagandistic features in the gentry's responses to slave insolence. This perspective rested on both formal religious doctrine and a less formal but equally compelling belief in a moral contract requiring an exchange of duties between masters and slaves. Endorsed righteously by planters, this contract called for paternalistic care by masters and childlike devotion by slaves.

The most formal version of paternalism, the doctrine of divine agency, represented a belief among members of the gentry like Catherine Carson that masters performed a priestly role as God's messengers to the slaves and that slaves sinned when they treated divine messengers disrespectfully. Masters could derive comfort about their hegemony over slaves from the self-induced belief that this regime was divinely ordained.

Other pronouncements of this doctrine more overtly display a rhetoric of self-persuasion and propaganda. From the sermons of Thomas Bacon and his successors to John Taylor's *Arator*, expressions of divine agency explicitly and continuously responded not to a heavenly call but to mundane pressures—including the need to rebuff abolitionists. Plantation mistresses like Keziah

Brevard might have preferred to maintain a purely moral tenor in their discussions of divine agency but they readily acknowledged their earthy distaste for abolitionism. In these instances, the gentry felt compelled to punish slaves who spoke insolently for civil heresy as much as moral lapses.

The literal version of paternalism—a call for happiness in extended plantation families that included slaves—was consistent both with domestic experience and religious doctrine. If masters and mistresses should be obeyed as parents, then slaves should be treated as children if only because children need to be disciplined for their own happiness. Moreover, as John Walker indicated in his plantation journals, a familial perspective included the hope that dutiful slaves were eligible for the same heavenly rewards as acknowledged biological children.

But slaves themselves rarely acknowledged a childlike attachment to their masters and mistresses. Without this confirmation, the gentry's call for happiness in the extended plantation family echoes with the same type of dominant voice that demands unconditional surrender from a besieged enemy. Claims by the gentry about a familial attachment to slaves remained unrequited, suggesting that they were not spontaneous declarations but tactical responses to moral challenges. These claims soothed guilty consciences and rebutted the negative testimony of slaves in their insolent speech.

Equally specious was the version of paternalism in which, notwithstanding an unequal and involuntary role for slaves, masters and slaves were said to enjoy bonds of friendship. Insolence made slaves liable for betraying this bond. The argument about bonds of friendship became a mainstay in defending the plantation system despite the argument's unrealistic and logically flawed character. At best, this argument was consistent with the gentry's pursuit of chivalry. Portraying themselves as champions and protectors of their slaves may have persuaded some masters that they were reenacting an antique role. In addition, regardless of their motives, slaves occasionally reinforced this notion by addressing their masters affectionately. While serving as Virginia's governor, David Campbell and members of his family received solicitous letters from their slaves back on the plantation. William S. Pettigrew received the same type of messages from slaves he had elevated to the posts of overseers on his North Carolina properties. However, this seemingly affectionate discourse can be distinguished from genuinely intimate messages to family members. Slaves were eminently capable of manipulating a master's feelings positively as well as negatively, especially when they were already being treated humanely. More could be gained from complimenting a distant master than reviling him. As a result, if members of the gentry wanted to persuade themselves that slaves betrayed bonds of friendship by their insolence, then material evidence was conspicuous in several sources.

The gentry's utterance of a moral perspective on slave insolence merits analysis for demonizing unruly slaves. Regardless of which version of paternalism a Southern partisan might endorse, insolent slaves could be decried as sinners. Although abusing a divine agent was clearly heinous, resisting parental authority or betraying a friend also violated the moral code. Unruly slaves were not merely villains in a secular sense—though not analogous to villeins in the common law tradition—they were portrayed as devils in a moral sense. Their insolence was particularly devilish if it led other slaves onto the path of evil. And they accomplished their despicable goal, despite shackles and whippings, by exercising a power of speech that could not be readily controlled.

Significant in this regard is the apparent lack of related discourse by overseers. Their discursive influence in general has largely escaped critical notice and so the lack of moral indictments of slaves in their narratives cannot be assessed conclusively. Yet the fact remains that nowhere in the letters, reports, and diaries of overseers analyzed in prior chapters does an immediate supervisor of slaves adopt a moral perspective on their insolence. Other than using the term "devil" pejoratively to depict an unruly slave, typically along with a racial epithet, overseers did not link insolence with immorality. These frontline supervisors appeared to experience frustration about lost productivity and anger over personal affronts when dealing with slave insolence but not moral outrage. Instead, the task of demonizing slaves usually fell to more distant critics. Aggrieved over slave insolence on a comparatively abstract level, these critics expressed suitably eternal and ephemeral concerns about an everyday, gritty problem.

Few pronouncements of the moral perspective were unreflective claims about a divinely inspired order in human affairs. Most were arguments that relied on *a priori* premises by which the gentry attempted to persuade themselves and others of a threat to the plantation system. Crafting a vision of warfare between good and evil, planters attempted to seize and hold the high ground. However, taken at their word, the gentry also acknowledged conversely that slaves could dislodge them by mere insolence. This argument, attributing an extraordinary power to slave speech, should not be dismissed until its underpinnings in other perspectives are examined.

The Social Perspective

From this perspective, slaves' personal affronts to the gentry entailed a larger social problem. The problem was solved when slaves performed rituals of deference and suppressed their personal identities by speaking and acting uniformly as a class. However, among the several double standards and disadvantages with which slaves had to contend was the lack of clear directions about how to perform the approved rituals. Indeed, the gentry themselves never clearly defined the acceptable bounds of social behavior. They were confounded by the bewildering number of ways in which a casual word or deed could be interpreted, and they were challenged by the need for legalistic precision in proscribing deviant behaviors. Nonetheless, slaves' failure to perform social rituals reinforced the bias that they were naturally inferior.

Slaves grossly violated the social ritual by becoming drunk and disorderly, although a double standard permitted more leeway to whites. From Thomas Jefferson to Tryphena Fox, masters and mistresses abhorred the deviance in their slaves' drinking. A social lubricant for whites, alcohol was typically forbidden to slaves because it lured them into loud talk and other conspicuous displays of individuality—deviant excesses all. The gentry preferred slaves to be silent and invisible in social settings, making it difficult if not impossible to discover their true identities.

Complaints and insults, even when uttered by sober slaves, were equally deviant. Recognizing the pitfalls of saying anything when they could not know which forms of speech were banned, slaves typically resorted to a fawning deference if not absolute silence. Poems and songs by slaves, although not addressed directly to white audiences or to any particular member of the gentry, also were perceived as threatening social stability. The degree to which the gentry perceived a corporate duty to sustain the social order by discouraging slaves' self-expression emerges clearly in the rare instances when slaves uttered complaints or insults: they could be punished by a white who overheard their insolence as well as by the whites being addressed. It was not as important to the gentry who punished slaves for social deviance as long as punishment would be administered.

Perceived affronts to white women also drew the gentry's wrath, whether or not a woman had been insulted to her face. The double standard afflicting slaves was illustrated clearly when male slaves defended their own women or female slaves themselves resisted exploitation, and then suffered for their words and deeds. Though consistent with the gentry's social norms, a slave's defense of female honor was insolent because it asserted an independent identity, an identity that belied complete erasure of individuality. The gentry knew that slaves were individuals but they abhorred the sights and sounds of this individuality.

So deep was this abhorrence that unspoken insolence was as troubling as its more conventional expressions. Firsthand observers, whether white or black, free or slave, uniformly attested to social rituals in which slaves surrendered sidewalks and doffed their hats to white passersby. Moreover, slaves could incite violent retaliation by wearing more stylish clothing or garments of better quality than whites. Slaves also had to monitor their bearing, gestures, and facial expressions or run the risk of affronting the gentry. More daunting to slaves than controlling their drinking, complaining, and other socially proscribed behaviors, was the need to control physical responses that would now be diagnosed as involuntary reflexes. In essence, they could not easily avoid insolence because the gentry found almost every sign of slave individuality to be distressing.

The gentry treated slave insolence as social deviance despite measuring themselves against different standards and despite failing to define clearly the words and deeds that slaves must avoid. Conformity was impossible because slaves would have needed to shed all outward displays of individuality—voluntary and involuntary—in order to avoid insolence. Unlike the gentry's claim to moral leadership, they could not claim social leadership as role models for slaves because of the obscure, double standards that were imposed. More readily than the propaganda derived from their moral perspective, the gentry derived self-persuasion from their social perspective. There was no propaganda value in arguing that slaves had no faces, no individual identities. Even casual observations by travel writers who were not unsympathetic to the South contradicted this notion. Rather, the gentry consoled themselves that their social ideals could be achieved if slaves would remain silent and invisible. Consistent with the treatment of slaves as morally suspect children, the social perspective also could be aligned with a widely endorsed business perspective.

The Business Perspective

The profit motive, when grafted onto a duty to protect the social order, ensured that planters and their business allies cared about the market as much as the polis. In resolving the problem of insolent slaves, social ideal was tempered with economic reality. From a business perspective, silence was golden and many slaveowners believed implicitly in an inverse ratio between impudence and a slave's value in the workplace. Moreover, widespread belief in slaves' cunning gradually reduced the effectiveness of their time-honored tactics for allaying the gentry's suspicions: smiling and bowing one's head might actually have the opposite effect even though these behaviors scarcely bespoke insolence.

Slaves' complaints and denials were disallowed because they were perceived to harm the efficient operation of plantations. Even apparently innocuous replies such as "I don't know" or "I forgot" might invite reprisals for signifying contempt. Denials of violating curfew or missing work were also sanctioned because, as slaves discovered, their master claimed ownership of their tongues as well as their time.

Assertions of independence or equality more explicitly challenged the gentry's mastery of slaves. Because of a perceived power in slave speech, masters and their overseers dealt harshly with these assertions regardless of the physical power of slaves. With rare exceptions, slaves made these assertions not to masters but to overseers. In response, overseers often felt that they had to decide between whipping the offending slaves, which very well could physically harm them and diminish their value as business assets, or conserving the slaveowner's human property, which could gradually result in a loss of control over the slaves. Only clever overseers found a middle ground in which they inflicted punishment tactically and with moderation.

For analogous reasons, slaves addressed the highly explicit insolence of insults and threats to plantation mistresses. These women made up another specially threatened class of interlocutors because, like overseers, their authority was limited if not illusory. They were bound by social and legal norms that made them subject to their husbands' authority, made them compete with one another for reputations of ladylike nobility and moral excellence, and made them particularly vulnerable to related insolence from slaves in the workplace. From Upper South to Deep South, mistresses faced taunts about their ignoble or impious characters that would never have been addressed to their fathers, brothers, or husbands. Slave insults were tantamount to threats because plantation mistresses cultivated their personal reputations at the same time they managed the manor house and executed other duties. Lacking their husbands' ultimate authority in the workplace, they toiled analogously to overseers in protecting their station in life as well as looking after profits.

Using an early version of the domino-effect argument, some members of the gentry persuaded themselves that they were defending the plantation system itself by literally stamping out impudent slaves. To this extent, the gentry promoted themselves as social heroes. However, most planters and their business associates restricted their attention to less lofty matters: the more time that slaves devoted to complaining, asserting their equality, and insulting their superiors, the less time they spent in seeding, weeding, and harvesting crops. In contrast to moral fulminations and social outcries, taking care of business did not demand thoughtful reflection by the gentry on the discursive threat posed by slaves. They were not condemned as sinners although their brutal treatment could easily be described as hellish. They were not denied an identity although, managed simplistically as bound laborers, slaves were viewed as little more than tools. The business environment prompted overseers and plantation mistresses to view slave insolence analogously. Genuinely concerned about profit margins but lacking authority and fearing diminution of their reputations, overseers and mistresses had little incentive to persuade themselves or others that an impudent slave was morally flawed or socially deviant. They were more anxious about immediate disruptions of the plantation routine and reverses in their personal fortunes, monetarily and reputably. These anxieties completed and compounded the driving force behind related legislation.

The Legislative Perspective

Colonial and territorial assemblies voiced concerns about race and speech, and early court records confirm these concerns, yet the first statute banning slave insolence was not enacted until 1806. More notorious and widely copied than this Tennessee statute was Virginia's 1819 version. Moreover, the slaves' acquisition of revolutionary ideology and language skills account only partially for the scope and timing of this legislation. Georgia had no relevant statute until 1861; South Carolina, Alabama, and Arkansas never passed such legislation. Additional clues can be found in the crisply bi-polar rhetoric used to express the legislative perspective and in the substantive antiphony of references to both black subordination and fear of slave revolts. Illuminated by the form and substance in other expressions of the gentry's mind, the legal history of slave insolence can be read more coherently.

Nowhere did the gentry completely ignore any of the four troubled dimensions of their regime but, in those jurisdictions where statutes banning slave insolence were enacted, the business perspective was dominant. In jurisdictions like South Carolina, Alabama, and Arkansas, where the gentry eschewed a legislative ban, the social and moral perspectives were dominant.

Keeping disorder to a minimum was clearly the legislators' motive in proscribing slave insolence. When Thomas Ruffin said in *State v. Mann* that North Carolina's high court had a duty to enforce slaves' subordination to the white race, he merely affirmed more than a century of legislative sentiment. The gentry saw the great mass of slaves as docile but, at the same time, feared that tumultuous meetings of slaves and allied mutterings were preludes to revolt. Despite the relatively weak correlation between their perceptions of servile insurrection and reality, the gentry proscribed threatening behavior by slaves, namely their lifting hands against whites, as early as the seventeenth century. These statutes were developed contemporaneously with proscriptions of seditious speech and riots. The next logical step was legislation against merely insolent speech in Tennessee, Virginia, North Carolina, Georgia, Florida, Mississippi, Louisiana, Texas, and Missouri.

The disorder that was perceived to follow from insolence posed a threat to personal safety but the gentry had little need of statutory authority to defend themselves physically against slaves. Instead, as expressed in their statutory language, they needed authority to preempt sedition and revolt because these were public rather than private threats. This was especially true when it was behavior by their neighbors' slaves—commercial property—that threatened the public peace. For example, as early as 1747, the Maryland assembly empowered constables to lash slaves if they behaved impudently when ordered to disperse. In effect, the gentry perceived that they needed legislative authority to apprehend and punish each other's slaves to preserve the peace.

The bond between peace and prosperity is axiomatic. Under peaceful conditions, markets were perceived to be more predictable, the process of supply and demand more stable, and the plantation system more secure. Thus, across most of the American South, legislation against slave insolence was a servant of the marketplace.

In contrast, the social and moral perspectives were prominent in jurisdictions where statutory bars to slave insolence were delayed or never enacted.

The Georgia gentry, for example, relied on the statutory defense of "sufficient cause or provocation" to legitimate their punishment of slaves until a statutory prohibition against slave insolence was enacted in 1861. In South Carolina, Alabama, and Arkansas, similar statutory defenses to slave beating were available. All that was required was a finding in the appropriate court that slaves had provoked white rage by their insolence. Legitimizing this form of self-help against insolent slaves put business assets at risk but soothed social and moral concerns.

The various and fluid perspectives on slave insolence underscore a singular regard for the power of speech. Ancient and modern theories of rhetoric admired by the gentry emphasized the necessary limits of insolent discourse. From Aristotle to Hugh Blair, the warning was clear: insulting and provocative speech should be used only by knowledgeable and properly motivated rhetors. Slaves might understand survival techniques in a sweltering environment as well as the methods to eradicate insects and blight in staple crops, but the gentry did not believe slaves possessed the higher order of knowledge in which rhetoric flourished. In addition, the slaves' motives for insolence could never be properly aligned with the purposes endorsed by classical sages and modern arbiters of taste. For them, insolent discourse was supposed to provide a mild corrective for social slips or a modest caution against silly behavior. Slaves, on the other hand, needed to correct profound injustices and issue serious warnings about their debased treatment. None of this would have made sense to reputable theorists and so, from the gentry's perspective, slaves forfeited access to the art of rhetoric.

Nonetheless, a thorny problem arose when slaves demonstrated their command of the insolent methods canonized in rhetorical theory. Their prowess was so conspicuous that they were ironically identified as artful and smooth-spoken in newspaper advertisements for their recapture. They composed poetry and music that infuriated the gentry, not because of artistic lapses but because these compositions elegantly condemned the plantation system.

Having denied the possibility of an artful insolence among slaves, the gentry faced a problem when slaves demonstrated rhetorical sophistication. In effect, the gentry was challenged to preserve a traditionally bright line between rhetoric and reality, style and substance. If the institution of slavery was as credible as they insisted, then slave insolence should not be as credible a threat as trespass or assault. Solving this problem required an addendum to the tortuous rhetoric of proslavery ideology. First, the gentry dismissed the insolent slave as an aberration—an argument that appeared reasonable in light of the infrequency with which slaves were impudent. Then, capitalizing on this apparent reasonableness, the gentry outlawed the insolent slave as a deviant. Never raised was the issue of how slaves designed and executed a type of discourse that they were not supposed to be capable of uttering.

In this sense, the gentry would have benefited from an understanding of code-switching as it is presently investigated by sociolinguists. Less obviously than gaining a proficiency in the gentry's language, slaves modified their verbal and nonverbal codes when interacting with planters, overseers, and other whites. These modifications or shifts were essential to accommodate the conflict that slaves would otherwise face in satisfying their dual needs of avoiding physical sanctions while maintaining spiritual integrity. They accomplished these negative and affirmative goals by expressing simultaneously a social deference and a personal resistance.

Today, simple observation reveals that white residents of the American South often imitate the standard dialect and intonation of their hosts while traveling in the North. Style shifting enables these travelers to avoid an unwarranted classification as rural hicks while, at the same time, gaining the satisfaction of outwitting their hosts. In addition to simple observation, social-scientific research reveals that black residents of the American South cultivate a similar but more expanded system of code-switching. They often shift styles when addressing whites, northern or southern, as well as when addressing other African Americans. Because the goals of slaves were not markedly different—both sets of goals have negative and affirmative dimensions—the question arises whether African American skill in code-switching has its roots in the covert insolence perfected by slaves.

Developing this skill would not have been as pressing a need for slaves if slaveowners themselves had not been so deeply impressed by the power of speech. Constitutionally protected for citizens in almost every instance by the end of the eighteenth century, freedom of speech did not become a major issue in American law until the early twentieth century. Attending critically to statutory prohibitions of slave insolence fills a historical gap and enhances our appreciation of related issues. Lacking the rights of citizens, slaves could not speak freely in any instance. Yet they possessed a power that could not be denied by themselves or their oppressors.

In a suitably peculiar inversion of their own constitution, members of the ruling class outlawed unruly slave speech as a prelude to insurrection. In fact, slaves resorted to the same nonverbal tactics to mask their effrontery that were later judicially canonized in *State v. Chaplinsky* as mitigating factors of liability in the "fighting words" doctrine. Critical study of legislation against slave insolence thus illuminates a device by which the gentry invoked yet another double standard and assailed slaves more fundamentally than with chains and whips.

So profound was this device that the gentry sensed their need to justify its invention elegantly and profusely. They claimed to promote business as usual when they enacted and enforced statutes regulating slave speech—legislation that would have been unconstitutional if applied to citizens and more intolerable than any British parliamentary acts of the prior century. They appealed to tenets of the social order, as well as a higher order, when they relied instead on statutory sanctions of self-help against slaves, thereby arrogating to themselves the role of custodians of nobility and piety. Their arguments and appeals wavered in tenor between the merely pragmatic and the outrageously self-serving: they argued, perhaps sincerely, that insolent slaves were business liabilities; more disingenuously they depicted insolent slaves as social deviants and sinners; as abolition gained momentum they crafted propaganda about dependent, childlike slaves who should be seen and not heard. No less an effort at justification was conscionable because despite their statutes, black codes, and plantation rules, their slaves—unlike other pieces of their property—could speak.

Notes

Abbreviations

ADAH	Alabama Department of Archives and History
HL	Hargrett Library, University of Georgia
KL	King Law Library, University of Georgia
LV	Library of Virginia
MDAH	Mississippi Department of Archives and History
SCDAH	South Carolina Department of Archives and History
SCL	South Caroliniana Library, University of South Carolina
SHC	Southern Historical Collection, University of North Carolina
TSLA	Tennessee State Library and Archives
VHS	Virginia Historical Society

Introduction

1. See, for example, James Oakes, "The Political Significance of Slave Resistance," reprinted in Paul Finkelman, ed., *Rebellions, Resistance, and Runaways within the Slave South* (New York: Garland Publishing, 1989), 309.

2. See, for example, Michael Mullin, *Africa in America: Slave Acculturation and Resistance in the American South and the British Caribbean, 1736–1831* (Urbana: University of Illinois Press, 1992), 235.

3. A. Leon Higginbotham Jr. and Greer C. Bosworth, "'Rather Than the Free': Free Blacks in Colonial and Antebellum Virginia," *Harvard Civil Rights-Civil Liberties Law Review* 26 (1991): 22.

4. Aristotle, *"Art" of Rhetoric* 2.2.1378b–1379a. 5–7, trans. John H. Freese, Loeb Classical Library (Cambridge, Mass.: Harvard University Press, 1982). Cf. *Aristotle on Rhetoric: A Theory of Civic Discourse*, trans. George A. Kennedy (New York: Oxford University Press, 1991), 125–26.

5. W. S. Jenkins, *Pro-Slavery Thought in the Old South* (Chapel Hill: University of North Carolina Press, 1935), 64–65.

6. Cf. Carl J. Richard, *The Founders and the Classics: Greece, Rome, and the American Enlightenment* (Cambridge, Mass.: Harvard University Press, 1994).

7. Hugh Blair, *Lectures on Rhetoric and Belles Lettres*, ed. Harold F. Harding (Carbondale: Southern Illinois University Press, 1965), 2:529.

8. George Campbell, *The Philosophy of Rhetoric*, ed. Lloyd L. Bitzer (Carbondale: Southern Illinois University Press, 1963), 21.

9. Campbell, *The Philosophy of Rhetoric*, 21.

10. Blair, *Lectures on Rhetoric and Belles Lettres*, 1:18.

11. Campbell, *The Philosophy of Rhetoric*, 23.

12. See the review of scholarly debates over Jefferson's ambivalent stance on slavery in *American Sphinx: The Character of Thomas Jefferson* by Joseph J. Ellis (New York: Alfred A. Knopf, 1997), 15–21, 145–48.

13. Willard S. Randall, *George Washington* (New York: Henry Holt and Co., 1997), 472.

14. See William E. Wiethoff, *A Peculiar Humanism: The Judicial Advocacy of Slavery in High Courts of the Old South, 1820–1850* (Athens: University of Georgia Press, 1996), 15–16.

15. *Parris v. Jenkins*, 2 Richardson 106, at 107 (S.C. 1845).

16. See a summary of the debate's history in Alden T. Vaughn, "The Origins Debate: Slavery and Racism in Seventeenth-Century Virginia," *Virginia Magazine of History and Biography* 97 (1989): 311–54, as well as in Michal J. Rozbicki, *Transformation of the English Cultural Ethos in Colonial America: Maryland 1634–1720* (Lanham, Md.: University Press of America, 1988), 132–34.

17. Quoted by Anne C. Loveland in *Southern Evangelicals and the Social Order 1800–1860* (Baton Rouge: Louisiana State University Press, 1980), 187.

18. Winthrop Jordan, "Modern Tensions and the Origins of American Slavery," *Journal of Southern History* 28 (1962): 30.

19. Alan Watson, *Slave Law in the Americas* (Athens: University of Georgia Press, 1989), 67.

20. Thomas D. Morris, *Southern Slavery and the Law, 1619–1860* (Chapel Hill: University of North Carolina Press, 1996), 246.

21. Cf. the reference to Michel Foucault's critique of intentionality by Mullin in *Africa in America*, 235.

22. Willie Lee Rose, "The Impact of the American Revolution of the Black Population," in *Legacies of the American Revolution*, ed. Larry R. Gerlach, James A. Dolph, and Michael L. Nicholls (Logan: Utah State University Press, 1978), 186.

23. Gerald W. Mullin has correlated slaves' degree of acculturation and familiarity with colonial affairs, along with their work routines, with their outward rebelliousness (*Flight and Rebellion: Slave Resistance in Eighteenth-Century Virginia* [New York: Oxford University Press, 1972], 36–390). More precisely, Michael Mullin has investigated the relationship "not between the degree of cultural change and amounts of overt rebelliousness, but between the varying types of acculturation and the form or shape that resistance in particular settings assumed" (*Africa in America*, 269). Sylvia R. Frey has specifically analyzed the "heightened awareness" and "intensified rebelliousness" of slaves after their experience of the American revolution (*Water from the Rock: Black Resistance in a Revolutionary Age* [Princeton, N.J.: Princeton University Press, 1991], 223). Elizabeth Fox-Genovese has made a particularly valuable contribution by surveying literature supporting her assertion that no one could "reasonably deny the impact of the Revolution and its message of liberty and equality for all on the imagination of Afro-American slaves" (*Within the Plantation Household: Black and White Women of the Old South* [Chapel Hill: University of North Carolina Press, 1988], 65, n. 50).

24. J. Hall Pleasants, ed., *Archives of Maryland* (Baltimore: Maryland Historical Society, 1930), 47:140.

25. 17 June 1783, reprinted in Lathan A. Windley, comp., *Runaway Slave Advertisements: A Documentary History from the 1730s to 1790* (Westport, Conn.: Greenwood Press, 1983), 2:284.

26. 2 Dec. 1783, reprinted in Windley, *Runaway Slave Advertisements*, 2:299.

27. 7 Feb. 1783; 5 Apr. 1783; 15 Oct. 1785—all reprinted in Windley, *Runaway Slave Advertisements*, 1:346–47, 347, 379–80.

28. 3 July 1781 and 22 Feb. 1782, reprinted in Windley, *Runaway Slave Advertisements*, 3:584, 595.

29. Bernard C. Steiner, ed., *Archives of Maryland* (Baltimore: Maryland Historical Society, 1924), 43:26–27, 125.

30. 25 Feb. 1777, reprinted in Windley, *Runaway Slave Advertisements*, 2:194.

31. Steiner, ed., *Archives of Maryland*, 48:512.

32. In the South, only Maryland permitted slave enlistment. See Benjamin Quarles, *The Negro in the American Revolution* (Chapel Hill: University of North Carolina Press, 1961), 56.

33. *Virginia Gazette and Weekly Advertiser*, 10 Dec. 1785, reprinted in Windley, *Runaway Slave Advertisements*, 1:234.

34. 31 May 1783, reprinted in Windley, *Runaway Slave Advertisements*, 1:349.

35. Steiner, ed., *Archives of Maryland*, 43:32.

36. Mullin, *Flight and Rebellion*, 37–38.

37. John W. Blassingame, *The Slave Community: Plantation Life in the Antebellum South*, rev. ed. (New York: Oxford University Press, 1979), 25.

38. Cf. Peter H. Wood, *Black Majority: Negroes in Colonial South Carolina from 1670 through the Stono Rebellion* (New York: Alfred A. Knopf, 1974), 287.

39. Fitzhugh to John Buckner, 3 Dec. 1681, reprinted in Richard B. Davis, ed., *William Fitzhugh and His Chesapeake World 1676–1701: The Fitzhugh Letters and Other Documents* (Chapel Hill: University of North Carolina Press, 1963), 105.

40. Steiner, ed., *Archives of Maryland*, 49:489–91.

41. *Virginia Gazette* 3 to 10 Oct. 1745, 14 to 21 Nov. 1745, and 14 to 21 Nov. 1745, reprinted in Windley, *Runaway Slave Advertisements*, 1:14–15.

42. *Virginia Gazette and Weekly Advertiser* 14 Jan. 1786, and *Virginia Independent Chronicle* 28 March 1787, reprinted in Windley, *Runaway Slave Advertisements*, 1:234 and 1:389.

43. *Maryland Gazette*, 15 June 1748 and 8 June 1748, reprinted in Windley, *Runaway Slave Advertisements*, 1:6–7.

44. *Maryland Journal and Baltimore Advertiser*, 2 April 1790 and 19 Feb. 1790, reprinted in Windley, *Runaway Slave Advertisements*, 2:405 and 2:403.

45. *Newbern Spectator and Literary Journal*, 10 June 1836, reprinted in Freddie L. Parker, ed., *Stealing a Little Freedom: Advertisements for Slave Runaways in North Carolina, 1791–1840* (New York: Garland Publishing, 1994), 782.

46. See Windley, *Runaway Slave Advertisements*, 4:6–11.

47. *Gazette of the State of Georgia*, 26 Apr. 1787, reprinted in Windley, *Runaway Slave Advertisements*, 4:148–49.

48. See the discussion and notes in Wood, *Black Majority*, 170–76.

49. Frey, *Water from the Rock*, 28.

50. Quoted in Blassingame, *The Slave Community*, 26, 29–30.

51. *Isham v. State*, 6 Howard 35, at 40 (Miss. 1841).

52. *Blanchard v. Dixon*, 4 La. Ann. 57 (1849).

53. Florian Coulmas, ed., *The Handbook of Sociolinguistics* (Cambridge, Mass: Blackwell Publishers, 1997).

54. Recent studies have typically focused on spoken language but Natalie Hess reprinted an intriguing literary variation in "Code Switching and Style Shifting as Markers of Liminality in Literature," *Language and Literature* 5 (1996): 5–18. Allied

analysis can be found in Hans-Jurgen Diller, "Code-Switching in Medieval English Drama," *Comparative Drama* 31 (1997): 506–37.

55. Jan-Petter Blom and John J. Gumperz, "Social Meaning in Linguistic Structures: Code-Switching in Norway," in *Directions in Sociolinguistics: The Ethnography of Speaking*, ed. John J. Gumperz and Dell Hymes (New York: Holt, Rinehart and Winston, 1972), 409–35.

56. For example, see Richard C. Doss and Alan M. Gross, "The Effects of Black English and Code-Switching on Intraracial Perceptions," *Journal of Black Psychology* 20 (1994): 282–93.

57. Cf. the criticism of selected accounts in Harriet Martineau, *Society in America* (London: Saunders and Otley, 1837) for relying on hearsay rather than personal observation, by Frances A. Kemble, *Journal of a Residence on a Georgia Plantation in 1838–1839*, ed. John A. Scott (New York: Alfred A. Knopf, 1961), 54, 65, 116–17.

58. Cf. Mullin, *Flight and Rebellion*, 40.

59. Cf. Marvin L. M. Kay and Lorin L. Cary, *Slavery in North Carolina, 1748–1775* (Chapel Hill: University of North Carolina Press, 1995), 122–23.

60. Marion W. Starling included an extensive bibliography of published slave narratives in *The Slave Narrative: Its Place in American History* (Boston: G.K. Hall and Co., 1981), 339–50. Gregory S. Sojka contributed an extensive review of critical scholarship in "Appendix Two: Black Slave Narratives—A Selected Checklist of Criticism," in *The Art of Slave Narrative: Original Essays in Criticism and Theory*, ed. John Sekora and Darwin T. Turner (Macomb, Ill.: Western Illinois University Press, 1982), 135–47.

61. See the brief but illustrative discussion in Charles H. Nichols' "Introduction" to *Many Thousand Gone: The Ex-Slaves' Account of Their Bondage and Freedom* (Leiden: E. J. Brill, 1963).

62. See the extensive discussion in John W. Blassingame, *Slave Testimony: Two Centuries of Letters, Speeches, Interviews, and Autobiographies* (Baton Rouge: Louisiana State University Press, 1977), xvii–lxv.

63. Cf. Robert S. Starobin, "Privileged Bondsmen and the Process of Accommodation: The Role of Houseservants and Drivers as Seen in Their Own Letters," *Journal of Social History* 5 (1971): 46–70. Also see the same author's *Blacks in Bondage: Letters of American Slaves* (New York: New Viewpoints-Franklin Watts, Inc., 1974).

Chapter 1: "Subordination Not Susceptible of Any Modification or Restriction"

1. John Rolfe to Sir Edwin Sandys, Jan. 1620, reprinted in Willie Lee Rose, ed. *Documentary History of Slavery in North America* (New York: Oxford University Press, 1976), 16.

2. A. Leon Higginbotham Jr. and Anne F. Jacobs, "The 'Law Only as an Enemy': The Legitimization of Racial Powerlessness through the Colonial and Antebellum Criminal Laws of Virginia," *North Carolina Law Review* 70 (1992): 975.

3. Thomas Cooper and David J. McCord, eds., *Statutes at Large of South Carolina* (Columbia: A. S. Johnston, 1836–1875), 7:343–47.

4. Watson, *Slave Law in the Americas*, 68. And see the analysis of the 1696 Code in M. Eugene Sirmans, "The Legal Status of the Slave in South Carolina, 1670–1740," *Journal of Southern History* 28 (1962): 464–67.

5. William H. Browne et al., eds., *Archives of Maryland* (Baltimore: Historical Society of Maryland, 1883), 1:533–34.

6. Browne, *Archives of Maryland*, 2:272.

7. William W. Hening, *Statutes at Large; Being a Collection of All the Laws of Virginia from the First Session of the Legislature in the Year 1619* (Richmond: Samuel Pleasants, 1810), 2:481.

8. James Walvin, *Slaves and Slavery: The British Colonial Experience* (Manchester: Manchester University Press, 1992), 32.

9. Quoted in Milton Cantor, "The Image of the Negro in Colonial Literature," *New England Quarterly* 36 (1963): 94, n. 11; and see the survey of related literature in John W. Blassingame, *The Slave Community: Plantation Life in the Antebellum South*, rev. ed. (New York: Oxford University Press, 1979), 227–28.

10. Ex Parte Boylston, 2 Strobhart 41, at 43 (S.C. 1847).

11. "Slaves. I. Their condition and relation to others," in Levi Pierce, Miles Taylor, and Wm. A. King, *The Consolidation and Revision of the Statutes of the State, of a General Nature* (New Orleans: Bee Office, 1852), 522.

12. Reprinted in Windley, *Runaway Slave Advertisements*, 2:52–53.

13. Reprinted in Parker, *Stealing a Little Freedom*, 212–13.

14. Ibid., 686.

15. Ibid., 592.

16. *Eden v. Legare*, 1 Bay 171 (S.C. 1791).

17. *State v. Mann*, 2 Devereux 263, at 264 and 266 (N.C. 1829).

18. 2 Devereux at 268.

19. *State v. Harden*, 2 Speers 152n, at 155n (S.C. 1832).

20. *State v. Maner*, 2 Hill 453 (S.C. 1834).

21. *Isham v. State*, 6 Howard 35, at 40, 42 (Miss. 1841).

22. *State v. Caesar*, 9 Iredell 391, at 405–06 (N.C. 1849).

23. 9 Iredell at 409 and 411.

24. 9 Iredell at 412, 414–15, 421, 423, 428.

25. Richmond Pearson to Ruffin, 18 Nov. 1852, reprinted in J. G. de Roulhac Hamilton, ed., *Papers of Thomas Ruffin* (Raleigh, N.C.: Edwards and Broughton, 1918), 2:352–53.

26. Receipt from Daniel G. Fowler for purchase of three slaves, 1 Sept. 1856, Richmond M. Pearson Papers 584, SHC; Application for Clemency, 16 Aug. 1865, Richmond M. Pearson Papers 584, SHC.

27. An Appeal to the Calm Judgment of North Carolinians, 20 July 1868, NCC.

28. Frederic Nash to Thomas Ruffin, 27 Dec. 1852 and 30 Jan. 1853, reprinted in Hamilton, *Ruffin Papers*, 2:370–71 and 380–82.

29. Anne, his wife, to Ruffin, 22 Oct. 1828, Thomas Ruffin Papers 641, SHC; Ruffin to Sterling, his son, 14 July 1833, reprinted in Hamilton, *Ruffin Papers* 2:81–82; Ruffin to Leonard Henderson, 31 July 1833, reprinted in Hamilton, *Ruffin Papers* 2:85; Ruffin to Joseph B.G. Roulhac, 13 May 1837 and 3 Oct. 1846, reprinted in Hamilton, *Ruffin Papers* 2:169–70 and 2:246–47; Ruffin to Joseph Pollock, 24 June 1852, reprinted in Hamilton, *Ruffin Papers* 2:328–30; Ruffin to James Renfro, 24 June 1852, reprinted in Hamilton, *Ruffin Papers* 2:330–31; and quoted language from Ruffin to Catherine, his daughter, 21 Jan. 1831, reprinted in Hamilton, *Ruffin Papers*, 2:23–25.

30. Cf. Patrick Brady, "Slavery, Race, and the Criminal Law in Antebellum North Carolina: A Reconsideration of the Thomas Ruffin Court," *North Carolina Central Law Journal* 10 (1979): 257.

31. Cf. Bertram Wyatt-Brown, *Southern Honor: Ethics and Behavior in the Old South* (New York: Oxford University Press, 1982), 406.

32. *Carr v. State*, 14 Ga. 358, at 360 (1853).

33. Cf. Mark V. Tushnet, *The American Law of Slavery 1810–1860: Considerations of Humanity and Interest* (Princeton, N.J.: Princeton University Press, 1981), 38; and the response to Tushnet's argument in Morris, *Southern Slavery and the Law*, 246.

34. James Horn, *Adapting to a New World: English Society in the Seventeenth-Century Chesapeake* (Chapel Hill: University of North Carolina Press, 1994), 349n. 24.

35. Horn, *Adapting to a New World*, 373–74.

36. Stephen S. Webb, *1767: The End of American Independence* (New York: Alfred A. Knopf, 1984), 36. Also generally see Horn, *Adapting to a New World*.

37. Henry R. McIlwaine, ed., *Minutes of the Council and General Court of Colonial Virginia* 2d ed. (Richmond: Virginia State Library, 1979), 12, 14.

38. Brown, *Archives of Maryland*, 1:23, 73.

39. Brown, *Archives of Maryland*, 7:104–5.

40. Herbert Aptheker, *American Negro Slave Revolts* (1943; reprinted New York: International Publishers, 1974), 340.

41. Emily Burke, *Reminiscences of Georgia* (n.p.: James M. Fitch, 1850).

42. Mary B. Chesnut, *A Diary from Dixie*, ed. Ben A. Williams (Boston: Houghton Mifflin, 1949).

43. Letter of 13 Oct. 1831, reprinted in Allie B. W. Webb, ed., *Mistress of Evergreen Plantation: Rachel O'Connor's Legacy of Letters 1823–1845* (Albany: State University of New York Press, 1983), 62–63.

44. John H. Bracey, August Meier, and Elliott Rudwick, eds., *American Slavery: The Question of Resistance* (Belmont, Calif.: Wadsworth Publishing, 1971).

45. See, for example, the rosters in Joseph C. Carroll, *Slave Insurrections in the United States 1800–1865* (New York: Negro Universities Press, 1968); and Thomas W. Higginson, *Black Rebellion: A Selection from Travellers and Outlaws* (New York: Arno Press, 1969).

46. Browne, *Archives of Maryland*, 19:193, 29:160–61; Cooper and McCord, *Statutes at Large*, 7:352.

47. Cooper and McCord, *Statutes at Large*, 7:352.

48. Anne E. Yentsch, *A Chesapeake Family and Their Slaves: A Study in Historical Archaeology* (Cambridge: Cambridge University Press, 1994), 178–79.

49. Blassingame, *The Slave Community*, 36–39.

50. Hening, *Statutes at Large*, 2:481.

51. See the survey of deliberations in the Executive Council of the Virginia colony in Darold D. Wax, "Negro Import Duties in Colonial Virginia," *Virginia Magazine of History and Biography* 79 (1971): 34.

52. Quoted in Winthrop D. Jordan, *White over Black: American Attitudes toward the Negro, 1550–1812* (Chapel Hill: University of North Carolina Press, 1968), 111.

53. Reprinted in Windley, *Runaway Slave Advertisements*, 1:45.

54. Reprinted in Windley, *Runaway Slave Advertisements*, 1:255.

55. Broadside "To the Public," 7 July 1812, Crenshaw and Miller Family Papers, OP-192/4, SHC.

56. Sirmans, 469–70.

57. Cooper and McCord, *Statutes at Large*, 7:352–96.

58. Browne, *Archives of Maryland*, 28:188–90.

59. Allen D. Candler and Lucian L. Knight, eds., *The Colonial Records of the State of Georgia* (Atlanta: Chas. P. Byrd, 1904–1916), 18:130–31.

60. Hening, *Statutes at Large*, 12:182; reenacted verbatim in 1792, *Statutes at Large of Virginia, from 1712 to 1806* (Richmond: Samuel Shepard, 1835), 1:123.

61. William Littell and Jacob Swigert, *A Digest of the Statute Law of Kentucky: Being a Collection of All the Acts of the General Assembly, of a Public and Permanent Nature, from the Commencement of the Government to May Session 1822* (Frankfort: Kendall and Russell, 1822), 1151.

62. Amos M. Thayer, *Laws of a Public and General Nature of the District of Louisiana, of the Territory of Louisiana, of the Territory of Missouri, and of the State of Missouri, up to the Year 1824* (Jefferson City: W. Lusk and Son, 1842), 1:29; *Laws of the State of Missouri* (St. Louis: E. Charles, 1825), 2:742.

63. Harry Toulmin, *Digest of the Laws of the State of Alabama* (Cahawba: Ginn and Curtis, 1823), 628, 631; Edward Scott, *Laws of the State of Tennessee Including Those of North Carolina Now in Force in this State from the Year 1715 to the Year 1820, Inclusive* (Knoxville: Heiskill and Brown, 1821), 2:959.

64. *Acts of the Legislative Council of the Territory of Florida* (Tallahassee: Joseph D. Davenport, 1828), 177–78.

65. See, for example, *Supplement to the Revised Code of the Laws of Virginia Being a Collection of All the Acts of the General Assembly of a Public and Permanent Nature, Passed since the Year 1819* (Richmond: Samuel Pleasants, 1833), 247; *Code of Virginia* (Richmond: William F. Ritchie, 1849), 754; *Code of Virginia*, 2d ed. (Richmond: Ritchie, Dunnavant and Co., 1860), 816.

66. See, for example, John J. Ormond, Arthur P. Bagby, and George Goldthwaite, *The Code of Alabama* (Montgomery: Britton and DeWolf, 1852), 238; Josiah Gould, ed., *A Digest of the Statutes of Arkansas Embracing All Laws of a General and Permanent Character, in Force at the Close of the Session of the General Assembly of 1856* (Little Rock: Johnson and Yerkes, 1858), 1033; *Acts and Resolutions Adopted by the General Assembly of Florida at Its Eleventh Session* (Tallahassee: Dyke and Carlisle, 1862), 39–40 [patrol regulations]; R. H. Clark, T. R. R. Cobb, and D. Irwin, *The Code of the State of Georgia* (Atlanta: John H. Seals, 1861), 920; C. A. Wickliffe, S. Turner, and S. S. Nicholas, *The Revised Statutes of Kentucky* (Frankfort: A. G. Hodges, 1852), 632–33; *Revised Code of the Statute Laws of the State of Mississippi* (Jackson: E. Barksdale, 1857), ch. 33, sec. 10, art. 50; Charles H. Hardin, *Revised Statues of the State of Missouri* (Jefferson City: James Lusk, 1856), 2:1474–75; Return J. Meigs and William F. Cooper, eds., *The Code of Tennessee Enacted by the General Assembly of 1857–58* (Nashville: E. G. Eastman and Co., 1858), 508–9; H. P. N. Gammel, comp., *The Laws of Texas 1822–1897* (Austin: Gammel Book Co., 1898), 3:15.

67. Daniel J. Flanigan, *The Criminal Law of Slavery and Freedom, 1800–1868* (New York: Garland Publishing, 1987), 142.

68. See, for example, Edmund S. Morgan, "Slavery and Freedom: The American Paradox," *Journal of American History* 59 (1972): 26.

69. Richard Hildreth, *Despotism in America: An Inquiry into the Nature, Results, and Legal Basis of the Slave-Holding System in the United States* (Boston: John P. Jewett and Co., 1854), 89.

70. Cf. the survey of rumors about insurrection in Blassingame, *The Slave Community*, 231–32.

71. 2 Strobhart at 46–47.

72. John B. O'Neall, *Biographical Sketches of the Bench and Bar of South Carolina* (Charleston: S. G. Courtenay and Co., 1859), 1:xix; *The Negro Law of South Carolina* (Columbia: John G. Bowman, 1848).

73. *Gordon v. Hines*, Warren County Circuit Court Minutes, 1856–1860, 174–76 (Nov. 3, 1858), quoted in Morris, *Southern Slavery and the Law*, 213.

74. *State v. Broadnax*, 61 N.C. 41–47 (1866).

75. Blassingame, *The Slave Community*, 237.

76. William W. Fisher III, "Ideology and Imagery in the Law of Slavery," *Chicago-Kent Law Review* 68 (1993): 1060.

77. Cf. Marvin L. M. Kay and Lorin L. Cary, *Slavery in North Carolina, 1748–1775* (Chapel Hill: University of North Carolina Press, 1995), 74.

78. Watson, *Slave Law in the Americas*, 65.

79. Hening, *Statutes at Large*, 2:481.

80. Hening, *Statutes at Large*, 3:459.

81. Littell and Swigert, *A Digest*, 2:1153.

82. Hening, *Statutes at Large*, 6:110.

83. B. W. Leigh, *Revised Code of the Laws of Virginia* (Richmond: Thomas Ritchie, 1819), 1:426–27.

84. *Code of Virginia* [1860], 816.

85. J. Steele and J. M'Campbell, *Laws of Arkansas Territory* (Little Rock: J. Steele, 1835), 437–38.

86. Thayer, *Laws of a Public and General Nature*, 1:30.

87. Toulmin, *Digest of the Laws*, 631.

88. Henry Bullard and Thomas Curry, comp., *A New Digest of the Statute Laws of the State of Louisiana, from the Change of Government to the Year 1841, Inclusive* (New Orleans: E. Johns and Co., 1842), 62; Peirce, Taylor, and King, *The Consolidation and Revision*, 545; U. B. Phillips, comp., *The Revised Statutes of Louisiana* (New Orleans: John Claiborne, 1856), 51.

89. *Revised Code of the Laws of Mississippi, in Which Are Comprised All Such Acts of the General Assembly of a Public Nature, as Were in Force at the End of the Year 1823* (Natchez: Francis Baker, 1824), 376; *Revised Code* [1857], ch. 33, sec. 10, art. 50.

90. *Acts of the Legislative Council:* 104.

91. Oliver C. Hartley, *Digest of the Laws of Texas* (Philadelphia: Thomas Cowperthwait and Co., 1850), 778; Gammel, *Laws of Texas*, 3:15.

92. *Revised Code of the Laws of Virginia* [1819], 427; Steele and M'Campbell, *Laws of Arkansas Territory*, 438; Thayer, *Laws of a Public and General Nàture*, 1:30; *Acts of the Legislative Council*, 104.

93. *Revised Code of the Statute Laws*, ch. 33, sec. 10, art. 50.

94. Toulmin, *Digest of the Laws*, 631.

95. Hartley, *Digest of the Laws of Texas*, 778; *Laws of Texas* [1853], 3:15; Williamson S. Oldham and George W. White, *Digest of the General Statute Laws of the State of Texas* (Austin: John Marshall and Co., 1859), 560–61.

96. Bernard C. Steiner, ed., *Archives of Maryland*, 44:650.

97. Browne, *Archives of Maryland*, 5:513.

98. Scott, *Laws of the State of Tennessee*, 2:959.

99. *State v. Charles* (May term 1841), Davidson County Circuit Court Minutes, Civil and Criminal, 1839–1841, vol. L–M, 332 (microfilm roll 527), TSLA.

100. Heiskill, *Statute Laws of the State of Tennessee*, 1:315.; R. L. Caruthers and A. O. P. Nicholson, *Compilation of the Statutes of Tennessee of a General and Permanent Nature from the Commencement of the Government to the Present Time* (Nashville: James Smith, 1836), 678; Meigs and Cooper, *Code of Tennessee*, 508–9.

101. Leigh, *Revised Code of the Laws of Virginia*, 1:426.

102. *Tholaball and Goad v. Cook* (Session of 2 Apr. 1729), Princess Anne County Minute Book 4 (1728–1737), 38, Microfilm 39, LV.

103. *Carter v. Tom* (Session of 9 Aug. 1745), Lancaster County Orders No. 9 (1743–1752), 75, Microfilm 28, LV.

104. *Code of Virginia* [1849], 754; *Code of Virginia* [1860], 816.

105. In *State v. Bill*, 13 Iredell 373, at 376 (N.C. 1852), Frederick Nash interpreted the Revised Statutes of 1836, ch. 11, sec. 41, as authorizing prosecutions in the magistrates' courts.

106. Bartholomew F. Moore and Asa Biggs, *Revised Code of North Carolina enacted by the General Assembly at the Session of 1854* (Boston: Little, Brown and Co., 1855), 570.

107. *State v. Tackett*, 1 Hawks 210, at 212–13, 216 (N.C. 1820).

108. *Revised Statutes of the State of Missouri* [1845], 1016.

109. *Williams v. Greenwade*, 3 Dana 432, at 435 (Ky. 1835).

110. *Revised Code of the Laws of Mississippi*, 376.

111. *Revised Code of the Statute Laws* [1857], ch. 33, sec. 10, art. 50.

112. *Acts of the Legislative Council* [1828], 104; John P. Duval, *Compilation of the Public Acts of the Legislative Council of the Territory of Florida Passed Prior to 1840* (Tallahassee: Samuel S. Sibley, 1839), 220.

113. Clark, Cobb, and Irwin, *The Code of the State of Georgia* [1861], 920.

114. Re Jeannot (1743), 12 *Louisiana Historical Quarterly* 143 (1930).

115. *Lemoine v. Raphael* (1745), 13 *Louisiana Historical Quarterly* 506 (1931).

116. Re Larue (1747), 13 *Louisiana Historical Quarterly* 367 (1931).

117. 1 *Martin's Digest* 640, cited in George M. Stroud, *A Sketch of the Laws Relating to Slavery in the Several States of the United States of America* (Philadelphia: Kimber and Sharpless, 1827), 98.

118. Bullard and Curry, *A New Digest*, 62.

119. Bullard and Curry, *A New Digest*, 62; Phillips, *The Revised Statutes*, 51.

120. Hartley, *Digest of the Laws of Texas*, 778; Gammel, *Laws of Texas*, 3:15.

121. Oldham and White, *Digest of the General Statute Laws*, 543, 560–61.

122. 2 Strobhart at 46, 47.

123. Cooper and McCord, *Statutes at Large*, 7:412; Benjamin James, *Digest of the Laws of South-Carolina, Containing the Public Statute Law of the State down to the Year 1822* (Columbia: Telescope Press, 1822), 388.

124. Watson, *Slave Law*, 71.

125. *Journal of the Commons House of Assembly, 1736–1739*, 221, and *Journal of the Commons House of Assembly, 1741–1742*, 16–17, reprinted in Peter H. Wood, *Black*

Majority: Negroes in Colonial South Carolina from 1767 through the Stono Rebellion (New York: Alfred A. Knopf, 1974), 287.

126. *White v. Chambers*, 2 Bay 70, at 71–75 (S.C. 1796).

127. *State v. Porter*, 3 Brevard 175, at 176–77 (S.C. 1815).

128. *Gray v. Court of Magistrates and Freeholders*, 3 McCord 175 (S.C. 1825).

129. *State v. Tom* (17 July 1846), Spartanburg District Magistrate Freeholders' Trial Papers, SCDAH.

130. 2 Speers at 155n.

131. *State v. Anthony* (16 Sept. 1848), Fairfield District Magistrate Freeholders' Trial Papers, SCDAH; *State v. John* (14 July 1849), Fairfield District Magistrate Freeholders' Trial Papers, SCDAH; *State v. Solomon* (Sole) (5 Feb. 1851), Fairfield District Magistrate Freeholders' Trial Papers, SCDAH. All of these cases are cited in Morris, *Southern Slavery and the Law*, 298.

132. *State v. Aleck, Bris, and Martin* (12 Apr. 1862), Anderson District Magistrate Freeholders' Trial Papers, SCDAH; cited in Morris, *Southern Slavery and the Law*, 274.

133. Hening, *Statutes at Large*, 4:132–33; 12:681.

134. Candler, *The Colonial Records*, 18:106.

135. Candler, *The Colonial Records*, 18:107.

136. Oliver H. Prince, *A Digest of the Laws of the State of Georgia* (Milledgeville: Grantland and Orme, 1822), 236.

137. Oliver H. Prince, *A Digest of the Laws of the State of Georgia* 2nd ed. (Athens: Oliver H. Prince, 1837), 656; William A. Hotchkiss, comp., *A Codification of the Statute Law of Georgia* 2d ed. (Augusta: Charles E. Grenville, 1848), 770.

138. James, *Digest of the Laws*, 381.

139. Ball and Roane, *Revised Statutes*, 246.

140. English, *A Digest* [1848], 332.

141. Alexander B. Meek, comp., *A Supplement to Aikin's Digest of the Laws of the State of Alabama* (Tuscaloosa: H. Olcott, 1841), 347.

142. Caruthers and Nicholson, *Compilation of the Statutes of Tennessee*, 678.

143. Meigs and Cooper, *Code of Tennessee* [1858], 513.

Chapter 2: The Master of Westover

1. See the catalog of "at the time the greatest private collection of books in colonial America" (ix) in Kevin J. Hayes, *The Library of William Byrd of Westover* (Madison, Wis.: Madison House, 1997).

2. Early descriptive projects such as Richard C. Beatty's *William Byrd of Westover* (1932; reprinted Hamden, Conn.: Archon Books, 1970) and Louis B. Wright's *The First Gentlemen of Virginia* (San Marino, Calif.: Huntington Library, 1940) have given way to richly interpretive studies such as Pierre Marambaud's *William Byrd of Westover 1674–1744* (Charlottesville: University Press of Virginia, 1971) and Kenneth A Lockridge's *The Diary, and Life, of William Byrd II of Virginia, 1674–1744* (Chapel Hill: University of North Carolina Press, 1987).

3. Henry R. McIlwaine, ed., *Executive Journals of the Council of Colonial Virginia* (Richmond: Virginia State Library, 1928), 3:221.

4. Lockridge, *The Diary*, 12–13.

5. Louis B. Wright, "William Byrd I and the Slave Trade," *Huntington Library Quarterly* 8 (1945): 379.

6. Byrd to Lord Tipparari, 18 Feb. 1718, *Another Secret Diary of William Byrd of Westover 1739–1741 with Letters and Literary Exercises 1696–1726*, ed. Maude H. Woodfin, trans. Marion Tinling (Richmond: Dietz Press, 1942), 324.

7. William Byrd II, "Will," *VHS*.

8. Cf. the utilitarian perspective found by Marambaud, *William Byrd*, 80.

9. Morgan, "Slavery and Freedom," 22.

10. William Byrd, "Commonplace Book" 14, Microfilm C66, *VHS*.

11. Entries for 21 and 24 Nov. 1710, *The Secret Diary of William Byrd of Westover 1709–1712*, ed. Louis B. Wright and Marion Tinling (Richmond: Dietz Press, 1941), 261–62.

12. William Byrd, "Commonplace Book" 14, Microfilm C66, *VHS*.

13. William Byrd, "Commonplace Book" 15, Microfilm C66, *VHS*.

14. Kenneth A. Lockridge, *On the Sources of Patriarchal Rage: The Commonplace Books of William Byrd and Thomas Jefferson and the Gendering of Power in the Eighteenth Century* (New York: New York University Press, 1992), 3.

15. William Byrd, "History of the Dividing Line," 46, Microfilm A19, *VHS*.

16. McIlwaine, *Executive Journals*, 3:234, 236, 243.

17. Henry R. McIlwaine, ed., *Journals of the House of Burgesses of Virginia 1702/3–1705, 1705–1706, 1710–1712* (Richmond: Virginia State Library, 1912), 281.

18. Entry of 5 Dec. 1711, *The Secret Diary*, 449.

19. McIlwaine, *Executive Journals*, 3:297.

20. Entry of 17 Dec. 1711, *The Secret Diary*, 455.

21. Entry of 7 October 1711, *The Secret Diary*, 425.

22. Byrd to Mr. Andrews, 10 Nov. 1739, Microfilm C62, *VHS*.

23. Byrd to Lord Egmont, 12 July 1736, Microfilm C62, *VHS*.

24. Byrd to Peter Bickford, 6 Dec. 1735, Microfilm C62, *VHS*.

25. Byrd to Lord Egmont, 12 July 1736, Microfilm C62, *VHS*.

26. Entry of 15 Oct. 1709, *The Secret Diary*, 94.

27. Virginia General Assembly, Judgment 1722, *VHS*.

28. Virginia General Assembly, Judgment 1723, *VHS*.

29. Entry of 30 Nov. 1720, *The London Diary (1717–1721) and Other Writings*, ed. Louis B. Wright and Marion Tinling (New York: Oxford University Press, 1958), 480.

30. Letter to Maxwell Clarke, 10 May 1862, Maxwell Troax Clarke Papers, Folder 1, SHC.

31. Lockridge, *On the Sources of Patriarchal Rage*, 95.

32. Lockridge, *The Diary*, 47.

33. Byrd to Lord Orrery, 5 July 1726, quoted in Susan Manning, "Industry and Idleness in Colonial Virginia: A New Approach to William Byrd II," *Journal of American Studies* 28 (1994): 174.

34. Entry of 23 Sept. 1711, *The Secret Diary*, 410.

35. Entry of 3 Feb. 1712, *The Secret Diary*, 480.

36. Entry of 27 Oct. 1711, *The Secret Diary*, 428.

37. Not all of Byrd's servants were slaves but his uniform references to them make it difficult to distinguish between the indentured and the enslaved. In context, Eugene appears to be the son of "negro quarter" Jenny as distinct from "house" Jenny. See *The Secret Diary*, 490 and 556.

38. Entry of 31 Dec. 1711, *The Secret Diary*, 462.

39. Entry of 22 May 1712, *The Secret Diary*, 533.
40. Entry of 12 Jan. 1711, *The Secret Diary*, 286.
41. Entry of 27 Feb. 1711, *The Secret Diary*, 307.
42. See, for example, the entry of 20 Dec. 1710, *The Secret Diary*, 274.
43. Entries of 1 Jan. 1712 and 10 May 1712, *The Secret Diary*, 463 and 528.
44. Entries of 18 June 1720 through 16 July 1720, *The London Diary*, 419–27.
45. Entry of 7 Aug. 1720, *The London Diary*, 436–37.
46. Entry of 12 April 1712, *The Secret Diary*, 514.
47. Entry of 22 Jan. 1711, *The Secret Diary*, 290.
48. Entry of 15 Mar. 1712, *The Secret Diary*, 501.
49. See, for example, self-reports of his ongoing affair with "Sarah" (or "Sally") at Westover during 1741, *Another Secret Diary*, 137, 155, 157, 168; see also his diary entries of assaults on "negro" girls at Williamsburg, *The Secret Diary*, 425, and *The London Diary*, 484.
50. According to Byrd's extant diaries, his nightly talks with his slaves began in April, 1720; see *The London Diary*, 395.
51. Entry of 22 Feb. 1709, *The Secret Diary*, 7.
52. Entry of 13 May 1709, *The Secret Diary*, 34–35.
53. Entry of 27 Feb. 1711, *The Secret Diary*, 419.
54. Byrd to Dunella, ca. 1710–1715, *Another Secret Diary*, 290–96.
55. Entry of 20 Feb. 1720, *The London Dairy*, 375.
56. Entry of 26 April 1720, *The London Diary*, 399.
57. Entry of 17 June 1720, *The London Diary*, 419.
58. Entries of 25 Feb. 1711 and 27 Feb. 1711, *The Secret Diary*, 306–7.
59. After his beating, Tom "marched off." Two days later, Byrd "wrote a letter" to him ordering him back to the plantation. The following day "Tom returned and promised fair, so [Byrd] took him into favor." Entries of 21–24 Jan. 1741, *Another Secret Diary*, 129–30.
60. Cf. Marambaud, *William Byrd*, 86–89.

Chapter 3: "A Perfect Understanding between a Master and a Slave"

1. Mullin, *Flight and Rebellion*, 38.
2. Wood, *Black Majority*, 287.
3. Allan Kulikoff, *Tobacco and Slaves: The Development of Southern Cultures in the Chesapeake, 1680–1800* (Chapel Hill: University of North Carolina Press, 1986), 389.
4. Mary Anderson, a former slave from North Carolina, quoted in Yetman, *Life under the "Peculiar Institution,"* 16.
5. Kay and Cary, *Slavery in North Carolina, 1748–1775*, 74.
6. Cf. generally Morton J. Horwitz, *The Transformation of American Law, 1780–1860* (New York: Oxford University Press, 1992).
7. Reprinted in Windley, *Runaway Slave Advertisements*, 2:212.
8. William Byrd to Dunella, reprinted in Woodfin and Tinling, *Another Secret Diary*, 290–96.
9. Philip Vickers Fithian, *Journal and Letters of Philip Vickers Fithian, 1773–1774: A Plantation Tutor of the Old Dominion*, ed. Hunter D. Parish (Williamsburg: Colonial Williamsburg Foundation, 1957), 129.
10. Reprinted in James O. Breeden, ed., *Advice among Masters: The Ideal in Slave Management in the Old South* (Westport, Conn.: Greenwood Press, 1980), 50.

11. Reprinted in Breeden, *Advice among Masters*, 31.

12. Cf. the argument for measuring analogous differences in perceptions of time "in degrees, not absolutes," in Mark M. Smith, *Mastered by the Clock: Time, Slavery, and Freedom in the American South* (Chapel Hill: University of North Carolina Press, 1997), 6.

13. Reprinted in Breeden, *Advice among Masters*, 43.

14. Kenneth S. Greenberg, "The Nose, the Lie, and the Duel in the Antebellum South," *American Historical Review* 95 (1990): 65.

15. *The Diary of Landon Carter of Sabine Hall, 1752–1778*, ed. Jack P. Greene (Charlottesville: University Press of Virginia, 1965), 1:310.

16. Landon Carter, *Diary*, 2:845.

17. Reprinted in Graham R. Hodges and Alan E. Brown, eds., *"Pretends to be Free:" Runaway Slave Advertisements from Colonial and Revolutionary New York and New Jersey* (New York: Garland Publishing, 1994), 92.

18. Reprinted in Windley, *Runaway Slave Advertisements*, 2:147; reprinted in Parker, *Stealing a Little Freedom*, 785.

19. *An Inquiry into the Law of Negro Slavery in the United States of America* (Philadelphia: J. W. Johnson and Co., 1858), 233.

20. Reprinted in Breeden, *Advice among Masters*, 34.

21. Holland N. McTyeire, C. F. Sturgis, and A. T. Holmes, *Duties of Masters to Servants* (1851; reprinted Freeport, N.Y.: Books for Libraries Press, 1971), 78.

22. Diary entry of 26 Jan. 1861, reprinted in John H. Moore, ed., *A Plantation Mistress on the Eve of the Civil War: The Diary of Keziah Goodwyn Hopkins Brevard, 1860–1861* (Columbia: University of South Carolina Press, 1993), 81.

23. Reprinted in Breeden, *Advice among Masters*, 87.

24. Quoted in Starobin, *Blacks in Bondage*, 33–34.

25. McTyeire, Sturgis, and Holmes, *Duties of Masters*, 140–43.

26. Ibid., 26.

27. Ibid., 132.

28. Quoted in Henry Louis Gates, Jr., ed. *The Classic Slave Narratives* (New York: Mentor, 1987), 266.

29. See the narratives cited in Norrece T. Jones Jr., *Born a Child of Freedom, Yet a Slave: Mechanisms of Control and Strategies of Resistance in Antebellum South Carolina* (Hanover, N.H.: Wesleyan University Press/University Press of New England, 1990), 52–53.

30. Quoted in James Redpath, *The Roving Editor: or, Talks with Slaves in the Southern States* (New York: A. B. Burdick, 1859), 41.

31. George P. Rawick, gen. ed., *The American Slave: A Composite Autobiography*, supplement, series 1 (Westport, Conn.: Greenwood Press, 1977), 9:1649, 2:119, 9:1614.

32. 18 A. 2d 754, at 762 (N. H. 1941).

33. *Chaplinsky v. New Hampshire*, 315 U.S. 568, at 573 (1942).

34. Bertram Wyatt-Brown, "The Mask of Obedience: Male Slave Psychology in the Old South," *American Historical Review* 93 (1988): 1249.

35. Reprinted in Windley, *Runaway Slave Advertisements*, 1:14, 20, 31, 283.

36. Reprinted in Windley, *Runaway Slave Advertisements*, 2:70, 72.

37. Kay and Cary, *Slavery in North Carolina*, 134.

38. Cf. Frey, *Water from the Rock*, 28.

39. Reprinted in Windley, *Runaway Slave Advertisements*, 3:307, 4:149.
40. Ibid., 4:64.
41. Ibid., 3:28, 715.
42. Ibid., 4:22, 159.
43. W. Robert Higgins, "Charleston: Terminus and Entrepot of the Colonial Slave Trade," *The African Diaspora: Interpretive Essays*, ed. Martin L. Kilson and Robert I. Rotberg (Cambridge, Mass.: Harvard University Press, 1976), 114–31.
44. See Parker, *Stealing a Little Freedom*, 80, 84–86, 154–55, 252–53, 268, 286, 299–300, 307–8, 370–71, 393, 396–97, 422, 424–25, 440–41, 444, 447–48, 455, 477–78, 480, 484–85, 488, 498, 515, 576, 593, 621–22, 627, 638, 649–50, 688–89, 696, 714, 720–21, 737–38, 776, 783, 788, 792, 795, 803–4, 810–13, 838–39, 848–49, 861, 865.
45. See Parker, *Stealing a Little Freedom*, 21, 46, 84, 113–14, 118–19, 122–23, 176, 232–33, 343, 384, 465, 528, 577–78, 583, 592, 596, 604–5, 620–21, 641, 755–56, 761, 789, 801, 825, 837, 854, 857.
46. Reprinted in Parker, *Stealing a Little Freedom*, 153–54.
47. Ibid., 346–47.
48. Ibid., 694, 787–88.
49. Reprinted in Windley, *Runaway Slave Advertisements*, 1:88, 103, 121, 401.
50. Ibid., 2:306–7, 377–78, 379, 405–6.
51. Ibid., 1:187, 272, 281.
52. Ibid., 2:273.
53. Ibid., 1:86–87, 1:152, 1:169, 1:184, 1:208, 1:229, 1:234, 1:281, 1:346, 1:347–48, 1:362–63, 1:376–77, 1:383, 1:389, 1:409, 2:159, 2:162–63, 2:298, 2:325–26, 2:338, 2:374, 2:402.
54. Ibid., 1:81, 2:237.
55. Ibid., 1:78, 406–7.
56. Ibid., 2:352, 359.
57. *Maryland Journal and Baltimore Advertiser*, 5 Oct. 1779, reprinted in Windley, *Runaway Slave Advertisements*, 2:232.
58. *Maryland Gazette*, 10 May 1787, reprinted in Windley, *Runaway Slave Advertisements*, 2:167–68.
59. *North Carolina Spectator and Western Advertiser*, 18 June 1830, reprinted in Parker, *Stealing a Little Freedom*, 807.
60. (Halifax and Tarboro) *Free Press*, 19 Sept. 1834, reprinted in Parker, *Stealing a Little Freedom*, 739.
61. *Virginia Gazette*, 9 Feb. 1769, reprinted in Windley, *Runaway Slave Advertisements*, 1:294.
62. *Maryland Journal and Baltimore Advertiser*, 26 Jan. 1779, reprinted in Windley, *Runaway Slave Advertisements*, 2:218.
63. *Virginia Gazette*, 12 Jan. 1775, reprinted in Windley, *Runaway Slave Advertisements*, 1:330.
64. Quoted in Rawick, *The American Slave* (1977), 1:150, 9:1409, 1396.
65. Browne, *Archives of Maryland*, 41:190–91.
66. Ibid., 41:205–6.
67. Quoted in Yetman, *Life under the "Peculiar Institution,"* 40.
68. *Carolina Observer* 24 Jan. 1828, reprinted in Parker, *Stealing a Little Freedom*, 582.

69. *Maryland Journal and Baltimore Advertiser* 12 Sept. 1783, reprinted in Windley, *Runaway Slave Advertisements*, 2:295.

70. *Virginia Gazette* 22 Sept. 1768, reprinted in Windley, *Runaway Slave Advertisements*, 1:289–90.

71. Benjamin Drew, *A North-Side View of Slavery: The Refugee, Or the Narratives of Fugitive Slaves in Canada* (1856; reprinted New York: Negro Universities Press, 1968), 68, 384.

72. Quoted in Breeden, *Advice among Masters*, 39.

73. Ibid., 83.

74. Robert Falls, a former slave from Tennessee, quoted in Yetman, *Life under the "Peculiar Institution,"* 116.

75. Frederick Law Olmsted, *A Journey in the Back Country in the Winter of 1853–4* (1860; reprinted New York: G. P. Putnam's Sons, 1907), 1:86–90.

76. Olmsted, *A Journey in the Back Country*, 2:224–25.

77. Journal of Thomas B. Chaplin, 19 Feb. 1849, quoted in Jones, *Born a Child of Freedom*, 89–90.

78. Quoted in William L. Katz, ed., *Five Slave Narratives* (New York: Arno Press, 1969), 20.

79. Sylvia R. Frey, "Shaking the Dry Bones: The Dialectic of Conversion," *Black and White Cultural Interaction in the Antebellum South*, ed. Ted Ownby (Jackson: University Press of Mississippi, 1993), 28.

80. Cf. Milton C. Sernett, *Black Religion and American Evangelism: White Protestants, Plantation Missions, and the Flowering of Negro Christianity, 1787–1865* (Metuchen, N.J.: Scarecrow Press, 1975), 108.

81. Quoted in Jones, *Born a Child of Freedom*, 158.

82. William Grimes, *Life of William Grimes*, quoted in Albert J. Raboteau, *Slave Religion: The "Invisible Institution" in the Antebellum South* (New York: Oxford University Press, 1978), 301–2.

83. Quoted in Katz, *Five Slave Narratives*, 6–8.

84. Quoted in Rawick, *The American Slave* (1977), 9:1499–1500.

85. Benjamin Drew, *A North Side View of Slavery—The Refugee: Or, Narratives of Fugitive Slaves in Canada*, quoted in Harvey Wish, ed., *Slavery in the South: First-Hand Accounts of the Ante-Bellum American Southland from Northern and Southern Whites, Negroes, and Foreign Observers* (New York: Farrar, Straus and Co., 1964), 112–13.

86. Cf. Redpath, *The Roving Editor*, 120.

87. Mattie G. Browne, *Autobiography of a Female Slave* (New York: Redfield, 1857), 102, 319.

88. Browne, *Autobiography*, 217.

89. Ibid., 213.

90. Ibid., 279.

91. Ibid., 256.

92. Rosalie Calvert to H. J. Stier, 20 Feb. 1805, reprinted in Margaret L. Callcott, ed., *Mistress of Riversdale: The Plantation Letters of Rosalie Stier Calvert 1795–1821* (Baltimore: Johns Hopkins University Press, 1991), 113.

93. Quoted in Gates, *The Classic Slave Narratives*, 265–66.

94. Quoted in Starobin, *Blacks in Bondage*, 33.

95. 32 Ala. 560 (1858).

96. *Jeff v. State*, 37 Miss. 321, at 321–22 (1859); see also *Jeff v. State*, 39 Miss. 593 (1860).

97. *Virginia Gazette or American Advertiser* 18 Dec. 1784, reprinted in Windley, *Runaway Slave Advertisements*, 1:130–31.

98. *Maryland Gazette* 25 Aug. 1780, reprinted in Windley, *Runaway Slave Advertisements*, 2:126–27.

99. *South-Carolina Gazette* 7 Nov. 1775, reprinted in Windley, *Runaway Slave Advertisements*, 3:345.

100. *South-Carolina and American General Gazette* 21 Feb. 1781, reprinted in Windley, *Runaway Slave Advertisements*, 3:577.

101. Quoted in Drew, *A North-Side View of Slavery*, 164.

102. Drew, *A North-Side View of Slavery*, 201.

103. Testimony of Albert Foster at a coroner's inquest, 5 July 1857, quoted in William K. Scarborough, *The Overseer: Plantation Management in the Old South* (Baton Rouge: Louisiana State University Press, 1966), 99.

104. William Jacobs to Mrs. Mary C. Weeks, 29 Nov. 1837, quoted in Scarborough, *The Overseer*, 99–100.

105. Charley Williams, a former slave, quoted in B. A. Botkin, *Lay My Burden Down: A Folk History of Slavery* (1945; reprinted Athens: University of Georgia Press, 1989), 11.

106. Quoted in Scarborough, *The Overseer*, 104–5.

107. Garnett Andrews, *Reminiscences of an Old Lawyer* (Atlanta: J. J. Toon, 1870), 45–46.

108. Fox-Genovese, *Within the Plantation Household*, 140.

109. Isaac Mason, *Life of Isaac Mason as a Slave* (1893; reprinted Miami: Mnemosyne Press, 1969), 26.

110. Quoted in Katz, *Five Slave Narratives*, 32–33.

111. Elam Tanner to John Hartwell Cocke, 9 April 1843 and 4 July 1845, reprinted in Randall M. Miller, ed., *"Dear Master:" Letters of a Slave Family* (Ithaca, N.Y.: Cornell University Press, 1978), 143–44.

112. Letter to John Hartwell Cocke, 8 July 1847, reprinted in Miller, *"Dear Master,"* 157.

113. Quoted in Rawick, *The American Slave* (1979), 1:20, 63.

114. Quoted in Katz, *Five Slave Narratives*, 15–16.

115. Quoted in Belinda Hurmence, ed., *My Folks Don't Want Me to Talk about Slavery: Twenty-One Oral Histories of Former North Carolina Slaves* (Winston-Salem, N.C.: John F. Blair, 1984), 88.

116. Quoted in Rawick, *The American Slave* (1977), 9:1561.

117. *White v. Chambers*, 2 Bay 70, 72 (S.C. 1796).

118. *Dave v. State*, 22 Ala. 23, at 24–26 (1853).

119. 17 Ark. 270 (1856).

120. Quoted in Frey, *Water from the Rock*, 229–30.

121. Former slaves quoted in Yetman, *Life under the "Peculiar Institution,"* 173–74, 302, 313, 240.

122. Olmsted, *A Journey in the Back Country*, 1:84–85.

123. Fox-Genovese, *Within the Plantation Household*, 24, 140.

124. Cf. Fox-Genovese, *Within the Plantation Household*, 196–207.

125. Reprinted in Botkin, *Lay My Burden Down*, 165.

126. Entry of 4 Feb. 1849, quoted in Leslie H. Owens, *This Species of Property: Slave Life and Culture in the Old South* (New York: Oxford University Press, 1976), 111.

127. Quoted in Harriet Martineau, *Society in America* (London: Saunders and Otley, 1837), 159.

128. Diary entries for 21 July 1828, 1829, and 15 Sept. 1833, quoted in Fox-Genovese, *Within the Plantation Household*, 23.

129. Diary entry of 15 Sept. 1860, reprinted in Moore, *A Plantation Mistress on the Eve of the Civil War*, 32.

130. Reprinted in Botkin, *Lay My Burden Down*, 165.

131. Tryphena Fox to her mother, 19 July 1858, reprinted in Wilma King, ed., *A Northern Woman in the South: Letters of Tryphena Blanche Holder Fox 1856–1876* (Columbia: University of South Carolina Press, 1993), 75.

132. Fox to her mother, 13 June 1859, reprinted in King, *A Northern Woman*, 89.

133. Fox to her mother, 16 Dec. 1860, reprinted in King, *A Northern Woman*, 107.

134. Fox-Genovese, *Within the Plantation Household*, 136.

135. Quoted in Gates, *The Classic Slave Narratives*, 204–5.

136. James Mars, *Life of James Mars, a Slave Born and Sold in Connecticut* (1869; reprinted Miami, Fla.: Mnemosyne Publishing Co., 1969), 24–25.

137. Solomon Northup, *Twelve Years a Slave*, reprinted in Gilbert Osofsky, ed., *Puttin' On Ole Massa: The Slave Narratives of Henry Bibb, William Wells Brown, and Solomon Northup* (New York: Harper and Row, 1969), 242.

138. Browne, *Archives of Maryland*, 45:104–5.

139. *Jacob v. State*, 3 Humphrey 493, at 494–95, 522 (Tenn. 1842).

140. *Nelson v. State*, 10 Humphrey 518, at 527, 519–20 (Tenn. 1850).

141. 10 Humphrey at 527, 530.

142. *Nelson v. Bondurant*, 26 Ala. 341, at 345 (1855).

143. *Brady v. Price*, 19 Texas 285–88 (1857).

144. *Williams v. Fambro*, 30 Ga. 232, at 233 (1860).

145. Scarborough, *The Overseer*, 38–44, 104, 40.

146. John S. Bassett, *The Southern Plantation Overseer as Revealed in His Letters* (1925; reprinted New York: Negro Universities Press, 1968) 274–75.

Chapter 4: The Polk Overseers

1. J. P. Erwin to Polk, 5 Aug. 1828, James K. Polk Papers, Ac. No. 71–59, V-K-1, Box 1, TSLA.

2. Cf. the related terms in Plowden C. J. Weston's contract with overseers on his South Carolina rice plantations during the 1850s, reprinted in Bassett, *The Southern Plantation Overseer*, 32.

3. Ephraim Beanland to Polk, 22 Dec. 1833, James K. Polk Papers, Microfilm 31, series 2, reel 4, *TSLA*.

4. A. O. Harris to Polk, 30 Dec. 1833, quoted in Bassett, *The Southern Plantation Overseer*, 56.

5. Beanland to Polk, 1 Feb. 1834, James K. Polk Papers, Microfilm 31, series 2, reel 5, *TSLA*.

6. Ibid., 13 Feb. 1834.

7. Ibid., 7 March 1834.

8. Ibid., 1 April 1834.

9. Ibid., 10 Oct. 1834, reel 6.
10. Ibid., 10 Sept. 1839, reel 15.
11. Ibid., 3 Nov. 1839, reel 16.
12. Ibid., 1 Nov. 1840, reel 18.
13. Ibid., 1 Feb. 1841.
14. Ibid., 1 April 1841, reel 19.
15. Ibid., 1 Sept. 1841.
16. Ibid., 13 Jan. 1851, series 9, reel 63.
17. Ibid., 10 Feb. 1851.
18. Ibid., 16 Apr. 1851.
19. Ibid., 10 June 1853, reel 64.
20. Ibid., 9 July 1853.
21. Ibid., 7 Jan. 1856.
22. Ibid., 13 Sept. 1856.
23. John Nevitt Plantation Journal, 543, Folders 3–10 (typescript of original), *SHC*.
24. Ibid., folder 3.
25. Beanland to Polk, 22 Dec. 1833, James K. Polk Papers, Microfilm 31, series 2, reel 4, *TSLA*.
26. A. O. Harris to Polk, 30 Dec. 1833, quoted in Bassett, *The Southern Plantation Overseer*, 56.
27. Harris to Polk, 3 Jan. 1834, quoted in Bassett, *The Southern Plantation Overseer*, 57.
28. Silas Caldwell to Polk, 4 Jan. 1834, James K. Polk Papers, Microfilm 31, series 2, reel 4, *TSLA*.
29. Beanland to Polk, 1 Feb. 1834, James K. Polk Papers, Microfilm 31, series 2, reel 5, *TSLA*.
30. Beanland to Polk, 6 Feb. 1834, James K. Polk Papers, Microfilm 31, series 2, reel 5, *TSLA*.
31. Albert F. McNeal to Polk, 15 June 1838, quoted in Bassett, *The Southern Plantation Overseer*, 111.
32. John I. Garner to Polk, 3 Nov. 1839, James K. Polk Papers, Microfilm 31, series 2, reel 16, *TSLA*.
33. Garner to Polk, 1 Nov. 1840, James K. Polk Papers, Microfilm 31, series 2, reel 18, *TSLA*.
34. Caldwell to Polk, 20 Oct. 1840, James K. Polk Papers, Microfilm 31, series 2, reel 18, *TSLA*.
35. William Bobbitt to Polk, 5 Apr. 1841, James K. Polk Papers, Microfilm 31, series 2, reel 19, *TSLA*.
36. John T. Leigh to Polk, 28 Sept. 1842, James K. Polk Papers, Microfilm 31, series 2, reel 20, *TSLA*.
37. Caldwell to Polk, 23 July 1841, quoted in Bassett, *The Southern Plantation Overseer*, 152.
38. Eliza Caldwell to Polk, 23 Aug. 1841, James K. Polk Papers, Microfilm 31, series 2, reel 19, *TSLA*.
39. Mary S. Jetton to Polk, 25 Sept. 1845, James K. Polk Papers, Ac. No. I-J-3, Box 1, Folder 10, *TSLA*.
40. Eliza Caldwell to Polk, 20 Nov. 1848, James K. Polk Papers, Ac. No. I-J-3, Box 1, Folder 4, *TSLA*.

41. Harlan Crenshaw to James A. Hamilton, 19 June 1841, Bullock-Hamilton Family Papers, 101, Folder 20, *SHC*.

42. Thomas Bell to Charles Hamilton, 19 June 1841, Bullock-Hamilton Family Papers, 191, Folder 20, *SHC*.

43. James A. Hamilton to Charles Hamilton, 15 Feb. 1842, Bullock-Hamilton Family Papers, 101, Folder 21, *SHC*.

44. Bell to James A. Hamilton, 20 July 1842, Bullock-Hamilton Family Papers, 101, Folder 21, *SHC*.

45. Bell to Hamilton, 24 June 1843, Bullock-Hamilton Family Papers, 101, Folder 22, *SHC*.

46. Robert Hamilton to Charles Hamilton, 10 Dec. 1842, Bullock-Hamilton Family Papers, 101, Folder 21, *SHC*.

Chapter 5: "An Offence Which Consists of Inconsistency"

1. Winthrop D. Jordan, *The White Man's Burden: Historical Origins of Racism in the United States* (New York: Oxford University Press, 1974), 13.

2. Tryphena Fox to her mother, 4 Jan. 1857, reprinted in King, *A Northern Woman*, 46–47.

3. In addition to the relevant works cited previously, I am indebted to Bertram Wyatt-Brown, *Honor and Violence in the Old South* (New York: Oxford University Press, 1986) 353–60; Barbara Welter, "The Cult of True Womanhood, 1820–1860," *American Quarterly* 28 (1966): 151–74, and the same author's *Dimity Convictions: The American Woman in the Nineteenth Century* (Athens: Ohio University Press, 1976); and Sally G. McMillen, *Southern Women: Black and White in the Old South* (Arlington Heights, Ill.: Harlan Davidson, 1992).

4. Frederick Law Olmsted, *The Slave States (Before the Civil War)*, ed. Harvey Wish (New York: Capricorn Books-G. P. Putnam's Sons, 1959), 43, 209.

5. Quoted in Blassingame, *Slave Testimony*, 729.

6. Quoted in Rawick, *The American Slave* (1977), 3:80.

7. H. C. Bruce, *The New Man: Twenty-Nine Years a Slave. Twenty-Nine Years a Free Man* (1895; reprinted New York: Negro Universities Press, 1969), 29–30, 66.

8. 2 Strobhart at 46.

9. 2 Strobhart at 44–46.

10. 13 Iredell 373, at 376.

11. Letter of 15 Feb. 1854, Francis Nash Papers 539, *SHC*.

12. 13 Iredell at 377.

13. *Virginia Gazette*, 14 Sept. 1769, reprinted in Windley, *Runaway Slave Advertisements*, 1:73.

14. *The Life of Gustavus Vassa*, reprinted in Gates, *The Classic Slave Narratives*, 20.

15. *Virginia Gazette*, 11 Nov. 1773 and 4 Nov. 1775, reprinted in Windley, *Runaway Slave Advertisements*, 1:323, 172.

16. *Virginia Gazette*, 15 Nov. 1775, reprinted in Windley, *Runaway Slave Advertisements*, 1:173.

17. *Virginia Gazette*, 19 June 1778, and *Virginia Gazette or American Advertiser*, 4 Dec. 1784, reprinted in Windley, *Runaway Slave Advertisements*, 1:272, 368.

18. *Virginia Gazette*, 10 July 1778, reprinted in Windley, *Runaway Slave Advertisements*, 1:193–94.

19. *Maryland Gazette,* 29 Nov. 1764, 16 May 1765, 9 Nov. 1769, and 17 June 1773, reprinted in Windley, *Runaway Slave Advertisements,* 2:56–59, 79–80, 99.

20. *Maryland Gazette,* 18 Dec. 1777, reprinted in Windley, *Runaway Slave Advertisements,* 2:121–22.

21. *Maryland Journal and Baltimore Advertiser,* 18 Feb. 1777 and 11 July 1783, reprinted in Windley, *Runaway Slave Advertisements,* 2:194, 287.

22. *Maryland Journal and Baltimore Advertiser,* 29 Oct. 1782, reprinted in Windley, *Runaway Slave Advertisements,* 2:274–75.

23. *Maryland Journal and Baltimore Advertiser,* 25 Mar. 1785, 16 Sept. 1785, and 7 Dec. 1790, reprinted in Windley, *Runaway Slave Advertisements,* 2:326, 336, 422–23.

24. *Maryland Journal and Baltimore Advertiser,* 13 July 1787, reprinted in Windley, *Runaway Slave Advertisements,* 2:366.

25. *Maryland Journal and Baltimore Advertiser,* 7 Aug. 1789, reprinted in Windley, *Runaway Slave Advertisements,* 2:394.

26. *North Carolina Gazette,* 31 Oct. 1795, reprinted in Parker, *Stealing a Little Freedom,* 11–12.

27. *Wilmington Gazette,* 3 June 1802, and *North Carolina Journal,* 14 Jan. 1805, reprinted in Parker, *Stealing a Little Freedom,* 149–50, 78.

28. *Western Carolinian,* 30 Oct. 1821 and 13 Sept. 1838, reprinted in Parker, *Stealing a Little Freedom,* 686–87, 716.

29. *Gazette of the State of Georgia.* 31 Aug. 1786, and *Georgia Gazette,* 22 Oct. 1789, reprinted in Windley, *Runaway Slave Advertisements,* 4:144, 171.

30. Letter to her mother, 28 June 1857, reprinted in King, *A Northern Woman* 56.

31. Olmsted, *A Journey in the Back Country* 61.

32. Tryphena Fox to her mother, 1 Nov. 1857, reprinted in King, *A Northern Woman,* 65.

33. Reprinted in Hurmence, *My Folks Don't Want Me to Talk about Slavery,* 2.

34. *Brunson v. Martin,* 17 Ark. 270 (1856).

35. Re Larue (1747), 13 *Louisiana Historical Quarterly* 367 (1931).

36. Quoted in Rawick, *The American Slave* (1977), 10:2372.

37. Redpath, *The Roving Editor,* 97.

38. W. B. Allen, quoted in Rawick, *The American Slave* (1977), 3:21.

39. Thomas H. Jones, *The Experience of Thomas H. Jones, Who Was a Slave for Forty-Three Years* (1849; reprinted Philadelphia: Rhistoric Publications, 1969), 16–17.

40. *State v. John* (S.C. July 14, 1849), Fairfield District Magistrate Freeholders' Trial Papers, SCDAH.

41. *State v. Jarrott,* 1 Iredell 76, at 77–80 (N.C. 1840).

42. *State v. Porter,* 3 Brevard 175 (S.C. 1815).

43. *Williams v. Greenwade,* 3 Dana 432 (Ken. 1835).

44. Redpath, *The Roving Editor,* 13–14.

45. *State v. Anthony* (S.C. Sept 16, 1848), Fairfield District Magistrate Freeholders' Trial Papers, SCDAH (cited in Morris, *Southern Slavery and the Law,* 298).

46. Frederick Law Olmsted, *The Cotton Kingdom: A Traveller's Observations on Cotton and Slavery in the American Slave States,* 2d ed. (New York: Mason Brothers, 1862), 1:47.

47. Browne, *Autobiography,* 168.

48. Quoted in Gates, *Classic Slave Narratives*, 72, 85.
49. Quoted in Starobin, *Blacks in Bondage*, 116–17.
50. *Journal of Nicholas Cresswell, 1774–1777*, quoted in Blassingame, *The Slave Community*, 115.
51. See Blassingame, *The Slave Community*, 116–21.
52. Reprinted in Starobin, *Blacks in Bondage*, 114.
53. Ibid., 115–16.
54. Quoted in Rawick, *The American Slave* (1977), 10:2008.
55. Quoted in Herbert Aptheker. "More on American Negro Slave Revolts," *Science and Society* 2 (1938): 389.
56. *Virginia Gazette*, 10 July 1778, reprinted in Windley, *Runaway Slave Advertisements*, 1:193–94.
57. Quoted in Rawick, *The American Slave* (1977), 9:1895.
58. Quoted in Yetman, *Life under the "Peculiar Institution,"* 313.
59. Quoted in Botkin, *Lay My Burden Down*, 194–95.
60. J. H. McNeill, Biographical Sketch, Ms. Sec. No. 719, II-H-1, Box 1, Folder 12, TSLA.
61. See generally Kenneth S. Greenberg, *Masters and Statesmen: The Political Culture of American Slavery* (Baltimore, Md.: Johns Hopkins University Press, 1985), 24–40.
62. See, for example, the editors' "Introduction: Reflections on Sex, Race, and Region," *The Devil's Lane: Sex and Race in the Early South*, ed. Catherine Clinton and Michele Gillespie (New York: Oxford University Press, 1997), xiv.
63. Compare, for example, the absence of this type of analysis in Joanne V. Hawks and Sheila L. Skemp, ed., *Sex, Race, and the Role of Women in the South* (Jackson: University Press of Mississippi, 1983) and Winthrop D. Jordan and Sheila L. Skemp, ed., *Race and Family in the Colonial South* (Jackson: University Press of Mississippi, 1987), with the attention paid to insolence ("A particularly important kind of insult is one directed at female members of a man's family.") in Richard E. Nisbett and Dov Cohen, *Culture of Honor: The Psychology of Violence in the South* (Boulder, Colo.: Westview Press, 1996), 5.
64. "Sketches-Biographical Questionnaires: Tennesseans," Ref., Ac. No. 210, Microfilm 485, *TSLA*.
65. 5 Humphrey 155, at 156, 160 (Tenn. 1844).
66. *State v. Tom* (S.C. 17 July 1846), Spartanburg District Magistrate Freeholders' Trial Papers, SCDAH.
67. *State v. Bill*, 13 Iredell 373, at 377 (N.C. 1852).
68. 1 Hawks 210, at 211–13 (N.C. 1820).
69. *Johnson v. Wideman*, 1 Rice 325, at 333–34 (S.C. 1839).
70. Reprinted in Blassingame, *Slave Testimony*, 434.
71. Quoted in Gates, *Classic Slave Narratives*, 388–89, 408.
72. Ibid., 302.
73. Quoted in Wish, *Slavery in the South*, 120.
74. *Life of Isaac Mason as a Slave* 1893; reprinted Miami, Fla.: Mnemosyne Publishing, 1969), 23.
75. *The Roving Editor*, 106.

76. Olmsted, *The Cotton Kingdom*, 47.

77. *Black Republican and Office-Holder's Journal*, Aug. 1865, 2, quoted in Smith, *Mastered by the Clock*, 155.

78. *Autobiography of James L. Smith* (1881; reprinted New York: Negro Universities Press, 1969) 26.

79. Quoted in Drew, *A North-Side View of Slavery*, 157.

80. Redpath, *The Roving Editor*, 105.

81. *Maryland Gazette* 20 June 1771, and *Maryland Journal and Baltimore Advertiser* 10 Aug. 1779, 21 Mar. 1780, 18 July 1783, and 13 July 1787, reprinted in Windley, *Runaway Slave Advertisements*, 2:88, 229, 237, 288, and 365.

82. *Raleigh Star* 28 Aug. 1818, and *Raleigh Register and North Carolina Weekly Advertiser* 28 Sept. 1820, 18 Feb. 1839, and 16 Aug. 1836, reprinted in Parker, *Stealing a Little Freedom*, 452, 277, 329, and 323.

83. *Virginia Gazette* 7 Sept. 1776, *Virginia Gazette and Weekly Advertiser* 25 May 1782, and *Maryland Journal and Baltimore Advertiser* 23 July 1782, 14 Jan. 1783, and 28 Mar. 1786, reprinted in Windley, *Runaway Slave Advertisements*, 1:178, 1:214, 2:265, 2:278, 3:344; *Raleigh Star* 15 Nov. 1816, *American Recorder*, 10 July 1818, *Raleigh Register and North Carolina Weekly Advertiser* 27 Apr. 1821, *Milton Gazette and Roanoke Advertiser* 31 July 1830, and *Charlotte Journal*, 10 June 1836, reprinted in Parker, *Stealing a Little Freedom*, 441, 553, 280, 746, 850.

84. *South Carolina Gazette* 24 Aug.–31 Aug. 1767, *Virginia Gazette* 9 Feb. 1769 and 23 Feb. 1769, and *Maryland Journal and Baltimore Advertiser* 26 Jan. 1779, reprinted in Windley, *Runaway Slave Advertisements*, 3:265, 1:294, 1:295, 2:218; *Edenton Gazette and North Carolina General Advertiser* 24 Nov. 1809 and 25 May 1810, *Western Carolinian* 20 Jan. 1834, and *Raleigh Star*, 29 May 1839, reprinted in Parker, *Stealing a Little Freedom*, 347, 350, 712, 506.

85. *Virginia Gazette* 26 Aug. 1775, 6 Sept. 1776, 7 Sept. 1776, and 19 June 1778, *Maryland Journal and Baltimore Advertiser* 24 May 1785, *Gazette of the State of Georgia* 6 July 1786, *Georgia Gazette* 22 Oct. 1789, and *Virginia Gazette and General Advertiser* 1 Dec. 1790, reprinted in Windley, *Runaway Slave Advertisements*, 1:171, 1:253, 1:178, 1:272, 2:329, 4:143, 4:171, 1:421; *Edenton Gazette and North Carolina General Advertiser*, 2 Mar. 1810, *Carolina Federal Republican*, 30 Apr. 1814, and *Fayetteville Gazette* 17 May 1820, reprinted in Parker, *Stealing a Little Freedom*, 349, 517, 672.

86. *Virginia Gazette* 10–17 Dec. 1736 and 7 Mar. 1766, reprinted in Windley, *Runaway Slave Advertisements*, 1:2 and 1:38.

Chapter 6: The Reluctant Mistress

1. Her own writings are the primary and best guides to her life's story. As explained in Frances Anne Kemble, *Journal of a Residence on a Georgian Plantation in 1838–1839*, ed. John A. Scott (New York: Alfred A. Knopf, 1961), the several biographies published in the 1930s are unreliable (409). Later biographies, including Winifred E. Wise, *Fanny Kemble: Actress, Author, Abolitionist* (New York: G. P. Putnam's Sons, 1966) and Dorothy Marshall, *Fanny Kemble* (New York: St. Martin's Press, 1977), are not significantly more helpful. I have relied on biographical sketches in Scott's edition of the *Journal* as well as in Frances A. Kemble and Frances A. Butler Leigh, *Principles and Privilege: Two Women's Lives on a Georgia Plantation*, ed. Dana D. Nelson (Ann Arbor: University of Michigan

Press, 1995). However, I have found J. C. Furnas, *Fanny Kemble: Leading Lady of the Nineteenth-Century Stage* (New York: Dial Press, 1982) to be the most valuable supplement to primary works.

2. For a brief account of this chronicle's influence, see Mildred Lombard, "Contemporary Opinions of Mrs. Kemble's *Journal of a Residence on a Georgia Plantation*," *Georgia Historical Quarterly* 14 (1930): 335–43.

3. Most subsequent citations refer to the 1961 edition by Scott; exceptional citations refer to another reprint (Chicago: Afro-Am Press, 1961).

4. See, for example, her explicit criticisms of Harriet Martineau's *Society in America* (1837) in Kemble's *Journal*, 54, 65, and 116–17.

5. Kemble to Anna Jameson, June 1835, *Records of Later Life* (London: Richard Bentley and Sons, 1882), 1:67.

6. *Journal*, 3–11.

7. *Journal*, 5–6.

8. Blake Allmendinger, "Acting and Slavery: Representations of Work in the Writings of Fanny Kemble," *Mississippi Quarterly* 41 (1988): 507.

9. Frances A. Kemble, *Records of a Girlhood* (New York: Henry Holt and Co., 1883), 291.

10. *Journal*, 260.
11. Ibid., 248.
12. Ibid., 174.
13. Ibid., 38–39.
14. Ibid., 343.
15. Ibid., 174.
16. Ibid., 155.
17. Ibid., 50.
18. Ibid., 66.
19. Ibid., 72–74.
20. Ibid., 85–86.
21. Ibid., 154.
22. Ibid., 159–61.

23. Cf. the analysis of belief "in the imminence of the millennium" among slaves, in Frey, "Shaking the Dry Bones," 28.

24. *Journal*, 118–19.

25. *Journal* (New York: Afro-Am Press, 1961), 226–27.

26. *Journal*, 210–11.

27. Ibid., 17.

28. *Further Records 1848–1883: A Series of Letters* (1891; reprint, New York: Benjamin Blom, 1972), 21.

29. Tryphena Fox to her mother, 16 Dec. 1860, reprinted in King, *A Northern Woman*, 107.

30. *Journal*, 40–41.

31. Ibid., 46.

32. Charles Ward to his mother, 15 May 1854, Misc. Letters 516/84, *SHC*.

33. *Journal*, 61–62.

34. Ibid., 62.

35. Ibid., 62.
36. Ibid., 80–81.
37. Ibid., 60.
38. Ibid., 84–85.
39. Ibid., 164.
40. Ibid., 102.
41. *Further Records*, 13.
42. *Journal*, 100.
43. Ibid., 117.
44. Sarah Alexander to Adam Leopold Alexander, 26 Apr. 1831, Alexander-Hillhouse Papers, Subcollection 1, Subseries 1.1, *SHC*.
45. Anna King to Lord King, 7 June 1852, Thomas Butler King Papers, Series 1, Box 10, Folder 240, *SHC*.
46. *Journal*, 93.
47. See an analysis of the persuasive use of this sale in abolitionist literature in Edward J. Piacentino, "Doesticks' Assault on Slavery: Style and Technique in *The Great Auction Sale of Slaves, at Savannah, Georgia*," *Phylon* 48 (1987): 196–203.

Chapter 7: "The Crowning Glory of This Age"

1. E. Brooks Holifield, *The Gentlemen Theologians: American Theology in Southern Culture, 1795–1860* (Durham, N.C.: Duke University Press, 1978), 110–11, 138–44.
2. Cf. Loveland, *Southern Evangelicals* 220. See, for example, the criticism of the lack of "regular, systematic religious instruction" of the slaves in Charles C. Jones, *The Religious Instruction of Negroes in the United States* (1842; reprinted New York: Negro Universities Press, 1969), 100.
3. Jones, *Religious Instruction* (1842), 130.
4. Entry of 31 June 1854, Everard Green Baker Papers, 41, Folder 2, *SHC*.
5. Mullin, *Africa in America*, 91, and see the specific analysis of "How and to what extent did conversion stifle or encourage slave resistance?" (243 ff.).
6. Alexander Glennie, *Sermons Preached on Plantations* (1844; reprinted Freeport, N.Y.: Books for Libraries Press, 1971), 35.
7. Jones, *Born a Child of Freedom*, 195.
8. See generally Cobb's *Inquiry into the Law of Negro Slavery* (1858). For a generation of allied criticism, cf. Eugene D. Genovese, *Roll, Jordan, Roll: The World the Slaves Made* (New York: Vintage Books, 1976), 3–7; James Oakes, *The Ruling Race: A History of American Slaveholders* (New York: Alfred A. Knopf, 1982) passim; and Joan E. Cashin, *A Family Venture: Men and Women on the Southern Frontier* (New York: Oxford University Press, 1991), 26–27.
9. Fox-Genovese, *Within the Plantation Household*, 101.
10. Quoted in Jones, *Born a Child of Freedom*, 197.
11. Thomas Jefferson provides a relevant case study; several slaves at Monticello were fathered by Jefferson's father-in-law. Cf. Ellis, *American Sphinx*, 151.
12. Drew G. Faust, "Culture, Conflict, and Community: The Meaning of Power on an Antebellum Plantation," *Journal of Social History* 14 (1980): 88.
13. Charles Joyner, "History as Ritual: Rites of Power and Resistance on the Slave Plantation," *Australian Journal of American Studies* 5 (1986): 224.

14. John Taylor, *Arator, Being a Series of Agricultural Essays, Practical and Political: In Sixty-Four Numbers*, Ed. M. E. Bradford (1818; reprint, Indianapolis: Liberty Classics, 1977), 185.

15. Catherine Carson to William S. Waller, 26 Jan. 1836, Carson Family Papers: Correspondence, Ac. No. 878, V-K-2, Box 4, Folder 5, *TSLA*.

16. J. H. McNeill, Biographical Sketch, Ms. Sec. No. 719, I-H-1, Box 1, Folder 12, *TSLA*.

17. John C. Inscoe, "Carolina Slave Names: An Index to Acculturation," *Journal of Southern History* 48 (1983): 527–54.

18. Emmaline Eve, quoted in Fox-Genovese, *Within the Plantation Household*, 135.

19. Quoted in Trezevant P. Yeatman Jr., "St. John's: A Plantation Church of the Old South," Duncan B. Cooper Papers, VIII-L-1–2, Ac. No. 72-153, Box 11, Folder 14, *TSLA*.

20. Joyner, "History as Ritual," 226.

21. "Sketches-Biographical Questionnaires: Tennesseans," *TSLA*.

22. *Virginia Gazette*, 19 Mar. 1772, reprinted in Windley, *Runaway Slave Advertisements*, 1:111; *North Carolina Minerva and Raleigh Advertiser* 9 Sept. 1814, reprinted in Parker, *Stealing a Little Freedom*, 118.

23. See, for example, Johnson V. Wideman, 1 Rice 325 (S.C. 1839).

24. Loveland, *Southern Evangelicals*, 189.

25. At the same time, I acknowledge that proslavery tracts such as Henry Hughes' 1854 *Treatise on Sociology* also asserted purely secular dimensions of the master's scope of control: "economic, political, and hygienic." Quoted in Faust, *The Ideology of Slavery*, 244.

26. Taylor, *Arator*, 183–84.

27. Entry of 29 Dec. 1710, Wright and Tinling, *The Secret Diary*, 278.

28. Reprinted in Breeden, *Advice among Masters*, 48–49.

29. *Archives of Maryland*, 1:80.

30. Jordan, *The White Man's Burden*, 51.

31. Quoted in Fox-Genovese, *Within the Plantation Household*, 135.

32. Quoted in Blassingame, *The Slave Community*, 85.

33. Thomas Bacon, *Laws of Maryland at Large* (Annapolis: Jonas Green, 1765).

34. Glennie, *Sermons Preached on Plantations*, 23–24.

35. Jones, *Religious Instruction* (1842), 16, 25.

36. Aptheker, *American Negro Slave Revolts*, 56.

37. Quoted in Jones, *Religious Instruction* (1842), 198–99.

38. See Loveland, *Southern Evangelicals*, 200–201.

39. Catoe Lones, Letter of 3 Mar. 1851, reprinted in Starobin, *Blacks in Bondage*, 54.

40. Reprinted in Breeden, *Advice among Masters*, 58.

41. Charles C. Jones, *Religious Instruction of the Negroes: An Address Delivered before the General Assembly of the Presbyterian Church, at Augusta, Ga., December 10, 1861* (Richmond: Presbyterian Committee of Publication, 1862), 6.

42. Entries of 13 Oct. 1860 and 26 Jan. 1861, reprinted in Moore, *A Plantation Mistress on the Eve of the Civil War*, 38–39, 81–82.

43. *Neal v. Farmer*, 9 Ga. 555, at 582 (1851).

44. John Livingston, ed., *Biographical Sketches of Eminent American Lawyers* (New York, 1852), 557.

45. J. C. Alford, William C. Dawson, Richard W. Habersham, Thos. Butler King, E. A. Nisbet, and Lott Warren, *Address*, 27 May 1840, p. 28, HL.

46. *The Address* (1861), HL.

47. Eugenius A. Nisbet to his wife, 23 July 1841, Nisbet Papers, Ms. 987, HL.

48. *A Lecture, Delivered before the Georgia Historical Society, in the Unitarian Church, Savannah, on Wednesday, 29th March, 1843* (Savannah: W. T. Williams, 1843), 12, 22–23, 29.

49. Mentioned by name in letters to his wife, 29 Nov. 1829, 2 Dec. 1830, 21 Oct. 1821, 23 Nov. 1832, 21 Nov. 1834, and 24 Nov. 1834, Nisbet Papers, Ms. 987, HL.

50. Cf. Browne, *Archives of Maryland*, 1:533–34.

51. Fox-Genovese, *Within the Plantation Household*, 101.

52. Reprinted in Breeden, *Advice among Masters*, 35.

53. *Southern Cultivator*, Aug. 1853, 226, quoted in Smith, *Mastered by the Clock*, 114.

54. Glennie, *Sermons Preached on Plantations*, 74.

55. John Walker Plantation Journals, 2300, SHC.

56. Ibid.

57. Ibid.

58. Letters of 11 Jan. 1836, 23 Mar. 1844, and 4 Sept. 1840, reprinted in Webb, *Mistress of Evergreen Plantation*, 185, 254, 224–25.

59. Diary entry of 12 Dec. 1853 and letter of 6 Aug. 1854, both quoted in C. W. Harper, "Black Aristocrats: Domestic Servants on the Antebellum Plantation," *Phylon* 46 (1985): 129.

60. Cf. Blassingame, *The Slave Community*, 87–89.

61. See Catoe Jones, Letter of 3 Sept. 1852, reprinted in Starobin, *Blacks in Bondage*, 47.

62. Entry of 8 Jan. 1861, reprinted in Moore, *A Plantation Mistress on the Eve of the Civil War*, 69–70.

63. Entries of 22 Feb. 1861, 27 Feb. 1861, 20 Jan. 1861, and 13 Feb. 1861, reprinted in Moore, *A Plantation Mistress on the Eve of the Civil War*, 93, 95, 77, 90.

64. Entries of 8 Jan. 1861 and 20 Feb. 1861, reprinted in Moore, *A Plantation Mistress on the Eve of the Civil War*, 69–70, 91–92.

65. Reprinted in Breeden, *Advice among Masters*, 59.

66. Pierce, Taylor, and King, *The Consolidation and Revision of the Statutes of the State*, 522.

67. *Tennent v. Dendy*, Dudley 83, at 86–87 (S.C. 1837).

68. *State v. Caesar*, 9 Iredell 391, at 401 (N.C. 1849).

69. *Jim v. State*, 15 Ga. 535, at 542–43 (1854).

70. 15 Ga. at 542.

71. Cf. Stephen F. Miller, *The Bench and Bar of Georgia: Memoirs and Sketches* (Philadelphia: J. B. Lippincott and Co., 1858), and Braswell D. Deen Jr. and William S. Henwood, *Georgia's Appellate Judiciary: Profiles and History* (Norcross: Harrison Co., 1987).

72. "The Duties of Christian Masters," in *Duties of Masters to Their Servants*, 143–44.

73. Ibid., 144–45.

74. Nehemiah Adams, *A South-Side View of Slavery: or, Three Months at the South, in 1854* (Boston: T. R. Marvin and B. B. Mussey and Co., 1854), 38.

75. Reprinted in Breeden, *Advice among Masters*, 35, 36, 41.

76. Kate S. Carney, diary entry of 15 July 1860, quoted in C. W. Harper, "House Servants and Field Hands: Fragmentation in the Antebellum Slave Community," *North Carolina Historical Review* 55 (1978): 49–50.

77. Letters of 1 Nov. 1837 and 18 Apr. 1838, David Campbell Papers, quoted in Robert S. Starobin, "Privileged Bondsmen and the Process of Accommodation: The Role of Houseservants and Drivers as Seen in Their Own Letters," *Journal of Social History* 5 (1971): 55, 57–58.

78. Letters of 5 July 1856, 2 Aug. 1856, 9 Aug. 1856, 27 Feb. 1858, 13 March 1858, and 20 March 1858, Pettigrew Family Papers, quoted in Starobin, "Privileged Bondsmen," 63.

79. "An Agricultural Address Delivered before the State Agricultural Society, 29th Dec. 1842," *Proceedings of the Agricultural Convention and of the State Agricultural Society of South Carolina from 1839 to 1845 — Inclusive* (Columbia: Summer and Carroll, 1846), 199–200.

80. *Biographical Sketches of the Bench and Bar of South Carolina*, xxiii–xxiv.

Chapter 8: The Judge and Patriarch

1. Letter of 13 Dec. 1851, Lumpkin Papers, Box 5, KL.

2. John Livingston, "Memoir of Joseph Henry Lumpkin," *United States Law Magazine*, July and August, 1851: 34.

3. Cf. the contemporary assertion that Lumpkin "abandoned politics" because he was a "religious man" in George White, *Historical Collections of Georgia: Containing the Most Interesting Facts, Traditions, Biographical Sketches, Anecdotes, etc. Relating to Its History and Antiquities, from Its First Settlement to the Present Time*, 3d ed. (New York: Pudney and Russell, 1855), 394.

4. Livingston, "Memoir of Joseph Henry Lumpkin," 34–38.

5. See Mason W. Stephenson and D. Grier Stephenson Jr., "'To Protect and Defend': Joseph Henry Lumpkin, the Supreme Court of Georgia, and Slavery," *Emory Law Journal* 25 (1976): 582.

6. Tushnet, *The American Law of Slavery*, 230; Flanigan, *The Criminal Law of Slavery*, 105.

7. Dean E. Ryman, comp., *Joseph Henry Lumpkin: An Unintentional Autobiography* (Atlanta, Ga.: Atlanta Bar Association, 1913), 15.

8. "Notes and Reflections — 1827," Lumpkin Papers, Ms. 192, Folder 1:2, HL.

9. Letter of 22 Feb. 1847 and letter from Justin Edwards, 15 Oct. 1847, Lumpkin Papers, Ms. 192, Folders 2:5 and 1:3, HL.

10. Announcements of 20 May 1848 and July 1853, Lumpkin Papers, Ms. 192, Folders 2:5 and 2:6, HL.

11. Form letter, 20 Oct. 1852, Lumpkin Papers, Ms. 192, Folder 1:10, HL.

12. Address Delivered before Hopewell Presbytery, the Board of Trustees of Oglethorpe University, and a Large Concourse of Ladies and Gentlemen, at the Methodist Church in the City of Milledgeville, after the Conclusion of the Ceremony of Laying the Cornerstone of Oglethorpe University, 31 Mar. 1837, 7, HL.

13. Poetic memorial on his birthday, 28 Dec. 1844, Lumpkin Papers, Box 5, KL.

14. Lumpkin to his daughter, Aug. 1854, Lumpkin Papers, Box 5, KL.

15. Quoted in Timothy S. Huebner, "Joseph Henry Lumpkin and Evangelical

Reform in Georgia: Temperance, Education, and Industrialization, 1830–1860," *Georgia Historical Quarterly* 75 (1991): 262–63.

16. Lumpkin to Callie, undated, Lumpkin Papers, Box 5, *KL*.

17. See, for example, his letter of 9 Sept. 1856, Lumpkin Papers, Box 5, *KL*.

18. Address Delivered before Hopewell Presbytery, 11, *HL*.

19. "Proceedings of the Supreme Court of Georgia in Commemoration of our late Chief Justice, Joseph Henry Lumpkin," 25 June 1867, Lumpkin Papers, Box 6, *KL*.

20. Letter of 24 Apr. 1856, Lumpkin Papers, Box 4, *KL*.

21. "Notes and Reflections—1827," Lumpkin Papers, Ms. 192, Folder 1:2, *HL*.

22. 14 Ga. 259 (1853).

23. 16 Ga. 496 (1854).

24. 18 Ga. 722 (1855).

25. Cf. Robert J. Cottrol, "Liberalism and Paternalism: Ideology, Economic Interest and the Business Law of Slavery," *American Journal of Legal History* 31 (1987): 367.

26. Letter of 20 Sept. 1859, Lumpkin Papers, Box 6, *KL*.

27. Letter of 14 Feb. 1856, Lumpkin Papers, Ms. 192, *HL*.

28. Cf. his letter of 18 Mar. 1856, Ms. 192, *HL*.

29. "Industrial Regeneration of the South" (1852), quoted in George M. Weston, "The Poor Whites of the South," 1 Feb. 1856, 49, a paper sponsored by the Republican Association of Washington, Carr Division of Lumpkin Papers, Ms. 192, Box 2, Folder 7, *HL*. Cf. Huebner, "Joseph Henry Lumpkin," 271.

30. Letter of 29 Oct. 1855, Lumpkin Papers, Box 4, *KL*.

31. Letter of 25 June 1856, Lumpkin Papers, Box 4, *KL*.

32. Livingston, "Memoir of Joseph Henry Lumpkin," 36–37.

33. Letter of 16 May 1852, Lumpkin Papers, Box 5, *KL*.

34. Letter to his daughter, 22 Sept. 1853, Lumpkin Papers, Box 5, *KL*.

35. 14 Ga. 185 (1853).

36. Letter of 29 June 1852, Lumpkin Papers, Box 5, *KL*.

37. Porter King to Callie (Lumpkin) King of 13 Feb. 1853, Lumpkin Papers, Box 5 *KL*.

38. See, for example, his letters of 15 Feb. 1853, 17 Feb. 1853, 20 Feb. 1853, 24 Feb. 1853, and 3 Mar. 1853, Lumpkin Papers, Box 5, *KL*.

39. *Scudder v. Woodbridge*, 1 Ga. 195, at 199 (1846).

40. *Gorman v. Campbell*, 14 Ga. 137, at 143 (1853).

Bibliography

Statutes

Acts and Resolutions Adopted by the General Assembly of Florida at Its Eleventh Session. Tallahassee: Dyke and Carlisle, 1862.
Acts of the Legislative Council of the Territory of Florida. Tallahassee: Joseph D. Davenport, 1828.
Aikin, John G. *Digest of the Laws of the State of Alabama*. Philadelphia: Alexander Towar, 1833.
Bacon, Thomas. *Laws of Maryland at Large*. Annapolis: Jonas Green, 1765.
Ball, McK., and Sam C. Roane, eds. *Revised Statutes of the State of Arkansas*. Boston: Weeks, Jordan and Co., 1838.
Browne, William H., et al., eds. *Archives of Maryland*. 72 vols. Baltimore: Historical Society of Maryland, 1883–1972.
Bullard, Henry A., and Thomas Curry. *A New Digest of the Statute Laws of the State of Louisiana, from the Change of Government to the Year 1841, Inclusive*. New Orleans: E. Johns and Co., 1842.
Candler, Allen D., and Lucian L. Knight, eds. *The Colonial Records of the State of Georgia*. 26 vols. Atlanta: Chas. P. Byrd, 1904–16.
Caruthers, R. L., and A. O. P. Nicholson. *Compilation of the Statutes of Tennessee of a General and Permanent Nature from the Commencement of Government to the Present Time*. Nashville: James Smith, 1836.
Clark, R. H., T. R. R. Cobb, and D. Irwin. *The Code of the State of Georgia*. Atlanta: John H. Seals, 1861.
Clay, C. C. *Digest of the Laws of the State of Alabama*. Tuscaloosa: Marmaduke J. Slade, 1843.
Code of Virginia. Richmond: William F. Ritchie, 1849.
Code of Virginia. 2d ed. Richmond: Ritchie, Dunnavant and Co., 1860.
Cooper, Thomas, and David J. McCord, eds. *Statutes at Large of South Carolina*. 14 vols. Columbia: A. S. Johnston, 1836–75.
English, E. H. *A Digest of the Statutes of Arkansas*. Little Rock: Reardon and Garritt, 1848.
Gammel, H. P. N., comp. *Laws of Texas 1822–1897*. 4 vols. Austin: Gammel Book Co., 1898.
Gould, Josiah, ed. *A Digest of the Statutes of Arkansas Embracing All Laws of a General and Permanent Character, in Force at the Close of the Session of the General Assembly of 1856*. Little Rock: Johnson and Yerkes, 1858.
Hardin, Charles H. *Revised Statutes of the State of Missouri*. 2 vols. Jefferson City: James Lusk, 1856.
Hartley, Oliver C. *Digest of the Laws of Texas*. Philadelphia: Thomas Cowperthwait and Co., 1850.
Haywood, John. *Manual of the Laws of North-Carolina*. Raleigh: J. Gales, 1819.
Haywood, John, and Robert L. Cobbs. *Statute Laws of the State of Tennessee of a Public and General Nature*. 2 vols. Knoxville: F. S. Heiskill, 1831.
Hening, William W. *Statutes at Large; Being a Collection of All the Laws of Virginia from*

the First Session of the Legislature in the Year 1619. 13 vols. Richmond and Philadelphia: Samuel Pleasants et al., 1809–1823.

Hotchkiss, William A. Comp. *A Codification of the Statute Law of Georgia*. 2d ed. Augusta: Charles E. Grenville, 1848.

Index to the Laws and Resolutions of the State of Maryland, from 1800–1813, Inclusive. Annapolis: J. Green, 1815.

Index to the Laws of Maryland, from the Year 1838 to the Year 1845, Inclusive. Annapolis: Riley and Davis, 1846.

James, Benjamin. *Digest of the Laws of South-Carolina, Containing the Public Statute Law of the State down to the Year 1822*. Columbia: Telescope Press, 1822.

Kilty, William. *Index to the Laws of Maryland, from the Year 1818 to 1825, Inclusive*. Annapolis: Jeremiah Hughes, 1827.

Kilty, William, Thomas Harris, and John N. Watkins. *The Laws of Maryland from the End of the Year 1799*. 6 vols. Annapolis: J. Green, n.d.

Laws of the State of Missouri. 2 vols. St. Louis: E. Charles, 1825.

Leigh, B. W. *Revised Code of the Laws of Virginia*. Richmond: Thomas Ritchie, 1819.

Littell, William, and Jacob Swigert. *A Digest of the Statute Law of Kentucky: Being a Collection of All the Acts of the General Assembly, of a Public and Permanent Nature, from the Commencement of the Government to May Sesssion, 1822*. 2 vols. Frankfort: Kendall and Russell, 1822.

McIlwaine, Henry R., ed. *Minutes of the Council and General Court of Colonial Virginia*. 2nd ed. Richmond: Virginia State Library, 1979.

Meek, Alexander B., comp. *A Supplement to Aikin's Digest of the Laws of the State of Alabama*. Tuscaloosa: H. Olcott, 1841.

Meigs, Return J., and William F. Cooper, eds. *Code of Tennessee Enacted by the General Assembly of 1857–8*. Nashville: E. G. Eastman and Co., 1858.

Moore, Bartholomew F., and Asa Biggs. *Revised Code of North Carolina Enacted by the General Assembly at the Session of 1854*. Boston: Little, Brown and Co., 1855.

Morehead, C. S., and Mason Brown. *A Digest of the Statute Laws of Kentucky*. Frankfort: Albert G. Hodges, 1834.

Nash, Frederick, James Iredell, and William H. Battle. *Revised Statutes of the State of North Carolina Passed by the General Assembly at the Session of 1836-7*. 2 vols. Raleigh: Turner and Hughes, 1837.

Oldham, Williamson S., and George W. White. *Digest of the General Statute Laws of the State of Texas*. Austin: John Marshall and Co., 1859.

Ormond, John J., Arthur P. Bagby, and George Goldthwaite. *The Code of Alabama*. Montgomery: Briton and DeWolf, 1852.

Parker, Mattie E. E., ed. *North Carolina Charters and Constitutions, 1578–1698*. Raleigh: Carolina Charter Tercentenary Commission, 1963.

Peirce, Levi, Miles Taylor, and Wm. W. King. *The Consolidation and Revision of the Statutes of the State, of a General Nature*. New Orleans: Bee Office, 1852.

Phillips, U. B., comp. *The Revised Statutes of Louisiana*. New Orleans: John Claiborne, 1856.

Potter, Hen., J. L. Taylor, and Bart Yancey. *Laws of the State of North-Carolina*. Raleigh: J. Gales, 1821.

Prince, Oliver H. *A Digest of the Laws of the State of Georgia*. Milledgeville: Grantland and Orme, 1822; and 2d ed., 1837.

———. *A Digest of the Laws of the State of Georgia*. 2d ed. Athens: Oliver H. Prince, 1837.

Revised Code of the Laws of Mississippi in Which Are Comprised All Such Acts of the General Assembly of a Public Nature, As Were in Force at the End of the Year 1823. Natchez: Francis Baker, 1824.

Revised Code of the Statute Laws of the State of Mississippi. Jackson: E. Barksdale, 1857.

Revised Statutes of the State of Missouri. St. Louis: Argus Office, 1835.

Revised Statutes of the State of Missouri. St. Louis: Chambers and Knapp, 1841.

Revised Statutes of the State of Missouri. St. Louis: J. W. Dougherty, 1845.

Rice, William. *Digested Index of the Statute Law of South-Carolina, from the Earliest Period to the Year 1836, Inclusive*. Charleston: J. S. Burges, 1838.

Scott, Edward. *Laws of the State of Tennessee Including Those of North Carolina Now in Force in This State from the Year 1715 to the Year 1820, Inclusive*. 2 vols. Knoxville: Heiskill and Brown, 1821.

Statutes at Large of Virginia, from 1712 to 1806. 3 vols. Richmond: Samuel Shepard, 1835.

Steele, J., and J. M'Campbell. *Laws of Arkansas Territory*. Little Rock: J. Steele, 1835.

Supplement to the Revised Code of the Laws of Virginia, Being a Collection of All the Acts of the General Assembly of a Public and Permanent Nature, Passed Since the Year 1819. Richmond: Samuel Shepard and Co., 1833.

Thayer, Amos M. *Laws of a Public and General Nature of the District of Louisiana, of the Territory of Louisiana, of the Territory of Missouri, and of the State of Missouri, up to the Year 1824*. 2 vols. Jefferson City: W. Lusk and Son, 1842.

Toulmin, Harry. *Digest of the Laws of the State of Alabama*. Cahawba: Ginn and Curtis, 1823.

Wickliffe, C. A., S. Turner, and S. S. Nicholas. *The Revised Statutes of Kentucky*. Frankfort: A. G. Hodges, 1852.

Cases

Austin v. State, 14 Ark. 555 (1854).
Benjamin v. Davis, 6 La. Ann. 472 (1851).
Bill v. State, 5 Humphreys 155 (Tenn. 1844).
Blanchard v. Dixon, 4 La. Ann. 57 (1849).
Bob v. State, 32 Ala. 560 (1858).
Bosworth v. Brand, 1 Dana 377 (Ky. 1833).
Brady v. Price, 19 Texas 285 (1857).
Brunson v. Martin, 17 Ark. 270 (1856).
Campbell ads. Atchison, S.C. Sup. Ct. (March, 1827).
Carr v. State, 14 Ga. 358 (1853).
Carter v. Tom (Session of 9 Aug. 1745), Lancaster County Orders No. 9 (1743–1752) 75, Microfilm 28, LV.
Chaplinsky v. New Hampshire, 315 U.S. 568 (1942).
Dave v. State, 22 Ala. 23 (1853).
Doss v. Birks, 11 Humphreys 431 (Tenn. 1850).
Eden v. Legare, 1 Bay 171 (S.C. 1791).
Ex Parte Boylston, 2 Strobhart 41 (S.C. 1847).
George v. State, 39 Miss. 570 (1860).

Gordon v. Hines, Warren County Circuit Court Minutes, 1856–1860, 174–76 (3 Nov. 1858).
Gray v. Court of Magistrates and Freeholders, 3 McCord 175 (S.C. 1825).
Grimke v. Houseman, 1 McMullen 131 (S.C. 1841).
Hooks v. Smith, 18 Ala. 338 (1850).
Isham v. State, 6 Howard 35 (Miss. 1841).
Jacob v. State, 3 Humphreys 493 (Tenn. 1842).
Jeff v. State, 37 Miss. 321 (1859).
Jeff v. State, 39 Miss. 593 (1860).
Jesse v. State, 20 Ga. 156 (1856).
Jim v. State, 15 Ga. 535 (1854).
Johnson v. Perry, 2 Humphreys 569 (Tenn. 1841).
Johnson v. Wideman, 1 Rice 325 (S.C. 1839).
Jolly v. State, 13 Smedes and Marshall 223 (Miss. 1849).
Lemoine v. Raphael, 13 *Louisiana Historical Quarterly* 506 (La. 1745).
Martin v. State, 25 Ga. 494 (1858).
Moran v. Davis, Ga. Sup. Ct. (April, 1855).
Neal v. Farmer, 9 Ga. 555 (1851).
Nelson v. Bondurant, 26 Ala. 341 (1855).
Nelson v. State, 11 Humphreys 518 (Tenn. 1850).
Parris v. Jenkins, 2 Richardson 106 (S.C. 1845).
Pyeatt v. Spencer, 4 Ark. 563 (1842).
Re Jeannot, 12 *Louisiana Historical Quarterly* 143 (La. 1743).
Re LaRue, 13 *Louisiana Historical Quarterly* 367 (La. 1747).
Scott v. State, 37 Ala. 117 (1861).
Singleton's Will, 8 Dana 315 (Ky. 1839).
State v. Aleck, Bris, and Martin (S.C. 12 April 1862), Anderson District Magistrate Freeholders' Trial Papers, SCDAH.
State v. Anthony (S.C. 16 Sept. 1848), Fairfield District Magistrate Freeholders' Trial Papers, SCDAH.
State v. Bill, 13 Iredell 373 (N.C. 1852).
State v. Broadnax, Phil. 41 (N.C. 1866).
State v. Caesar, 9 Iredell 391 (N.C. 1849).
State v. Charles (Tenn. May 1841), Davidson County Circuit Court Minutes, Civil and Criminal, 1839–41, vol. L–M, 352, TSLA.
State v. Fuentes, 5 La. Ann. 427 (1850).
State v. Harden, 2 Speers 152n (S.C. 1832).
State v. Jarrott, 1 Iredell 76 (N.C. 1840).
State v. John (S.C. 14 July 1849), Fairfield District Magistrate Freeholders' Trial Papers, SCDAH.
State v. Jowers, 11 Iredell 555 (N.C. 1850).
State v. Maner, 2 Hill 453 (S.C. 1834).
State v. Mann, 2 Devereux 263 (N.C. 1829).
State v. Porter, 3 Brevard 175 (S.C. 1815).
State v. Solomon (Sole) (S.C. 5 Feb. 1851), Fairfield District Magistrate Freeholders' Trial Papers, SCDAH.
State v. Tackett, 1 Hawks 210 (N.C. 1820).

State v. Tom (S.C. 17 July 1845), Spartanburg District Magistrate Freeholders' Trial Papers, *SCDAH*.
State v. Will, 1 Devereux and Battle 121 (N.C. 1834).
Tennent v. Dendy, Dudley 83 (S.C. 1837).
Tholaball and Goad v. Cook (Session of 2 Apr. 1729), Princess Anne County Minute Book 4 (1728–1737) 38, Microfilm 39, *LV*.
White v. Chambers, 2 Bay 70 (S.C. 1796).
Williams v. Fambro, 30 Ga. 232 (1860).
Williams v. Greenwade, 3 Dana 432 (Ky. 1835).
Willis v. Bruce, 8 B. Monroe 548 (Ky. 1848).

Newspaper Advertisements

Hodges, Graham R., and Alan E. Brown, eds. *"Pretends to Be Free": Runaway Slave Advertisements from Colonial and Revolutionary New York and New Jersey*. New York: Garland Publishing, 1994.
Parker, Freddie L., ed. *Stealing a Little Freedom: Advertisements for Slave Runaways in North Carolina, 1791–1840*. New York: Garland Publishing, 1994.
Windley, Lathan A., comp. *Runaway Slave Advertisements: A Documentary History from the 1730s to 1790*. 4 vols. Westport, Conn.: Greenwood Press, 1983.

Narratives

Adams, Nehemiah. *A South-Side View of Slavery: or, Three Months at the South, in 1854*. Boston: T. R. Martin, 1854.
Alexander, Sarah. Letter to Adam Leopold Alexander, 26 Apr. 1831. Alexander-Hillhouse Papers, *SHC*.
Alford, J. C., William C. Dawson, Richard W. Habersham, Thos. Butler King, E. A. Nisbet, and Lott Warren. *Address*, 27 May 1840, *HL*.
Andrews, Garnett. *Reminiscences of an Old Lawyer*. Atlanta, Ga.: J. J. Toon, 1870.
Armstrong, Orland K., ed. *Old Massa's People: The Old Slaves Tell Their Story*. Indianapolis, Ind.: Bobbs-Merrill Co., 1931.
Ball, Charles. *Fifty Years in Chains; or, the Life of an American Slave*. New York: H. Dayton, 1858.
Bassett, John S., ed. *The Southern Plantation Overseer As Revealed in His Letters*. 1925; reprint, New York: Negro Universities Press, 1968.
Bayliss, John F., ed. *Black Slave Narratives*. London: MacMillan Co., 1970.
Bell, Thomas. Letter to Charles E. Hamilton, 19 June 1841. Bullock-Hamilton Family Papers, *SHC*.
———. Letter to James A. Hamilton, 20 July 1842. Bullock-Hamilton Family Papers, *SHC*.
———. Letter to Charles E. Hamilton, 24 June 1843. Bullock-Hamilton Family Papers, *SHC*.
Bierce, Lucius V. *Travels in the Southland 1822–1823: The Journal of Lucius Verus Bierce*. Ed. George W. Knepper. Columbus: Ohio State University Press, 1966.
Blassingame, John W., ed. *Slave Testimony: Two Centuries of Letters, Speeches, Interviews, and Autobiographies*. Baton Rouge: Louisiana State University Press, 1977.
Botkin, B. A., ed. *Lay My Burden Down: A Folk History of Slavery*. 1945; reprint, Athens: University of Georgia Press, 1989.

Breeden, James O., ed. *Advice among Masters: The Ideal in Slave Management in the Old South.* Westport, Conn.: Greenwood Press, 1980.

Brevard, Keziah G. H. *A Plantation Mistress on the Eve of the Civil War: The Diary of Keziah Goodwyn Hopkins Brevard, 1860–1861.* ed. John H. Moore. Columbia: University of South Carolina Press, 1993.

Brown, John. *Slave Life in Georgia: A Narrative of the Life, Sufferings, and Escape of John Brown, a Fugitive Slave.* Ed. F. N. Boney. Savannah: Beehive Press, 1991.

Browne, Mattie G. *Autobiography of a Female Slave.* New York: Redfield, 1857

Bruce, H. C. *The New Man: Twenty-Nine Years a Slave. Twenty-Nine Years a Free Man.* 1895; reprint, New York: Negro Universities Press, 1969.

Bullock-Hamilton Family Papers. 101, SHC.

Burke, Emily. *Reminiscences of Georgia:* James M. Fitch, 1850.

Byrd, William, II. "Commonplace Book," Microfilm C66, VHS.

———. "History of the Dividing Line," Microfilm A19, VHS.

———. Letter to Lord Egmont, 12 July 1736, reprinted in *American Historical Review* 1 (1895): 88–90.

———. Letters. Microfilm C62, VHS.

———. *The Westover Manuscripts: Containing The History of the Dividing Line betwixt Virginia and North Carolina; A Journey to the Land of Eden, A.D. 1733; and a Progress to the Mines.* Petersburg, Va: Edmund and Julian C. Ruffin, 1841.

———. "Will," VHS.

Byrd, William. *Another Secret Diary of William Byrd of Westover, 1739–1741, with Letters and Literary Exercises, 1696–1726,* ed. Maude H. Woodfin. Trans. Marion Tinling. Richmond: Dietz Press, 1942.

———. *The Correspondence of the Three William Byrds of Westover, Virginia 1684–1776.* 2 vols. Ed. Marion Tinling. Charlottesville: Virginia Historical Society, 1977.

———. *The London Diary (1717–1721) and Other Writings.* Ed. Louis B. Wright and Marion Tinling. New York: Oxford University Press, 1958.

———. *The Prose Works of William Byrd of Westover: Narratives of a Colonial Virginia.* Ed. Louis B. Wright. Cambridge: Belknap-Harvard University Press, 1966.

———. *The Secret Diary of William Byrd of Westover 1709–1712.* Ed. Louis B. Wright and Marion Tinling. Richmond, Va.: Dietz Press, 1941.

[Calvert, Rosalie Stier]. *Mistress of Riversdale: The Plantation Letters of Rosalie Stier Calvert 1795–1821.* Ed. Margaret L. Callcott. Baltimore, Md.: Johns Hopkins University Press, 1991.

Carson, Catherine. Letter to William S. Waller, 26 Jan. 1836. Carson Family Papers—Correspondence, Ac. No. 878, V-K-2, TSLA.

[Carter, Landon]. *The Diary of Landon Carter of Sabine Hall, 1752–1778.* 2 vols. Ed. Jack P. Greene. Charlottesville: University Press of Virginia, 1965.

[Carter, Robert]. *Letters of Robert Carter 1720–1727: The Commercial Interests of a Virginia Gentleman.* Ed. Louis B. Wright. San Marino, Calif.: Huntington Library, 1940.

Chesnut, Mary B. *A Diary from Dixie.* Ed. Ben A. Williams. Boston: Houghton Mifflin, 1949.

Clarke, Colin. Letter to Maxwell Clarke, 10 May 1862. Maxwell Troax Clarke Papers, SHC.

Clay-Clopton, Virginia. *A Belle of the Fifties: Memoirs of Mrs. Clay, of Alabama,*

Covering Social and Political Life in Washington and the South, 1853–66. New York: Doubleday, Page and Co., 1905.

Cobb, Thomas R. R. *An Inquiry into the Law of Negro Slavery in the United States of America*. Philadelphia: T. and J. W. Johnson and Co., 1858.

Crenshaw, Charles. Broadside "To the Public," 7 July 1812. Crenshaw and Miller Family Papers, OP-192/4, SHC.

Crenshaw, Harlan. Letter to James A. Hamilton, 19 June 1841. Bullock-Hamilton Family Papers, SHC.

Drago, Edmund L., ed. *Broke by the War: Letters of a Slave Trader*. Columbia: University of South Carolina Press, 1991.

Drew, Benjamin. *A North-Side View of Slavery: The Refugee or the Narratives of Fugitive Slaves in Canada*. 1856; reprinted, New York: Negro Universities Press, 1968.

Ducas, George, and Charles Van Doren., eds. *Great Documents in Black American History*. New York: Praeger Publishers, 1970.

Fairbank, Calvin. *Rev. Calvin Fairbank: During Slavery Times*. 1890; reprint, New York: Negro Universities Press, 1969.

Featherstonhaugh, G. W. *Excursion through the Slave States, from Washington on the Potomac to the Frontiers of Mexico; with Sketches of Popular Manners and Geological Notices*. 1844; reprinted, New York: Negro Universities Press, 1968.

[Fithian, Philip Vickers]. *Journal and Letters of Philip Vickers Fithian, 1773–1774: A Plantation Tutor of the Old Dominion*. Ed. Hunter D. Parish. Williamsburg, Va.: Colonial Williamsburg Foundation, 1957.

[Fitzhugh, William]. *William Fitzhugh and His Chesapeake World, 1676–1701*. Ed. Richard B. Davis. Chapel Hill: University of North Carolina Press, 1963.

[Fontaine, John]. *The Journal of John Fontaine: An Irish Huguenot Son in Spain and Virginia 1710–1719*. Ed. Edward P. Alexander. Williamsburg, Va.: Colonial Williamsburg Foundation, 1972.

[Fox, Tryphena B. H.]. *A Northern Woman in the South: Letters of Tryphena Blanche Holder Fox 1856–1876*. Ed. Wilma King. Columbia: University of South Carolina Press, 1993.

Frazier, Thomas R., ed. *Afro-American History: Primary Sources*. New York: Harcourt, Brace and World, 1970.

Gallay, Alan., ed. *Voices of the Old South: Eyewitness Accounts, 1528–1861*. Athens: University of Georgia Press, 1994.

Gates, Henry Louis, Jr., ed. *The Classic Slave Narratives*. New York: Mentor, 1987.

Glennie, Alexander. *Sermons Preached on Plantations*. 1844; reprint, Freeport, N.Y.: Books for Libraries Press, 1971.

Greeley, Horace. *A History of the Struggle for Slavery Extension or Restriction in the United States from the Declaration of Independence to the Present Day*. New York: Dix, Edwards and Co., 1856.

Halliburton, Warren J., ed. *Historic Speeches of African Americans*. New York: Franklin Watts, 1993.

Hamilton, James A. Letter to Charles E. Hamilton, 15 Feb. 1842. Bullock-Hamilton Family Papers, SHC.

Hamilton, Robert. Letter to Charles E. Hamilton, 10 Dec. 1842. Bullock-Hamilton Family Papers, SHC.

[Harrower, John]. *The Journal of John Harrower: An Indentured Servant in the Colony of Virginia, 1773–1776*. Ed. Edward M. Riley. Williamsburg, Va.: Colonial Williamsburg Foundation, 1963.

Higginson, Thomas W. *Black Rebellion: A Selection from Travellers and Outlaws*. New York: Arno Press, 1969.

Hildreth, Richard. *Despotism in America: An Inquiry into the Nature, Results, and Legal Basis of the Slave-Holding System in the United States*. Boston: John P. Jewett and Co., 1854.

———. *The White Slave; Or, Memoirs of a Fugitive*. 1852; reprint, New York: Arno Press, 1969.

Hurmence, Belinda, ed. *Before Freedom: 48 Oral Histories of Former North and South Carolina Slaves*. New York: Mentor, 1990.

———. *Before Freedom, When I Just Can Remember: Twenty-Seven Oral Histories of Former South Carolina Slaves*. Winston-Salem, N.C.: John F. Blair, 1989.

———. *My Folks Don't Want Me to Talk about Slavery: Twenty-One Oral Histories of Former North Carolina Slaves*. Winston-Salem, N.C.: John F. Blair, 1984.

———. *We Lived in a Little Cabin in the Yard*. Winston-Salem, N.C.: John F. Blair, 1994.

Ingraham, J. H., ed. *The Sunny South; or, The Southerner at Home, Embracing Five Years' Experience of a Northern Governess in the Land of the Sugar and the Cotton*. Philadelphia: G. G. Evans, 1860.

Jackson, Margaret Y., ed. *The Struggle for Freedom: Phase I As Revealed in Slave Narratives of the Pre-Civil War Period (1840–1860)*. Chicago: Adams Press, 1976.

Jefferson, Thomas. *The Life and Selected Writings of Thomas Jefferson*. Ed. Adrienne Koch and William Peden. New York: Modern Library, 1944.

———. *Notes on the State of Virginia*. Ed. William Peden. Chapel Hill: University of North Carolina Press, 1955.

Jones, Charles C. *The Religious Instruction of Negroes in the United States*. 1842; reprint, New York: Negro Universities Press, 1969.

———. *Religious Instruction of the Negroes: An Address Delivered before the General Assembly of the Presbyterian Church, at Augusta, Ga., December 10, 1861*. Richmond, Va.: Presbyterian Committee of Publication, 1862.

Jones, Thomas H. *The Experience of Thomas H. Jones, Who Was a Slave for Forty-Three Years*. Philadelphia: Rhistoric Publications, 1969.

Journal Devoted to Subjects Moral, Speculative, and Commonplace. Everard Green Baker Papers, SHC.

Katz, William L., ed. *Five Slave Narratives*. New York: Arno Press, 1969.

Kearney, Belle. *A Slaveholder's Daughter*. 1900; reprint, New York: Negro Universities Press, 1969.

Kemble, Frances A. *Further Records 1848–1883: A Series of Letters*. 1891; reprint, New York: Benjamin Blom, 1972.

———. *Journal of a Residence on a Georgian Plantation in 1838–1839*. Ed. John A. Scott. 1863; reprint, New York: Alfred A. Knopf, 1961.

———. *Journal of a Residence on a Georgian Plantation in 1838–1839*. 1863; reprint, Chicago: Afro-Am Press, 1969.

———. *Records of a Girlhood*. New York: Henry Holt and Co., 1883.

———. *Records of Later Life*. 3 vols. London: Richard Bentley and Sons, 1882.

Kemble, Frances A., and Frances A. B. Leigh. *Principles and Privilege: Two Women's Lives on a Georgia Plantation.* Ann Arbor: University of Michigan Press, 1995.
King, Anna. Letter to Lord King, 7 June 1852. Thomas Butler King Papers, *SHC.*
[Laurens, Henry]. *The Papers of Henry Laurens.* Ed. Philip M. Hamer. Columbia: University of South Carolina Press, 1968.
[Lee, Richard Henry]. *The Letters of Richard Henry Lee.* Ed. James C. Ballagh. New York: Da Capo Press, 1970.
Lester, Julius, ed. *To Be a Slave.* New York: Dial Press, 1968.
Loguen, Jermain W. *The Rev. J. W. Loguen, as a Slave and as a Freeman: A Narrative of Real Life.* Syracuse, N.Y.: J. G. K. Truair and Co., 1859.
Lumkpkin, Joseph Henry. Address Delivered before Hopewell Presbytery, the Board of Trustees of Oglethorpe University, and a Large Concourse of Ladies and Gentlemen, at the Methodist Church in the City of Milledgeville, after the Conclusion of the Ceremony of Laying the Cornerstone of Oglethorpe University (31 Mar. 1837), *HL.*
———. Papers. Ms. 192, Folders 1–2, *HL.*
———. Papers. Boxes 4–6, *KL.*
Mackie, J. Milton. *From Cape Cod to Dixie and the Tropics.* 1864; reprint, New York: Negro Universities Press, 1969.
Mallard, R. Q. *Plantation Life before Emancipation.* Richmond: Whittet and Shepperson, 1892.
Mars, James. *Life of James Mars, a Slave Born and Sold in Connecticut.* 1869; reprint, Miami, Fla.: Mnemosyne Publishing Co., 1969.
Martineau, Harriet. *Society in America.* London: Saunders and Otley, 1837.
Mason, Isaac. *Life of Isaac Mason as a Slave.* 1893; reprint, Miami, Fla.: Mnemosyne Press, 1969.
McIlwaine, Henry R., ed. *Executive Journals of the Council of Colonial Virginia.* 6 vols. Richmond: Virginia State Library, 1928.
———. *Journals of the House of Burgesses of Virginia 1702/3–1705, 1705–1706, 1710–1712.* Richmond: Virginia State Library, 1912.
McNeill, J. H. Biographical Sketch of Dr. James G. Carson. Sec. No. 719, II-H-1, *TSLA.*
McTyeire, Holland N., C. F. Sturgis, and A. T. Holmes, eds. *Duties of Masters to Servants.* Freeport, N.Y.: Books for Libraries Press, 1971.
Miller, Randall M., ed. *"Dear Master:" Letters of a Slave Family.* Ithaca, N.Y.: Cornell University Press, 1978.
Nash, Frederick. Letter of 15 Feb. 1854. Francis Nash Papers, *SHC.*
Nevitt, John. Plantation Journal. 543, *SHC.*
Nichols, Charles H., ed. *Many Thousand Gone: The Ex-Slaves' Account of Their Bondage and Freedom.* Leiden: E. J. Brill, 1963.
[O'Connor, Rachel]. *Mistress of Evergreen Plantation: Rachel O'Connor's Legacy of Letters 1823–1845.* Ed. Allie B. W. Webb. Albany: State University of New York Press, 1983.
Olmsted, Frederick Law. *The Cotton Kingdom: A Traveller's Observations on Cotton and Slavery in the American Slave States.* 2 vols. New York: Mason Brothers, 1862.
———. *A Journey in the Back Country in the Winter of 1853–4.* 2 vols. 1860; reprint, New York: G. P. Putnam's Sons, 1907.
———. *The Papers of Frederick Law Olmsted: Vol. II, Slavery in the South 1852–1857.* Ed. Charles E. Beveridge and Charles C. McLaughlin. Baltimore, Md.: Johns Hopkins University Press, 1977.

———. *The Slave States (Before the Civil War)*. Ed. Harvey Wish. New York: Capricorn Books-G. P. Putnam's Sons, 1959.

O'Neall, John B. *Biographical Sketches of the Bench and Bar of South Carolina*. Charleston: S. G. Courtenay and Co., 1859.

Osofsky, Gilbert, ed. *Puttin' On Ole Massa: The Slave Narratives of Henry Bibb, William Wells Brown, and Solomon Northup*. New York: Harper and Row, 1969.

Pearson, Richmond M. An Appeal to the Calm Judgment of North Carolinians, 20 July 1868, NCC.

———. Papers. SHC.

Polk, James K. Papers. Ac. No. 71–59, V-K-1, *TSLA*.

———. Papers. Ac. No. I-J-3, *TSLA*.

———. Papers. Microfilm 31, Series 2 and 9, *TSLA*.

Pope, John. *A Tour through the Southern and Western Territories of the United States of North-America*. 1792; reprint, Gainesville: University Press of Florida, 1979.

Randolph, Peter. *From Slave Cabin to the Pulpit*. Boston: James H. Earle, 1893.

Rawick, George P. Gen., ed. *The American Slave: A Composite Autobiography*. Supplement, Series 1. 12 vols. Westport, Conn.: Greenwood Press, 1977.

———. *The American Slave: A Composite Autobiography*. Supplement, Series 2. 10 vols. Westport, Conn.: Greenwood Press, 1979.

Redpath, James. *The Roving Editor: Or, Talks with Slaves in the Southern States*. New York: A. B. Burdick, 1859.

Rose, Willie L. *A Documentary History of Slavery in North America*. New York: Oxford University Press, 1976.

Ruffin, Thomas. Papers. SHC.

[Ruffin, Thomas]. *Papers of Thomas Ruffin*. 4 vols. Ed. J. G. de Roulhac. Raleigh, N.C.: Edwards and Broughton, 1918.

Schwaab, Eugene L., and Jacqueline Bull. *Travels in the Old South: Selected from Periodicals of the Time*. 2 vols. Lexington: University Press of Kentucky, 1973.

[Seabury, Cardine]. *The Diary of Cardine Seabury, 1854–1863*. Ed. Suzanne L. Bunkers. Madison: University of Wisconsin Press, 1991.

Semmes, Ralph, ed. *Baltimore as Seen by Visitors 1783–1860*. Studies in Maryland History. No. 2. Baltimore: Maryland Historical Society, 1953.

Sketches-Biographical Questionnaires: Tennesseans. Ac. No. 210, Microfilm 485, *TSLA*.

Smith, James L. *Autobiography of James L. Smith*. 1881; reprint, New York: Negro Universities Press, 1969.

Starobin, Robert S., ed. *Blacks in Bondage: Letters of American Slaves*. New York: New Viewpoints-Franklin Watts, Inc., 1974.

Stearns, Charles. *The Black Man of the South and the Rebels*. 1872; reprint, New York: Klaus Reprint Co., 1969.

Sterling, Dorothy, ed. *Speak Out in Thunder Tones: Letters and Other Writings by Black Northerners, 1787–1865*. Garden City, N.J.: Doubleday and Co., 1973.

Stirling, James, ed. *Letters from the Slave States*. 1857; reprint, New York: Negro Universities Press, 1969.

Taylor, John. *Arator: Being a Series of Agricultural Essays, Practical and Political: In Sixty-Four Numbers*. Ed. M. E. Bradford. 1818; reprint, Indianapolis: Liberty Classics, 1977.

Thomas, Ella G. C. *The Secret Eye: The Journal of Ella Gertrude Clanton Thomas, 1848–1889*. Ed. Virginia I. Burr. Chapel Hill: University of North Carolina Press, 1990.

Thompson, John. *The Life of John Thompson, a Fugitive Slave; Containing His History of 25 Years in Bondage, and His Providential Escape, Written by Himself.* 1856; reprinted, New York: Negro Universities Press, 1968.

Torrey, Jesse. *American Slave Trade*. 1822; reprint, Westport, Conn.: Negro Universities Press, 1971.

Tyler, Ronnie C., and Lawrence R. Murphy, ed. *The Slave Narratives of Texas*. Austin: Encino Press, 1974.

Virginia General Assembly. Judgments 1722 and 1723, VHS.

Ward, Charles. Letter to his mother, 15 May 1854. Misc. Letters, 516/84, SHC.

Williams, James. *Life and Adventures of James Williams, A Fugitive Slave, with a Full Description of the Underground Railroad.* 3d ed. 1874; reprint, Saratoga, Calif.: R. and E. Research Associates, 1969.

Wish, Harvey, ed. *The Slave States (Before the Civil War)*. New York: Capricorn Books-G. P. Putnam's Sons, 1959.

———. *Slavery in the South: First-Hand Accounts of the Ante-Bellum American Southland from Northern and Southern Whites, Negroes, and Foreign Observers.* New York: Farrar, Straus and Co., 1964.

Yeatman, Trezevant P. Jr. "St. John's: A Plantation Church of the Old South." Duncan B. Cooper Papers, Ac. No. 72–153, VIII-L-1–2, *TSLA*.

Yetman, Norman R., ed. *Life under the "Peculiar Institution:" Selections from the Slave Narrative Collection.* New York: Holt, Rinehart and Winston, 1970.

Related Scholarship

Books

Abzug, Robert H., and Stephen E. Maizlish, eds. *New Perspectives on Race and Slavery in America: Essays in Honor of Kenneth M. Stampp.* Lexington: University Press of Kentucky, 1986.

Aptheker, Herbert. *American Negro Slave Revolts.* 1943; reprint, New York: International Publishers, 1974.

Aristotle. *"Art" of Rhetoric.* Trans. John H. Freese. Loeb Classical Library. Cambridge: Harvard University Press, 1982.

Aristotle on Rhetoric: A Theory of Civic Discourse. Trans. George A. Kennedy. New York: Oxford University Press, 1991.

Armstrong, Margaret. *Fanny Kemble: A Passionate Victorian.* New York: Macmillan Co., 1938.

Bardaglio, Peter W. *Reconstructing the Household: Families, Sex, and the Law in the Nineteenth-Century South.* Chapel Hill: University of North Carolina Press, 1995.

Barnett, Hollander. *Slavery in America: Its Legal History.* London: Bowes and Bowes, 1962.

Beatty, Richard C. *William Byrd of Westover.* 1932; reprint, Hamden, Conn.: Archon Books, 1970.

Berry, Mary F. *Black Resistance/White Law: A History of Constitutional Racism in America.* Rev. ed. New York: A. Lane, 1994.

Billings, Warren M., ed. *The Old Dominion in the Seventeenth Century: A Documentary History of Virginia, 1606–1689.* Chapel Hill: University of North Carolina Press, 1975.

Blair, Hugh. *Lectures on Rhetoric and Belles Lettres.* 2 vols. Ed. Harold F. Harding. Carbondale: Southern Illinois University Press, 1965.

Blassingame, John W. *The Slave Community: Plantation Life in the Antebellum South.* Rev. ed. New York: Oxford University Press, 1979.

Bobbe, Dorothie. *Fanny Kemble.* New York: Minton, Balch and Co., 1931.

Bowman, Shearer D. *Masters and Lords: Mid-Nineteenth Century U.S. Planters and Prussian Junkers.* New York: Oxford University Press, 1993.

Bracey, John H. Jr., August Meier, and Elliott Rudwick, ed. *American Slavery: The Question of Resistance.* Belmont, Calif.: Wadsworth Publishing, 1971.

Campbell, George. *The Philosophy of Rhetoric.* Ed. Lloyd L. Bitzer. Carbondale: Southern Illinois University Press, 1963.

Carroll, Joseph C. *Slave Insurrections in the United States 1800–1865.* 1938; reprint, New York: Negro Universities Press, 1968.

Cashin, Joan E. *A Family Venture: Men and Women on the Southern Frontier.* New York: Oxford University Press, 1991.

Clinton, Catherine, and Michele Gillespie, ed. *The Devil's Lane: Sex and Race in the Early South.* New York: Oxford University Press, 1997.

Cooper, William J. *The South and the Politics of Slavery 1828–1856.* Baton Rouge: Louisiana State University Press, 1978.

Cope, Robert S. *Carry Me Back—Slavery and Servitude in Seventeenth Century Virginia.* Pikeville, Ky.: Pikeville College Press, 1973.

Coulmas, Florian, ed. *The Handbook of Sociolinguistics.* Cambridge, Mass.: Blackwell Publishers, 1997.

Coyle, Betty W. W. *The Treatment of Slaves and Servants in Colonial Virginia.* M.A. thesis. College of William and Mary, 1974.

Craven, Frank W. *The Southern Colonies in the Seventeenth Century.* Baton Rouge: Louisiana State University Press, 1949.

———. *White, Red, and Black: The Seventeenth Century Virginian.* Charlottesville: University of Virginia Press, 1971.

Davis, David B. *Slavery and Human Progress.* New York: Oxford University Press, 1984.

———. *The Problem of Slavery in Western Culture.* Ithaca, N.Y.: Cornell University Press, 1966.

Dillon, Merton L. *Slavery Attacked: Southern Slaves and Their Allies 1619–1865.* Baton Rouge: Louisiana State University Press, 1990.

Driver, Leota S. *Fanny Kemble.* Chapel Hill: University of North Carolina Press, 1933.

Eaton, Clement. *The Mind of the Old South.* Baton Rouge: Louisiana State University Press, 1967.

Elkins, Stanley M. *Slavery: A Problem in American Institutional and Intellectual Life.* Chicago: University of Chicago Press, 1959.

Ellis, Joseph J. *American Sphinx: The Character of Thomas Jefferson.* New York: Alfred A. Knopf, 1997.

Falkowski, James E. *Indiana Law/Race Law—A Five-Hundred-Year History.* New York: Praeger, 1992.

Finkelman, Paul, ed. *Colonial Southern Slavery.* New York: Garland Publishing, 1989.

———. *The Culture and Community of Slavery.* New York: Garland Publishing, 1989.

———. *Race and Criminal Justice.* New York: Garland Publishing, 1992.
———. *Rebellions, Resistance, and Runaways within the Slave South.* New York: Garland Publishing, 1989.
———. *Southern Slavery at the State and Local Level.* New York: Garland Publishing, 1989.
Flanigan, Daniel J. *The Criminal Law of Slavery and Freedom, 1800–1868.* New York: Garland Publishing, 1987.
Fox-Genovese, Elizabeth. *Within the Plantation Household: Black and White Women of the Old South.* Chapel Hill: University of North Carolina Press, 1988.
Franklin, John H. *The Militant South, 1800–1861.* Cambridge: Belknap Press-Harvard University Press, 1956.
Frey, Sylvia R. *Water from the Rock: Black Resistance in a Revolutionary Age.* Princeton, N.J.: Princeton University Press, 1991.
Furnas, J. C. *Fanny Kemble: Leading Lady of the Nineteenth-Century Stage.* New York: Dial Press, 1982.
Genovese, Eugene D. *The Political Economy of Slavery.* New York: Pantheon Books, 1966.
———. *Roll, Jordan, Roll: The World the Slaves Made.* New York: Pantheon Books, 1966.
———. *The Southern Front: History and Politics in the Cultural War.* Columbia: University of Missouri Press, 1995.
———. *The Southern Tradition: The Achievement and Limitations of an American Conservatism.* Cambridge, Mass.: Harvard University Press, 1994.
Greenberg, Kenneth S. *Masters and Statesmen: The Political Culture of American Slavery.* Baltimore, Md.: Johns Hopkins University Press, 1985.
Gumperz, John J., and Dell Hymes, ed. *Directions in Sociolinguistics: The Ethnography of Speaking.* New York: Holt, Rinehart and Winston, 1972.
Hawks, Joanne V., and Sheila L. Skemp, ed. *Sex, Race, and the Role of Women in the South.* Jackson: University Press of Mississippi, 1983.
Hayes, Kevin J. *The Library of William Byrd of Westover.* Madison, Wis.: Madison House, 1997.
Henretta, James A., Michael Kammen, and Stanley N. Katz, ed. *The Transformation of Early American History: Society, Authority, and Ideology.* New York: Alfred A. Knopf, 1991.
Hepperly, Ira W., comp. *Ancestors and Descendants of Robert Lumpkin and His Wife Elizabeth (Forrest) Lumpkin.* Phillipsburg, Kans.: Robert Lumpkin Family Association, 1969.
Hoffer, Peter C., ed. *Africans Become Afro-Americans: Selected Articles on Slavery in the American Colonies.* New York: Garland Publishing, 1988.
Holifield, E. Brooks. *The Gentlemen Theologians: American Theology in Southern Culture, 1795–1860.* Durham, N.C.: Duke University Press, 1978.
Horn, James. *Adapting to a New World: English Society in the Seventeenth-Century Chesapeake.* Chapel Hill: University of North Carolina Press, 1994.
Horwitz, Morton J. *The Transformation of American Law, 1780–1860.* New York: Oxford University Press, 1992.
Jenkins, W. S. *Pro-Slavery Thought in the Old South.* Chapel Hill: University of North Carolina Press, 1935.
Jernegan, Marcus W. *Laboring and Dependent Classes in Colonial America, 1607–1783.* 1931; reprint, New York: Frederick Ungar Publishing, 1960.
Jones, Norrece T. Jr. *Born a Child of Freedom, Yet a Slave: Mechanisms of Control and Strategies of Resistance in Antebellum South Carolina.* Hanover, N.H.: Wesleyan University Press/University Press of New England, 1990.

Jordan, Winthrop D. *The White Man's Burden: Historical Origins of Racism in the United States*. New York: Oxford University Press, 1974.

———. *White over Black: American Attitudes toward the Negro, 1550–1812*. Chapel Hill: University of North Carolina Press, 1968.

Jordan, Winthrop D., and Sheila L. Skemp, ed. *Race and Family in the Colonial South*. Jackson: University Press of Mississippi, 1987.

Kay, Marvin L. M., and Lorin L. Cary. *Slavery in North Carolina, 1748–1775*. Chapel Hill: University of North Carolina Press, 1995.

Kulikoff, Allan. *Tobacco and Slaves: The Development of Southern Cultures in the Chesapeake, 1680–1800*. Chapel Hill: University of North Carolina Press, 1986.

Land, Aubrey C., Lois G. Carr, and Edward C. Papenfuse. Eds. *Law, Society, and Politics in Early Maryland: Proceedings of the First Conference of Maryland History, June 14–15, 1974*. Baltimore, Md.: Johns Hopkins University Press, 1977.

Livingston, John, ed. *Biographical Sketches of Eminent American Lawyers*. New York, 1852.

Lockridge, Kenneth A. *The Diary, and Life, of William Byrd II of Virginia, 1674–1744*. Chapel Hill: University of North Carolina Press, 1987.

———. *On the Sources of Patriarchal Rage: The Commonplace Books of William Byrd and Thomas Jefferson and the Gendering of Power in the Eighteenth Century*. New York: New York University Press, 1992.

Lovejoy, Paul E., and Nicholas Rodgers, ed. *Unfree Labour in the Development of the Atlantic World*. Portland, Ore.: Frank Cass, 1994.

Loveland, Anne C. *Southern Evangelicals and the Social Order, 1800–1860*. Baton Rouge: Louisiana State University Press, 1980.

Lumpkin, Ben Gray, and Martha Neville Lumpkin. Comps. *The Lumpkin Family of Virginia, Georgia, and Mississippi*. Clarkesville, Tenn.: privately printed, 1973.

Main, Gloria L. *Tobacco Colony: Life in Early Maryland, 1650– 1720*. Princeton, N.J.: Princeton University Press, 1982.

Marambaud, Pierre. *William Byrd of Westover 1674–1744*. Charlottesville: University Press of Virginia, 1971.

Marshall, Dorothy. *Fanny Kemble*. New York: St. Martin's Press, 1977.

Morgan, Edmund S. *American Slavery, American Freedom: The Ordeal of Colonial Virginia*. New York: Norton, 1975.

Morris, Thomas D. *Southern Slavery and the Law, 1619–1860*. Chapel Hill: University of North Carolina Press, 1996.

Morton, Louis. *Robert Carter of Nomini Hall: A Virginia Tobacco Planter of the Eighteenth Century*. Williamsburg: Colonial Williamsburg, 1941.

Mullin, Gerald W. *Flight and Rebellion: Slave Resistance in Eighteenth-Century Virginia*. New York: Oxford University Press, 1972.

Mullin, Michael. *Africa in America: Slave Acculturation and Resistance in the American South and the British Caribbean, 1736–1831*. Urbana: University of Illinois Press, 1992.

Nash, Gary B. *Race and Revolution*. Madison, Wis.: Madison House Publishers, 1990.

Nisbet, Richard E., and Dov Cohen. *Culture of Honor: The Psychology of Violence in the South*. Boulder, Colo.: Westview Press, 1996.

Oakes, James. *The Ruling Race: A History of American Slaveholders*. New York: Alfred A. Knopf, 1982.

Olshausen, George. *American Slavery and After*. San Francisco: Olema Press, 1983.

Owens, Leslie H. *This Species of Property: Slave Life and Culture in the Old South.* New York: Oxford University Press, 1976.

Ownby, Ted, ed. *Black and White Cultural Interaction in the Antebellum South.* Jackson: University Press of Mississippi, 1993.

Patterson, Orlando. *Slavery and Social Death: A Comparative Study.* Cambridge: Harvard University Press, 1982.

Phillips, Ulrich B. *American Negro Slavery: A Survey of the Supply, Employment and Control of Negro Labor as Determined by the Plantation Regime.* 1918; reprint, Gloucester, Mass.: Peter Smith, 1959.

Price, Richard, ed. *Maroon Societies: Rebel Slave Communities in the Americas.* 2d ed. Baltimore, Md.: Johns Hopkins University Press, 1979.

Raboteau, Albert J. *Slave Religion: The "Invisible Institution" in the Antebellum South.* New York: Oxford University Press, 1978.

Randall, Willard S. *George Washington.* New York: Henry Holt and Co., 1997.

Richard, Carl J. *The Founders and the Classics: Greece, Rome, and the American Enlightenment.* Cambridge, Mass.: Harvard University Press, 1994.

Rozbicki, Michal J. *Transformation of the English Cultural Ethos in Colonial America: Maryland 1634–1720.* Lanham, Md.: University Press of America, 1988.

Ryman, Dean E., comp. *Joseph Henry Lumpkin: An Unintentional Autobiography.* Atlanta: Atlanta Bar Association, 1913.

Scarborough, William K. *The Overseer: Plantation Management in the Old South.* Baton Rouge: Louisiana State University Press, 1966.

Sekora, John, and Darwin T. Turner, ed. *The Art of Slave Narrative: Original Essays in Criticism and Theory.* Macomb, Ill.: Western Illinois University Press, 1982.

Shaw, Robert B. *A Legal History of Slavery in the United States.* Potsdam, N.Y.: Northern Press, 1991.

Stampp, Kenneth M. *The Peculiar Institution: Slavery in the Antebellum South.* New York: Alfred A. Knopf, 1956.

Starling, Marion W. *The Slave Narrative: Its Place in American History.* Boston: G. K. Hall, 1981.

Sternett, Milton C. *Black Religion and American Evamgelism: White Protestants, Plantation Missions, and the Flowering of Negro Christianity, 1787–1865.* Metuchen, N.J.: Scarecrow Press, 1975.

Tate, Thad W., and David L. Ammerman, ed. *The Chesapeake in the Seventh Century: Essays on Englo-American Society.* Chapel Hill: University of North Carolina Press, 1979.

Tushnet, Mark V. *The American Law of Slavery 1810–1860: Considerations of Humanity and Interest.* Princeton, N.J.: Princeton University Press, 1981.

Walvin, James. *Slaves and Slavery: The British Colonial Experience.* Manchester: Manchester University Press, 1992.

Watson, Alan. *Slave Law in the Americas.* Athens: University of Georgia Press, 1989.

Webb, Stephen S. *1676: The End of American Independence.* New York: Alfred A. Knopf, 1984.

Welter, Barbara. *Dimity Convictions: The American Woman in the Nineteenth Century.* Athens: Ohio University Press, 1976.

White, George. *Historical Collections of Georgia: Containing the Most Interesting Facts, Traditions, Biographical Sketches, Anecdotes, etc. Relating to Its History and Antiquities, from Its First Settlement to the Present Time.* 3d ed. New York: Pudney and Russell, 1855.

Wiecek, William M. *The Sources of Antislavery Constitutionalism in America, 1760–1848.* Ithaca, N.Y.: Cornell University Press, 1977.

Wiethoff, William E. *A Peculiar Humanism: The Judicial Advocacy of Slavery in High Courts of the Old South, 1820–1850.* Athens: University of Georgia Press, 1996.

Wineman, Walter R. *The Landon Carter Papers in the University of Virginia Library: A Calendar and Biographical Sketch.* Charlottesville: University of Virginia Press, 1962.

Wise, Winifred E. *Fanny Kemble: Actress, Author, Abolitionist.* New York: G. P. Putnam's Sons, 1966.

Wister, Fanny K., ed. *Fanny the American Kemble: Her Journals and Unpublished Letters.* Tallahassee, Fla.: South Pass Press, 1972.

Wood, Betty. *Slavery in Colonial Georgia, 1730–1775.* Athens: University of Georgia Press, 1984.

Wood, Peter H. *Black Majority: Negroes in Colonial South Carolina from 1670 through the Stono Rebellion.* New York: Alfred A. Knopf, 1974.

Wright, Louis B. *The First Gentlemen of Virginia.* San Marino, Calif.: Huntington Library, 1940.

Wyatt-Brown, Bertram. *Honor and Violence in the Old South.* New York: Oxford University Press, 1986.

———. *Southern Honor: Ethics and Behavior in the Old South.* New York: Oxford University Press, 1982.

Yentsch, Anne E. *A Chesapeake Family and Their Slaves: A Study in Historical Archeaology.* Cambridge, Mass.: Cambridge University Press, 1994.

Zubrow, Marcia S., ed. *Pimsleur's Checklists of American Legal Publications.* Littleton, Colo.: Fred B. Rothman and Co., 1992.

Zweiben, Beverly. *How Blackstone Lost the Colonies: English Law, Colonial Lawyers, and the American Revolution.* New York: Garland Publishing, 1990.

Articles/Chapters

Allmendinger, Blake. "Acting and Slavery: Representations of Work in the Writings of Fanny Kemble." *Mississippi Quarterly* 41 (1988): 507–13.

Aptheker, Herbert. "More on American Negro Slave Revolts." *Science and Society* 2 (1938): 386–91.

Baine, Rodney M. "Indian Slavery in Colonial Georgia." *Georgia Historical Quarterly* 79 (1995): 418–24.

Bauer, Raymond A., and Alica H. Bauer. "Day to Day Resistance to Slavery." in *American Slavery: The Question of Resistance*, ed. John H. Bracey, August Meier and Elliott Rudwick (Belmont, Calif.: Wadsworth Publishing, 1971), 37–60.

Blom, Jan Petter, and John J. Gumperz. "Social Meaning in Linguistic Structures: Code-Switching in Norway." in *Directions in Sociolinguistics: The Ethnography of Speaking*, ed. John J. Gumperz and Dell Hymes (New York: Holt, Rinehart and Winston, 1972), 409–35.

Brady, Patrick. "Slavery, Race, and the Criminal Law in Antebellum North Carolina: A Reconsideration of the Thomas Ruffin Court." *North Carolina Central Law Journal* 10 (1979): 248–60.

Breen, T. H. "A Changing Labor Force and Race Relations in Virginia, 1660–1710." *Journal of Social History* 7 (1973): 3–25.

Bush, Jonathan A. "Free to Enslave: The Foundations of Colonial American Slave Law." *Yale Journal of Law and the Humanities* 5 (1993): 417–70.

Cannon, Carl L. "William Byrd II of Virginia." *The Colophon.* New Series. 3 (1938): 291–302.

Cantor, Milton. "The Image of the Negro in Colonial Literature." *New England Quarterly* 36 (1963): 452–77.

Chaplin, Joyce E. "Slavery and the Principle of Humanity: A Modern Idea in the Early Lower South." *Journal of Social History* 24 (1990): 299–315.

Cottrol, Robert J. "Liberalism and Paternalism: Ideology, Economic Interest and the Business Law of Slavery." *American Journal of Legal History* 31 (1987): 359–73.

Degler, Carl N. "Slavery and the Genesis of American Race Prejudice." *Comparative Studies in Society and History* 2 (1959): 49–66.

Diller, Hans-Jurgen. "Code-Switching in Medieval English Drama." *Comparative Drama* 31 (1997): 506–37.

Doss, Richard C., and Alan M. Gross. "The Effects of Black English and Code-Switching on Intraracial Perceptions." *Journal of Black Psychology* 20 (1994): 282–93.

Edwards, John C. "Slave Justice in Four Middle Georgia Counties." *Georgia Historical Quarterly* 57 (1973): 265–73.

Elkins, Stanley. "Slave Personality and the Concentration Camp Analogy." in *American Slavery: The Question of Resistance*, ed. John H. Bracey, August Meier and Elliott Rudwick (Belmont, Calif.: Wadsworth Publishing, 1971), 74–85.

Epstein, Dena J. "Slave Music in the United States before 1860." *Music Library Association Notes* 20 (1965): 195–212, 377–90.

Faust, Drew G. "Culture, Conflict and Community: The Meaning of Power on an Ante-Bellum Plantation." *Journal of Social History* 14 (1980): 83–97.

Fisher, William W. III. "Ideology and Imagery in the Law of Slavery." *Chicago-Kent Law Review* 69 (1993): 1051–86.

Frederickson, George M., and Christopher Lasch. "Resistance to Slavery." in *American Slavery: The Question of Resistance*, ed. John H. Bracey, August Meier and Elliott Rudwick (Belmont, Calif.: Wadsworth Publishing, 1971), 179–92.

Frey, Sylvia R. "Shaking the Dry Bones: The Dialectic of Conversion." in *Black and White Cultural Interaction in the Antebellum South*, ed. Ted Ownby (Jackson: University Press of Mississippi, 1993), 23–44.

Garfield, Deborah M. "Speech, Listening, and Female Sexuality in Incidents in the Life of a Slave Girl." *Arizona Quarterly* 50.2 (1994): 19–49.

Genovese, Eugene D. "Rebelliousness and Docility in the Negro Slave: A Critique of the Elkins Thesis." in *American Slavery: The Question of Resistance*, ed. John H. Bracey, August Meier and Elliott Rudwick (Belmont, Calif.: Wadsworth Publishing, 1971), 99–118.

Greenberg, Kenneth S. "The Nose, the Lie, and the Duel in the Antebellum South." *American Historical Review* 95 (1990): 57–74.

Gross, Ariela. "Pandora's Box: Slave Character on Trial in the Antebellum Deep South." *Yale Journal of Law and the Humanities* 7 (1995): 267–315.

Handlin, Oscar, and Mary F. Handlin. "Origins of the Southern Labor System." *William and Mary Quarterly.* 3d series. 7 (1950): 199–222.

Harper, C. W. "Black Aristocrats: Domestic Servants on the Antebellum Plantation." *Phylon* 46 (1985): 123–35.

———. "House Servants and Field Hands: Fragmentation in the Antebellum Slave Community." *North Carolina Historical Review* 55 (1978): 42–59.

Hess, Natalie. "Code Switching and Style Shifting as Markers of Liminality in Literature." *Language and Literature* 5 (1996): 5–18.

Higginbotham, A. Leon Jr., and Greer C. Bosworth. "'Rather than the Free': Free Blacks in Colonial and Antebellum Virginia." *Harvard Civil Rights-Civil Liberties Law Review* 26 (1991): 17–66.

Higginbotham, A. Leon, Jr., and Anne F. Jacobs. "The 'Law Only As Enemy': The Legitimization of Racial Powerlessness through the Colonial and Antebellum Criminal Laws of Virginia." *North Carolina Law Review* 70 (1992): 969–1070.

Higgins, W. Robert. "Charleston: Terminus and Entrepot of the Colonial Slave Trade." in *The African Diaspora: Interpretive Essays*. Ed. Martin L. Kilson and Robert I. Rotberg. Cambridge, Mass.: Harvard University Press, 1976.

Huebner, Timothy S. "Joseph Henry Lumpkin and Evangelical Reform in Georgia: Temperance, Education, and Industrialization, 1830–1860." *Georgia Historical Quarterly* 75 (1991): 254–74.

Ingersoll, Thomas N. "Slave Codes and Judicial Practice in New Orleans." *Law and History Review* 13 (1995): 23–62.

Inscoe, John C. "Carolina Slave Names: An Index to Acculturation." *Journal of Southern History* 48 (1983): 527–54.

Johnson, Whittington B. "The Origin and Nature of African Slavery in Seventeenth Century Maryland." *Maryland Historical Magazine* 73.3 (1978): 236–45.

Jordan, Winthrop. "Modern Tensions and the Origins of American Slavery." *Journal of Southern History* 28 (1962): 18–30.

Joyner, Charles. "History as Ritual: Rites of Power and Resistance on the Slave Plantation." *Australian Journal of American Studies* 5 (1986): 1–9.

Livingston, John. "Memoir of Joseph Henry Lumpkin." *United States Law Magazine* July and August, 1851: 34–43.

Lombard, Mildred. "Contemporary Opinions of Mrs. Kemble's *Journal of a Residence on a Georgia Plantation*." *Georgia Historical Quarterly* 14 (1930): 335–43.

Manning, Susan. "Industry and Idleness in Colonial Virginia: A New Approach to Wiliam Byrd II." *Journal of American Studies* 28 (1994): 169–90.

Morgan, Edmund S. "Slavery and Freedom: The American Paradox." *Journal of American History* 59 (1972): 5–29.

Morris, Thomas D. "Slaves and the Rules of Evidence in Criminal Trials." *Chicago-Kent Law Review* 68 (1993): 1209–40.

Oakes, James. "The Political Significance of Slave Resistance," reprinted in Finkelman, *Rebellions, Resistance, and Runaways within the Slave South*, 309–27.

Piacentino, Edward J. "Doestick's Assault on Slavery: Style and Technique in *The Great Auction Sale of Slaves, at Savannah, Georgia*." *Phylon* 48 (1988): 196–203.

Reid, John P. "Lessons of Lumpkin: A Review of Recent Literature om Law, Comity, and the Impending Crisis." *William and Mary Law Review* 23 (1982): 571–624.

Russell, Marion. "American Slave Discontent." *Journal of Negro History* 31 (Oct. 1946): 411–34.

Sojka, Gregory S. "Appendix Two, Black Slave Narratives: A Selected Checklist of Criticism." in *The Art of Slave Narrative: Original Essays in Criticism and Theory*, ed. John Sekora and Darwin T. Turner (Macomb, Ill.: Western Illinois University Press, 1982), 135–47.

Sirmans, M. Eugene. "The Legal Status of the Slave in South Carolina, 1670–1740." *Journal of Southern History* 28 (1962): 462–73.

Stampp, Kenneth M. "A Troublesome Property." in *American Slavery: The Question of Resistance*, ed. John H. Bracey, August Meier and Elliott Rudwick (Belmont, Calif.: Wadsworth Publishing, 1971), 61–72.

Starobin, Robert S. "Privileged Bondsmen and the Process of Accommodation: The Role of Houseservants and Drivers As Seen in Their Own Letters." *Journal of Social History* 5 (1971): 46–70.

Stephenson, Mason W., and D. Grier Stephenson Jr. "'To Protect and Defend': Joseph Henry Lumpkin, the Supreme Court of Georgia, and Slavery." *Emory Law Journal* 25 (1976): 579– 608.

Vaughan, Alden T. "The Origins Debate: Slavery and Racism in Seventeenth-Century Virginia." *Virginia Magazine of History and Biography* 97 (1989): 311–54.

Wax, Darold D. "Negro Import Duties in Colonial Virginia." *Virginia Magazine of History and Biography* 79 (1971): 29–44.

Welter, Barbara. "The Cult of True Womanhood, 1820–1860." *American Quarterly* 28 (1966): 151–74.

Wiecek, William M. "The Statutory Law of Slavery and Race in the Thirteen Mainland Colonies of British America." *William and Mary Quarterly*. 3d series. 34 (1977): 258–80.

Wish, Harvey. "American Slave Insurrections before 1861." in *American Slavery: The Question of Resistance*, ed. John H. Bracey, August Meier and Elliott Rudwick (Belmont, Calif.: Wadsworth Publishing, 1971), 21–36.

Wood, Betty. "'Until He Shall Be Dead, Dead, Dead': The Judicial Treatment of Slaves in Eighteenth-Century Georgia." *Georgia Historical Quarterly* 71 (1987): 377–98.

Wright, Louis B. "William Byrd I and the Slave Trade." *Huntington Library Quarterly* 8 (1945): 379–87.

Wyatt-Brown, Bertram. "The Mask of Obedience: Male Slave Psychology in the Old South." *American Historical Review* 93 (1988): 1228–52.

INDEX

Adams, Nehemiah, 145n. 4
Alabama: case law of, 70–71, 76–77, 82; statutes of, 24–25, 28, 29, 30, 39, 167–68
Alexander, Sarah (plantation mistress), 127
Allen, Leonard (former slave), 110
Andrews, Garnett, 74
Aristotle, 1–2, 168
Arkansas: case law of, 77, 105; statues of, 28, 29, 30, 39, 167–68

Bacon, Thomas, 16, 137, 161
Bacon's rebellion, 21, 25, 28, 42, 43, 45
Beanland, Ephraim (overseer), 86–90, 92–93, 96
Bell, Thomas (planter), 95
Bethell, Mary (plantation mistress), 142
Blackman, G. D. (overseer), 91
Blair, Hugh, 2, 168
Bobbit, William, 92, 94
Bolton, James (former slave), 102
Branch, Jacob (former slave), 65
Bratton, George W. (overseer), 86, 89, 93
Brevard, Keziah (plantation mistress), 60, 79, 138, 142–43, 161–62
Browne, Mattie Griffith (former slave), 69–70, 107
Bruce, H. C. (former slave), 102
Burke, Emily, 21
Butler, Pierce (planter), 117, 120–22, 128
Byrd, Lucy (plantation mistress), 48, 50–51
Byrd, William II (planter): biographical sketch of, 42–43; commonplaces of, 43–44; perspective on divine agency of, 136; perspective on insolent slaves of, 47–52; perspective on rebellious slaves of, 44–46

Caldwell, Eliza, 92, 94–95
Caldwell, Silas M., 89, 92–94, 96
Calvert, Rosalie (plantation mistress), 70
Campbell, Governor David (planter), 146, 162
Campbell, George, 2
Campbell, Virginia, 146
Carney, Kate S. (plantation mistress), 146
Carson, Catherine (plantation mistress), 134–35, 161
Carson, James G. (planter), 110, 134–35
Carter, Landon (planter), 59, 71–72
Carter, Robert (planter), 58
Channing, William Ellery, 117–18
Chesnut, Mary, 22
Childress, John W. (planter), 92
Cobb, Thomas R. R., 60, 133
Cocke, John Hartwell (planter), 74
code-switching, 7, 169

Colcock, Judge Charles J., 36
Coleman, Daniel (overseer), 73
Cozart, Willis (former slave), 76
Crenshaw, Charles, 23–24
Crenshaw, Harlan (overseer), 95–96
Cresswell, Nicholas, 107

Deadfoot, Peter (slave), 66
Dismukes, Isaac H. (overseer), 87, 89–90, 94
divine agency, 136–40
Douglas, Hattie (former slave), 75
Douglass, Frederick (former slave), 61, 70, 115

English language, slaves' acquisition of, 5–7
Eve, Emmaline, 135n. 18, 136

family, ideal of, 140–44
"fighting words," doctrine of, 61, 169
Fithian, Philip Vickers, 58
Florida, statutes of, 25, 29, 30, 33, 167
Fort, Judge Joel B., 110, 135
Fox, Tryphena (plantation mistress), 79–80, 101, 105, 123, 164
friendship, bonds of, 144–47
Fugitive Blacksmith, 68

Garner, John I. (overseer), 86–87, 89, 91, 93–94
Gayle, Sarah (plantation mistress), 79
Georgia: case law of, 83, 138–39, 144, 151–54, 155–58; statutes of, 24, 33, 38–39, 167–68
Glennie, Alexander, 133, 137, 141n. 54
Green, Judge Nathan, 81–82
Grimes, William (former slave), 68

"Hail Columbia," parody of, 109
Hamilton, Charles (planter), 95
Hamilton, James A. (planter), 95
Hamilton, Robert (planter), 95
Harris, A. O., 92–93
Harris, Judge William L., 71
Hazard, Thomas B. (overseer), 91
Hedgbeth, Thomas (former slave), 113
Henderson, Francis, 114
Hicks, Edward (former slave), 69
Hildreth, Richard, 25
Holmes, A. T., 60, 145
Holmes, John (former slave), 72
Horton, George Moses (slave), 108

Incidents in the Life of a Slave Girl, 112

Jackson, President Andrew (planter), 86
Jefferson, President Thomas (planter), 2, 104, 164

Jeter, Jeremiah, 3
Jetton, Mary S., 94
Johnson, Eli (former slave), 66
Jones, Catoe (slave), 142n. 61
Jones, Charles C., 137–38
Jones, Thomas (former slave), 106

Kemble, Frances Anne (plantation mistress): biographical sketch of, 117; criticism of planters by, 126–27; criticism of slave law by, 119–20; criticism of slave music by, 126; criticism of slaves' appearance by, 123–25; criticism of slaves' suffering by, 121–22; estimate of slaves' deceitfulness by, 120–21; reactions to slave insolence by, 127
Kentucky: case law of, 26, 32–33, 106; statutes of, 24, 27, 29, 32
King, Anna (plantation mistress), 128, 142
King, Porter (planter), 157

Leigh, John T. (planter), 92, 94
Little, John (former slave), 72–73
Louisiana: case law of, 7, 33–34; statutes of, 16, 24, 28, 29, 30, 34, 167
Lumpkin, Callie, 149, 155
Lumpkin, Judge Joseph Henry: biographical sketch of, 149–51; personal advocacy of black subordination by, 155–58; sentiments on divine agency of, 153–54; sentiments on paternalism of, 151–53;

Mairs, John A. (overseer), 87, 90–91, 94
Mars, James (former slave), 80
Martin, James (overseer), 77, 105
Martin, Sella (slave), 102
Martineau, Harriet, 117n. 4, 133
Maryland: case law of, 65, 81; statutes of, 15–16, 22, 24, 31, 167
Mason, Isaac (former slave), 74, 113
Mathew, Theobald, 150
Mayo, G. W. (overseer), 86, 89, 93
McLeod, Norman (overseer), 91–92
McGaffey, Henry L. (former slave), 65
McKlennan, Abe (former slave), 65
McNeal, Albert F., 92–93
Melville, Joseph L. (planter), 60
Miller, Harriet (former slave), 68–69
Mississippi: case law of, 6, 18, 71; statutes of, 29, 30, 33, 167
Missouri, statutes of, 24, 32, 167
Montgomery, Rube (former slave), 76
Moore, George, 92

Nash, Judge Frederic, 19, 20, 103
Nat, stereotype of, 26
Nevitt, John (planter), 91–92
Nichols, Christopher (former slave), 66
Nisbet, Judge Eugenius A., 138–40
North Carolina: case law of, 17, 19–20, 26, 32, 103, 111, 143–44, 167; statutes of, 23, 32, 167
Northup, Solomon (former slave), 80

O'Connor, Rachel (plantation mistress), 22, 142
Olmsted, Frederick Law, 66–67, 78, 101, 105, 107, 113
O'Neall, Judge John B., 18, 25–26, 35, 102–3, 143–44, 146–47

Parker, Ann (former slave), 105
paternalism, myth of, 133–36
Patterson, Delicia (former slave), 78
Pearson, Judge Richmond M., 18–19, 20, 143–44
Pettigrew, William S. (planter), 60, 70, 146, 162
"Pluto Jumbo," 114
Polk, President James K. (planter), 86–90, 92–94, 96
Polk, Janie, 135
Polk, Leonidas, 135
Polk, Sarah (plantation mistress), 86, 90, 94–95
Polk, William (planter), 89, 92
Prince, Mary (former slave), 80
Purvis, Miles (overseer), 91

Redpath, James, 105, 113, 114
research methods, criticism of, 10–11
Revolutionary war; compensation for captured slaves during, 4; advertisements for runaway slaves during, 3–4; slaves' experience of, 4–5;
Rollins, Joe (former slave), 109
Ruffin, Judge Thomas, 17–18, 19, 167
Rutledge, Judge John, 17

Sambo, sterotype of, 26
Sandiford, J. H. (planter), 67
Sharkey, Judge William L., 18, 25
Skipwith, George (slave), 74–75
Slave behavior, gentry's perception of: affronts to women, 110–13; assertions of independence or equality, 71–77; deceitfulness, 59–60; insults, 105–10; denials, 64–71; downcast looks, 62–64; drunkenness, 103–5; nonverbal cues, 113–15; revolts, 21–22, 77; silence, 60–63, 68; smiling, 61–62; threats, 77–84; tumultuous meetings, 23–24
Smith, James L. (former slave), 114
Snow, Susan (former slave), 108–9
South Carolina: case law of, 17, 18, 25–26, 35–37, 76, 102–3, 106, 111, 112, 143; statutes of, 15, 22, 24, 26, 39, 167–68
speech, power of, 3, 10, 119, 163, 168–69
Spotswood, Governor Alexander, 23, 42
Starnes, Judge Ebenezer A., 144
Stroyer, Jacob (former slave), 67, 74–75

Taylor, John, 134, 136, 139, 161
Taylor, Judge John Louis, 32
Tennessee: case law of, 31, 81–82, 110–11; statutes of, 24, 31–32, 40, 166–67
Texas: case law of, 82–83; statutes of, 29, 30, 34–35, 167
Thornwell, James Henley, 136
Throgmorton, Isaac (former slave), 112
Tims, J. T. (former slave), 78
Turley, Judge William, 110–11

Vassa, Gustavus (former slave), 104, 107
Virginia: case law of, 21, 32; statutes of, 16, 23–25, 27, 29, 30, 32, 38, 166–67

Waddel, Moses, 136
Walker, James, 92–93
Walker, John (planter), 141–42, 162
Ward, Charles, 124
Wardlaw, Judge John, 3, 16, 103
Warfield, Susanna (plantation mistress), 78–79
Washington, President George (planter), 2
Weston, Plowden C. J. (planter), 96
White, Mingo (former slave), 78, 110
Williams, Charley (former slave), 73
Wilson, Temple (former slave), 105